APPLE KITCHEN COOK BOOK

BY DEMETRIA TAYLOR

POPULAR LIBRARY • NEW YORK

ABOUT THE AUTHOR

Demetria Taylor holds a master's degree in Home Economics, is a Registered Dietitian and is a nationally known authority in the food field. Following eight years at Good Housekeeping Institute, she went to *McCall's Magazine* as head of their kitchens.

For many years now, Miss Taylor has been a free-lance food editor and consultant. She is in charge of the work of the Apple Kitchen and has been food editor for *Parade Magazine* under the name Beth Merriman for many years. She is also home economist for several associations concerned with food.

Miss Taylor is the author of other cook books, including *The Cook's Blessings,* published in 1965 by Random House, *From Soup to Nuts, The Fondue Cook Book,* and *The Fondue Party Cook Book,* all three under the Beth Merriman by-line, and published by Grosset and Dunlap. In addition she has written many recipe booklets and brochures.

POPULAR LIBRARY EDITION

A project of the International Apple Institute, 2430 Pennsylvania Avenue, N.W., Washington, D.C., 20037

TABLE OF CONTENTS

EVERYBODY
LOVES APPLES!

This book is dedicated to the incomparable apple, loveliest, most versatile, most delicious of fruits.

The apple tree is a vision of beauty from springtime, when pink and white blossoms crowd its branches and make the air fragrant with their special perfume, through summer, dressed in leaves that have given the name "apple green" to the world of color, into autumn, when its boughs droop under the weight of scarlet or golden fruit ripening to perfection in the slanting rays of the September sun. Even in winter the gnarled, bare branches of an apple tree have a peculiar beauty of their own, an air of secret awareness of life soon to be renewed.

An apple tree left to its own devices is a friendly tree, its low branches inviting a child to climb into a magic leafy retreat above the level of curious eyes. Once I knew such a tree, on a farm in Duxbury, Massachusetts—my own special apple tree, with a couple of shelves to hold my books and a comfortable seat with a back to lean against. Perhaps the reason children don't care much about reading today is because they lack the privacy dear to a child's heart, at its best in the shady boughs of an apple tree! I'd like to recommend to apple growers that one tree be planted near the house, just for the children's pleasure, and left free of the pruner's ministrations so necessary in the orchard.

Legends and Folklore

Apples are as old as mankind, and just as soon as man learned to write he began their recorded history. Many of our most fascinating stories, fables and legends are woven around apples. Was it an apple that tempted Adam in the Garden of Eden? The Bible doesn't say so, but down through the centuries we have credited the apple with man's downfall, probably because its superlative beauty and flavor would make it difficult to resist!

1

King Solomon, in his wisdom, hailed the apple as a fruit of healing. Ages later, in Devonshire, this saying arose: "Ate an apfel avore gwain to bed. Makes the doctor beg his bread." And today we claim, with substantial evidence to support it, that "an apple a day keeps the doctor away."

Greek and Roman myths abound in stories about the apple, symbol of love and beauty. Even today we refer to something or someone we prize as "the apple of our eye."

An apple was the cause of the Trojan War. It all began because Eris, Goddess of Discord, was miffed when she was not invited to the wedding of Peleus and Thetis. To avenge this snub, she had an artisan make an apple of solid gold, inscribed "To the Fairest." And on the day of the nuptials she tossed it among the guests. Three goddesses claimed it— Hera, Athena and Aphrodite. To put an end to their squabbling, Paris was called upon to judge what may have been the first beauty contest.

It appears that even goddesses were not above bribery. Hera promised Paris power and riches in return for the apple. Athena offered glory and renown as a warrior. But Aphrodite held out a reward no man could resist, the fairest of all earthly women for a wife—Helen of Troy. Unfortunately Helen was already married to Menelaus, King of Sparta, who failed to appreciate her abduction by Paris. So began a war that lasted ten long years!

It is said that when Zeus and Hera were married in the Garden of the Gods, a wonderful tree bearing golden apples sprang from the earth. These apples had "a taste of honey" and cured all illnesses.

Atalanta, beautiful goddess and huntress, was also fleet of foot. She challenged every man who sought her hand to a race, promising that if he won she would marry him, but if he lost, he must die. Because she was so beautiful, many men accepted the terms, and as many died, until one, called Hippomemes, bethought himself to pray to Aphrodite before the race. She answered his prayers by giving him three golden apples. Following her instructions, he dropped them, one by one, during the race. Each time, Atalanta was tempted beyond her strength and stopped to retrieve the apple, thus losing the race and winning a husband.

British folklore, too, is filled with praise of apples. An ancient Saxon coronation benediction reads, "Bless oh Lord the courage of this Prince and prosper the works in his hands and may this land be filled with apples."

In Herefordshire, Devonshire and Cornwall the old custom of "wassailing" the apple orchards on Christmas Eve still persists. The farmers walk in procession to a chosen tree in each orchard where an incantation is spoken and a bowl of cider dashed against the trunk of the tree, thus insuring a fruitful harvest.

Superstitions follow on legends, and in Devonshire this "cure" for warts may still be in use today: Halve an apple, rub it on warts, tie it back together again and bury it. The warts will vanish!

In Lincolnshire a poultice of rotten apples was once recommended for rheumatism. (Fresh apples in the diet would have been more effective!) And in Cornwall, in 1562, a clergyman treated every illness with a diet of apples and milk.

Apple History

To go back to the Garden of Eden, most scholars agree that apples may well have originated in Southwest Asia, credited by Biblical savants as being the site of the Garden!

Carbonized remains of apples have been found by archeologists in prehistoric lake dwellings in Switzerland, going back to the Iron Age. There is also evidence to show that apples were eaten and preserved by slicing and sun-drying during the Stone Age in Europe.

In the earliest annals of China, Egypt and Babylon we find apples mentioned, and we know that man understood the art of budding and grafting fruit trees as long as twenty centuries ago.

When Caesar's Roman legions invaded Britain they introduced apples to those isles. Another Roman, Cato, who lived and wrote in the third century B.C., speaks of seven apple varieties, while Pliny, in the first century A.D., names 36 varieties. In the centuries that followed, apple orchards were planted all over Europe.

When the first settlers arrived in America they brought apple seeds with them. The first apple crop in the New World was harvested from trees planted by the Pilgrims.

In 1647 Governor Stuyvesant of New York (then New Amsterdam) brought a grafted apple tree from Holland and the trunk of this tree stood on the corner of Third Avenue and 13th Street until a dray knocked it down in 1866.

The first commercial apple tree nursery was established in Flushing, Long Island, in 1730.

When covered wagons lumbered over wilderness trails traveling westward, they carried apple trees and "scion wood" for grafting as part of their cargo.

Back East the Pennsylvania Dutch became expert at drying sliced apples, which they called "schnitz." They also made (and still make) fine cider, while their apple recipes have won renown for generations.

Farther South, in the Appalachian area, apple orchards were begun at about the same time as the New England plantings. George Washington and Thomas Jefferson were two famous apple growers in Virginia.

Today the annual apple crop in the United States is approximately 145 million bushels. Most of this fruit comes from 35 or more of the 50 states—states which offer a temperate climate, ample moisture and sunlight, well-drained soil, and a winter season during which the trees can rest.

Apples are produced around the globe. Australia, New Zealand, China, Japan, Israel, and many other nations of the Middle and Far East produce substantial volumes, while production continues in Europe and in the Americas.

The Story of Johnny Appleseed

Almost everyone thinks that Johnny Appleseed is the mythical hero of a charming American legend. Actually, this is the nickname of a real person, John Chapman, who was born in Massachusetts in 1774.

As a youth, John followed his father's trade of carpentry. He drifted away from his birthplace and eventually migrated to Pittsburgh. Here he listened avidly to tales about the pioneers who were trekking westward, and to stories of life on the frontier.

Ignoring the disdainful laughter of those in whom he confided, he ultimately set out alone with a sack of apple seeds gathered from cider press refuse, an axe, a short-handled hoe and a Bible, to follow an urge to teach religion and to plant apple trees.

His possessions were few. Often he wore only a burlap coffee sack for clothing. Bareheaded and often barefoot, even when the weather was freezing, a saucepan on his head when it stormed, he traveled unarmed, often over the dangerous wilderness trails. Sometimes friendly Indians gave him moccasins. He was a welcome guest at homesteads where he stopped and he showed his appreciation by making toys for the children, by telling stories, and by reading aloud from his Bible.

Johnny Appleseed was a gentle man, a student of Sweden-borgian philosophy. He never harmed a living thing, and had an almost mystical love of nature. Above all, he had a deep love and respect for all mankind, including the Indian tribes he encountered in his travels.

John Chapman, the beloved "Johnny Appleseed," died in the early spring of 1845 near Ft. Wayne, Indiana, while tending one of his numerous frontier apple nursery plantings. He was 71 years of age. A friend of everyone he met, an honored guest wherever he stayed, respected and beloved throughout the 10,000 square miles of frontier country he traveled, he is remembered today as one of that rare and truly good breed of men who devote their lives to their fellow men with no thought of reward.

A Word About Apples, Health and Nutrition

Ask anyone who is eating an apple, "What's so great about apples?" and you'll probably elicit a reply like, "They're great —I just like them, that's all." Press the question further and the respondent may elaborate, "because they're good . . . and good for you."

Enjoyment and good health . . . an unbeatable testimonial for nature's most nearly perfect fruit.

But what about the health and nutrition values of apples? What about the old "apple a day" adage; is it true?

Apples are a major member of the fruit and vegetable group of the four essential food groups which nutritionists recommend.

While apples are not a major source of any one specific nutrient they contain modest amounts of a number of the important nutrients. For this reason and their universal flavor appeal, versatility, convenience and year around availability, nutritionists and dietitians rate them highly.

Apples are low in calories, the food energy unit supplied by carbohydrates, fats and proteins. Apples are for slimming . . . one average apple supplies only about 80 calories. The energy that is supplied, however, comes from quickly available fruit sugars. Hence they meet one of the prime qualifications for snacks. They fill you up, not out, and provide quick energy.

Not all food and diet values can be measured in terms of precisely named nutrients. Apples, for example, provide bulk in the diet for the proper functioning of the body's digestive and regulatory systems. Pectin and hemicellulose and the acid and alkaline balance contribute to this. They are catalytic and contribute to fighting body toxins, aiding digestion and pepping up the entire body system.

Apples are an excellent source of pectin, which is associated with helping keep cholesterol levels in balance, a relationship felt to be significant in helping to prevent or reduce the dangers of coronary heart disease.

The relatively high potassium and low sodium ratio in apples is also significant in some cardiac and renal problems as well as in diets for overweight persons.

Studies have shown that persons eating apples regularly have fewer headaches and other illnesses associated with nervous tension; and also show a reduced incidence of colds and other minor upper respiratory ailments.

Apples are "Nature's Toothbrush." The mild fibrous texture of the apple for detergent action; its juice content; its delightful aroma and mouth-watering appeal to induce salivary activity, all combine to make the apple an ideal dentifrice and natural "toothbrush." Studies have shown a marked reduction in dental caries when apples are eaten regularly in lieu of or following excessive amounts of candies, pastries and other foods which leave sticky residues between and around the teeth.

While much research remains to be done to analyze and understand all the many ways apples contribute to better health and nutrition, the age-old adage, "an apple a day . . . ," is true enough and is being more and more strongly confirmed.

People eat apples primarily for sheer enjoyment, but health and nutrition are important motivations too, and for good reason: They're the all around, year around health fruit and "glow" fruit. They are good for the teeth, the stomach, the skin and the complexion, the nerves, the smile and overall good health.

SPEAKING OF APPLES

About the Growing of Apples

Apples do not reproduce "true" from seed. In other words, the fruit from a tree grown from the seed of an apple will not produce fruit quite like the apple from which the seed came. Thus, every apple seed produces a new variety. It is hardly surprising, then, that we have had 2,500, and more, different apple varieties mentioned in American horticultural literature. And these 2,500 were mostly from early Colonial days. Apple growers perpetuated a desirable variety by budding and grafting live buds from the tree bearing this fruit to a new seedling or another tree. Thus, wanted varieties could be grown for a much longer time than the life span of the original seedling tree. This is why we have apple varieties today that trace their ancestry literally from tree to tree—generation to generation—back to Colonial days. (See pp. 15–29.)

Apple growing is a science called pomology. The perfect shape, beautiful color and distinctive flavor of each variety is not simply a matter of chance, but rather the result of the knowledge and efforts by many people.

Apple orchards need year-round care by trained people. The trees are planted 50 to 400 or more per acre, depending on the size of the tree at maturity.

Efficient management and care mean a better yield per acre, usually 600 or more bushels at harvest time. When there is a lavish bloom in the spring and a good "set" of fruit, some of the apples must be thinned out to give those remaining on the branches a chance to grow to a good size and take on good color.

Budding and grafting, planting, pruning, insect and disease control, pollination, irrigation and thinning are some of the many facets of the science and profession of apple growing. The orchardist must be a jack-of-all-trades and a master of them, too.

Harvesting, storing, packing and marketing are also vital factors in getting quality apples to the consumer in the best possible condition. For more about storage see pp. 12–13.

Apples and Hospitality

The fruit bowl has been a warm and friendly expression of hospitality almost since the beginning of recorded history.

Fresh fruit and cheese, long a standard final course on European menus, served after the "sweet," has become popular in America too.

Today the apple bowl and cheese tray have become a popular, sophisticated and delightful final course for lunch or dinner. (See p. 175.)

After a hearty meal when a rich dessert is often declined, a cold, crisp fresh apple with assorted cheeses provides a perfect final touch and satisfies without satiating. Simple to prepare, easy to serve, apples have a way of saying "We're glad you came and hope you'll come again."

Fresh apples are available the year around. They come ready to serve, colorfully packaged by Mother Nature in an assortment of varieties to satisfy every taste. Just refrigerate, then polish and serve when you're ready.

America's Favorite Pie—Apple

Pie is a favorite American dessert, and many regions have their own specialties, but the all-national top favorite, as proved by many surveys, is *apple* pie.

Who made the first apple pie, and when? No one seems to know for sure. We do know that pastry originated in the Golden Age of Greece and that the Romans carried home the recipe after conquering the Greeks. After that it traveled through Europe wherever the Romans went and was adapted to native customs and available foods.

In early times pies were heavy and hearty, usually served as a main dish. Chaucer wrote of a "coke" (cook) who could "wel bake a pie," but in his day the ingredients in one pie would be marrow bones, sparrows, vegetables, nuts, dates, oysters, eggs, fruits, spices, wine, butter and sugar baked in a huge pan under a thick layer of pastry!

We do know that apple pie was in great favor as a dessert in the time of Elizabeth I, because it is mentioned in the literature of those years.

Oliver Cromwell, that fanatical Puritan who held sway in England in the mid 1600s, banned all pies throughout the Commonwealth because they gave people pleasure, and therefore must be wicked! When Charles II became king in 1660, his subjects not only welcomed him with enthusiasm but welcomed the return of their beloved pies as well!

Robert Oliver, in his book *An Apple A Day,* emphasizes the love of the English for apple pies. He tells a story about the Earl of Dudley, a multimillionaire who lived in the early 1800s and who "could not dine comfortable without an apple pie." Once, at a grand dinner party, he was greatly annoyed because no apple pie was served and kept up a steady, audible murmur: "God bless my soul! No apple pie."

Henry Mayhew, an English author, after interviewing thousands of London's "street people," published a book in 1851 called *Mayhew's London.* In it he writes of the "piemen" who once sold all sorts of small pies on the streets, including apple pie. He tells us that "pie shops" eventually almost destroyed their trade and that they then frequented summer fairs, races, public houses and taverns as the best sources of customers.

English settlers in this country found no familiar apple trees here, and soon seedlings were being brought over to supply the lack. In a cook book by Amelia Simmons, published in 1796, the author urged families to set out apple trees, and gives recipes for apple pies.

Before the days of refrigerated storage, apples were peeled, cored, quartered and hung on cords in the kitchen to dry. These dried apples were used all winter long to make pies. From the moment apples were available, New Englanders ate apple pie for breakfast, and in some rural areas the custom persists. Once when Emerson was twitted about this, he asked, "What is pie for?"

In Colonial times pies were not beautiful or fancy, but they were good. The custom of baking pies in round, shallow pans rather than in deep square or oblong pans originated here for reasons of economy, in order to stretch scarce food supplies. Some cooks still insist that "take-off crusts" give apple pies an even better flavor. Sliced apples are arranged in a pastry-lined pie pan, and the top crust is laid on top, but not sealed to the undercrust. When the pie is done, the top crust is gently lifted off, sugar and spices are added, and the top crust put back in place.

In France, a fruit "pie" is round but has straight sides. The shell is made with pastry, and the fruit topped with a glaze. In Germany, what is called a fruit "kuchen" is made with a bottom crust of cookie-like pastry, filled with concentric circles of fruit, then baked and glazed. And so it goes —to each his own. But here in America we cling to our version: a two-crust apple pie baked in a round pan. Served warm, topped with a scoop of ice cream if you like, there is no dessert, however exotic, that can compare with it for superb flavor.

Apple Juice and Apple Cider

"Cider Apples"
When God had made the oak trees,
And the beeches and the pines,
And the flowers and the grasses,
And the tendrils of the vines;
He saw that there was wanting
A something in His plan,
And He made the little apples
The little cider apples,
The sharp, sour cider apples,
To prove His love for man.
Author unknown

Colonists from Europe brought with them the "know-how" for making apple juice and apple cider. Apple juice is natural, unfermented juice, often misnamed *sweet cider*. Fresh apple juice stays sweet for several days under refrigeration. It is often flash pasteurized at temperatures not exceeding 160°F. and bottled or canned for later utilization.

Cider is fermented or partially fermented apple juice.

Apple juice and apple cider were produced in large volume by the early colonists and during the early years of American growth and development because cider had long been a popular beverage in Europe. Then, too, a great number of seedling apple trees produced fruit (some sweet, some very tart) that was of little value except when blended with other apples to make cider.

Limited storage and limited refrigeration for apples were additional reasons for making them into cider. Boiled cider (cider syrup) and dried apples were other means of preserving apples for future use.

The best apple cider is generally made with late fall maturing apple varieties because they usually contain more fruit sugars and flavor. Most good apple juice, sweet cider and hard cider are made from blends of a number of varieties.

Like haying time, silo filling time, corn husking bees, barn raisings and maple sugar time, cider making and the cider mill were a colorful part of early America.

Apple cider and apples were substitutes for currency in those days. The wealth of a town was sometimes measured in terms of the number of barrels of cider put down for the winter, and no farmer ever felt that he had completed his fall work until several barrels of cider were put into the cellar for the winter months.

Today, thanks to modern technology, good sweet apple cider and apple juice are available in food stores everywhere the year around, and are doubtless of better quality than our forebears enjoyed.

Buying and Handling Apples

In the retail food store apples are marketed in bulk, by the pound, in polyethylene bags of three, four, and five pounds, and in film-wrapped trays of two or more apples in each "over-wrap" or tray package.

Almost all apples are graded for marketing, and the package is identified with a U.S. Department of Agriculture grade of U.S. No. 1, U.S. Fancy, or U.S. Extra Fancy. Differences in grade are a matter of color, uniformity of size and shape, and minor superficial blemishes such as russeting, scratches and scars, which occur in production.

In selecting apples, check for bruising. Apples bruise easily, and a minor amount of bruising is almost impossible to prevent in shipping and handling. Bruises soon lead to decay, however, and excessive bruising usually means that the apples have been poorly handled and will decay more rapidly after you have taken them home. Over-ripe apples, however, are not usually marketed, and you can feel reasonably secure in purchasing most apples on display. They should appear bright and fresh looking. The green "ground color," or background color, when visible on varieties that are not a solid red color, should be a yellow-green. If too "grass green" in appearance, the apples may be too immature and will have a starchy, green taste.

If the ground color is a faded yellow-green, the apples may be overmature and will be soft and mealy with loss of juice and flavor. Today many apples are waxed to enhance appearance. The wax is safe and made with approved materials.

In storing apples at home, keep them cool. Whenever possible, reserve supplies should be refrigerated. Keep them in the hydrator or in the polyethylene bag in which you purchased them, to maintain proper humidity and to prevent them from absorbing other food flavors. Serve apples cold or at room temperature, as preferred.

The Refrigerated Storage of Apples

The life cycle of an apple begins following fertilization and the start of a tiny green apple. From this moment on, its growth and development progresses to a peak point of optimum ripeness or maturity, then continues on the down side of the cycle until it finally spoils and decomposes.

Apples are harvested, as nearly as is possible and practicable, at optimum maturity. They are alive and continue to respire and age after being picked from the tree. The rate of respiration and maturation is directly related to temperature. The higher the temperature, the more rapid the rate of respiration and aging and the loss of optimum quality for eating. Apples kept at room temperature, for example, respire and age far more rapidly than they do in the refrigerator.

Because of their high water content, apples keep best in a reasonably moist atmosphere. A dry atmosphere tends to draw moisture from the fruit. Therefore the refrigerator hydrator is the best place to store them.

To preserve fresh apples and extend their availability for many weeks longer than their normal life span, huge refrigerators, or cold storages as they are called, are filled at harvest time each fall.

The first apple storages in America, back in Colonial days, and for many years thereafter, were called common storages or root cellars. They maintained temperatures above freezing, but were cool and moist. Late fall apple varieties, or "winter" varieties, could be kept in reasonably good condition all winter long in such storages.

The cellars of early American homes, with dirt floors, and later, concrete floors, provided excellent household storages for apples. Today, with the advent of central heating and dry, heated basements, this is no longer true.

One of the first American commercial cold storage plants for apples was built in Niagara County, New York, in 1870. Ice, packed in sawdust, lining the walls, provided the first refrigerant. It was not until 1915 and thereafter that mechanical refrigeration took over.

While refrigeration extended the life cycle of a number of apple varieties, making them available for market for several months longer, February and March usually marked the end of the cold storage season.

In France, early in the 1800s, Jacques Berard, in research he was conducting, found that harvested fruits used oxygen and gave off carbon dioxide and that in an atmosphere largely or completely deprived of oxygen, they cease to ripen. He demonstrated that, if not totally deprived of oxygen, they were not suffocated and that the ripening process could be restored upon restoration of oxygen. While Berard's research was fifty years or more ahead of the practical and commercial development of mechanical refrigeration, it was the beginning of *Controlled Atmosphere Storage*. This type of storage re-apportions the air in storage areas for apples in a way that slows the maturation rate to a point well below that of refrigeration alone and extends the crisp, flavorful life of fresh apples for additional months. With Controlled Atmosphere Storage fresh apples can now be kept, nearly harvest-time fresh, almost the year around.

In 1940, the only controlled atmosphere storage plants in the United States were in eastern New York State, due largely to R. M. Smock's intensive work at Cornell University. Today, nearly 20 million bushels of apples, largely in New York, Michigan and Washington, but increasingly in all apple-producing sections of the U.S. and Canada, are stored in controlled atmosphere. This volume, plus twice as many more in regular refrigerated storage, effectively "stretch" the apple season from September into May and June of the following spring and summer, when a new crop blossoms forth and little green apples begin the cycle all over again.

Processed Apple Products

Nearly one-half the apple crop in America each year is processed into convenient apple products: apple cider, apple juice, applesauce, canned and frozen pie-sliced apples, apple pie filling, whole baked apples, apple butter, dehydrated sliced apples and applesauce and others.

Canned applesauce is the most popular and the most universally available processed product. It is packaged in number 10 size cans (approximately one gallon) for restaurants and other institutional users and in a range of consumer sizes of glass jars and cans. Applesauce is usually made from a blend of two or more apple varieties. McIntosh, Golden Delicious and Gravenstein are three varieties from which popular single variety applesauce is increasingly available.

Commercially prepared applesauce is usually not seasoned, because it would be too difficult to please everyone. However, it is an easy matter to "season to taste" and to experiment with many flavor combinations.

Canned pie-sliced apples and apple pie filling are also available in most food stores and are quick and easy to use for pies and other pastries, for toppings for ice cream and other desserts and many other uses.

Apple juice, by itself and blended with other fruit juices, is increasingly popular and available year-round in all food stores. Sweet apple cider, fresh pressed at harvest time each fall, is still one of the most popular of all apple products. With refrigeration and freezing today, it is available for a much longer period than in the past.

Recipes for Quantity Service

The following recipes can be easily adapted for quantity service by a simple process of multiplication. In other words, you can double, triple, etc. your ingredients, using these equivalents. See index for recipes.

3 teaspoons = 1 tablespoon
16 tablespoons = 1 cup
1 cup = 8 fluid ounces
2 cups = 1 pint

2 pints = 1 quart
4 quarts = 1 gallon
1 1-pound can = 2 cups, approximately

Apple-Crowned Pork Chops
Apple-Smothered Pork Chops
Baked Pork Chops Normandy
Sweet and Pungent Pork Chops
Apple-Stuffed Sausage Roll
Chicken Apple Scallop
Scalloped Apples and Cheese
Apple Cheese Salad
Apple Salmon Salad Bowl
Apple Potato Salad
Chicken Fruit Salad
Dutch Salad
Waldorf Salad Supreme
Apple Sour Cream Slaw
Fruit and Vegetable Slaw
Waldorf Salad

Cranberry Waldorf Salad
French Toast Sandwich Caledonia
Grilled Applesauce Sandwich
Patio Sandwiches
Apple-Topped Muffins
Yams with Apples
Baked Apples in Foil
Honey Baked Apples
Apple Bread Pudding
Danish Apple Pudding 1 & 2
Applesauce Cup Cake
Apple Lemon Snow
Old-Fashioned Apple Pan Dowdy
Old-Fashioned Apple Slump

KNOW YOUR APPLES

It's fun to "know your apples"—and smart too—for full enjoyment of this delightful and versatile fruit is not to be found in any single variety, but in selection and choice for flavor enjoyment and cooking triumphs.

When it is understood that every seedling apple tree bears fruit that differs from every other seedling apple tree, the numbers of named varieties is not surprising. Of the millions of seedling trees that have produced fruit over the centuries, probably fewer than 8,000 produced fruit of such note that the variety was named, recorded and propagated. Of these, fewer than a thousand attained lasting recognition. Today, about fifty varieties represent most of the apple production throughout the world.

Nowadays nursery stock of apple cultivars from all over the world is shipped to all parts of the world. When America was colonized, only species of the wild crab apple were native to the New World. The apple as we know it came to America from Europe and to Europe from the Middle East. A comparative few of the best varieties were propagated for many generations and, indeed, are still produced today.

In 1872, Downing's *Fruits and Fruit Trees in America* listed and described over 1,000 named apple varieties of American origin.

The demands of present day mass marketing and food distribution, the need for large volumes of uniform and consistent supply, the preferences of the consuming public, the economic demand for high annual yields and efficient production of quality fruit that handles, stores and ships well—these and other reasons have eliminated most of the varieties of yesteryear.

It is now well over 300 years since the *Roxbury Russet*, one of the earliest known American cultivars, was first propagated. The *Rhode Island Greening, Winesap, Baldwin, Newtown Pippin* or *Yellow Newtown*, and others known in the early 1700s are still produced commercially today. And a number that were "discovered" at about the time of the Declaration of Independence and in the years prior to the Civil War, are still important commercial cultivars today: *Jonathan, McIntosh, Northern Spy, Rome Beauty, York Imperial, Grimes Golden* and others.

Many of the old favorites of the 1700s and early 1800s, however, like the *Roxbury Russet, Golden Russet, Black Gillflower* or *Sheepnose*; the *Bonum, Chenango, Pound Sweet, Esopus Spitzenburg, Winter Banana, Snow, Smokehouse, Wolf River, Sweet Bough,* and many, many others, while still produced, some even in limited commercial volume, are mostly produced only in "collectors' orchards"—for nostalgic reasons and hobby interests. The names of many of these bespeak the esteem in which they were held: *Seek-No-Further, Nonesuch,* and other superlative descriptive terms.

Horticultural history buffs delight in researching the origins of the names of the old varieties, many of which witness to historical events, places and names.

Even today, however, of the fifteen most important commercial varieties grown, only *Stayman, Delicious, Golden Delicious* and *Cortland* originated since 1850; and only *Cortland* is a product of the scientific plant breeder. All the others are of chance seedling origin.

Today, although most of the old chance seedling selections have gone, modern plant breeding and scientific evaluation and selection of apple cultivars to meet today's need are introducing many superb new selections. Modern commercial fruit farming has placed increased interest and emphasis on seeking out and propagating natural *bud sports* or mutations of major varieties that produce more highly colored fruit. Better yields, more efficient tree size and other growth characteristics are other factors that have accelerated the search for improved variations of all major varieties today.

A few of the many newer, scientifically developed hybrids, or crosses, of other varieties that are gaining popularity include *Kendall*, a cross between *McIntosh* and *Zusoff*; *Spartan*, a cross between *McIntosh* and *Yellow Newtown*; *Idared*, a cross between *Jonathan* and *Wagener*; *Jondel*, a cross between *Jonathan* and *Delicious*; and many others.

It's fun to "Know Your Apples"; exciting to know that this colorful, flavorful and versatile fruit keeps turning up in new and delightful varieties; and, best of all, fun to experience the many flavors and many wonderful ways to serve and enjoy all of them.

Delicious

Delicious, or *Red Delicious* as it is generally called, is the major volume variety produced in the United States, and an increasingly popular variety throughout the world. A chance seedling, it was discovered by Hiatt at Peru, Iowa, in 1872. He found it near an old *Yellow Bellflower* apple tree and because of this surmised that this variety may have been one of the parents. It was cut down twice because it was growing out of the row of other trees. Each time it sprouted up and grew more vigorously than before. Hiatt finally let it grow, and bear fruit, and it was first named "Hawkeye." In 1895 Stark Brothers, a commercial nursery, purchased all rights to the variety and renamed it Delicious. This was one of the first varieties owned and marketed exclusively by a commercial nursery. Hiatt had won prizes with the "Hawkeye" at local horticultural shows. Stark Brothers' representatives first noticed it at one of these shows, and after some difficulty, located the owner and the tree and arranged for its purchase. Today there are more named color sports and strains and tree types of Delicious than of any other variety. Most of the Delicious production today is of these variously named sports of Delicious.

Golden Delicious

Is the *Golden Delicious* a direct descendant of the golden apple of Greek Mythology? We can't prove it, but it's a nice bit of fanciful conjecture! The Greek Gods would have cherished it.

Actually, it was discovered on the Anderson Mullins farm in Clay County, West Virginia, in 1914. Another chance seedling, careful research strongly indicates that it probably came from the *Grimes Golden* variety, pollenated by the *Golden Reinette* variety. Bearing trees of both of these old varieties grew near where the new seedling was discovered. The Reinette is of English origin and was also known as English Pippin. The Grimes Golden is of native West Virginia origin in the late 1700s. Fruit from the original tree of Grimes Golden was sold to New Orleans traders in about the year 1800 and the variety soon became highly prized for its delicate dessert quality and was planted extensively in the Appalachian area.

Fruit from this single seedling tree attracted considerable attention locally, both for its flavor and its excellent keeping quality. It was first called *Mullens' Yellow Seedling*. In the spring of 1914, Mullens sent some of the fruit to Stark Brothers Nursery. This nursery, looking for a companion variety for the already popular Delicious, soon purchased the Mullens' Yellow Seedling tree and renamed it Golden Delicious.

Today, it is the second major volume variety in the United States, a major variety in Europe, and increasing in popularity throughout the world. In the United States, the Golden Delicious is produced in nearly all of our apple-producing states, from Maine to North Carolina and from Virginia to the state of Washington. In Canada, too, it is grown to some extent in all apple-producing provinces.

McIntosh

John McIntosh was the youngest son of a Scottish family that emigrated to America about 1776 and settled in the Mohawk Valley of New York near Schenectady. John was born there in 1777. In 1796, following a disagreement with his parents, he left home and emigrated to Ontario, Canada. He operated a farm along the St. Lawrence River, and in 1811, exchanged farms with his brother-in-law, Edward Doran. It was on this farm, near what is now Dundela, Ontario, that the *McIntosh* apple had its origin.

John salvaged some young seedling apple trees that had grown up in the brush on a section of the farm and transplanted them to a garden area near his home. By 1830, only one of the transplanted trees had survived. The fruit from this tree, however, was greatly admired by the McIntosh family and all who sampled it for its aroma and spritely flavor. John planted seeds from the fruit and sold the seedlings to other settlers in the area. Like all seedlings, none resembled the parent tree. In 1835, however, a wanderer and peddler came through the area who knew how to graft and bud fruit trees. Out of this learning and experience John McIntosh developed an apple tree nursery and began propagating trees that now produced fruit identical to the parent tree. As his farming operation expanded, his wife, Hannah, took over the nursery, and as a result of this, the McIntosh apple was first called "granny's apple" by neighbors and fellow settlers who purchased trees at the McIntosh nursery.

A son. Allan, who continued the nursery business, named the variety McIntosh Red. A younger brother, Sandy, and Allan's youngest son, Harvey, continued the nursery and orchard in the years to follow. Relatives in New York and Vermont planted the variety and extolled its virtues. Through their interest as well as the nursery business itself, the McIntosh apple variety became well known and spread throughout the northeastern United States by the time the original tree, damaged by fire, finally died in 1910 after over 100 years of productive life and a three-generation nursery business dedicated to it.

The *Fameuse* or *Snow* apple variety, a popular variety in the 1700s and 1800s, has long been believed to have been one of the parents of the original seedling McIntosh. More recent horticultural scholars, sleuthing the possible origin of the variety, cite *Fall St. Lawrence*, and *Alexander*, as being two varieties grown in that area in the 1700s and early 1800s that may well have spawned the McIntosh. No one knows for certain.

Crosses of other varieties with McIntosh have created a number of new and promising hybrids, some already well known, including *Cortland, Spartan, Melba, Macoun, Niagara, Puritan* and many others.

McIntosh grows and matures to its crisp, juicy aromatic best in the cooler, late season apple-producing areas of the United States and Canada—around the Great Lakes and in New England states.

Ontario, Quebec, New Brunswick, New York, Michigan, Wisconsin and Minnesota all produce excellent McIntosh. Even in these states and provinces, however, the finest and best-colored fruit are produced where the temperatures remain coolest throughout the summer and fall.

Most aromatic of all our apple varieties, a bowl of McIntosh apples on a table imparts an orchard-fresh aroma to the entire house.

Rome Beauty

In the fall of 1816, a fruit grower, Joel Gillett, brought a number of young apple trees from Putnam's nursery at Marietta, Ohio, to a farm near Proctorville. (Putnam's nursery, started by Rufus Putnam in 1796, preceded Johnny Appleseed's travels in the Ohio Valley country and included a number of eastern apple varieties for which Putnam had brought scion wood from the colonies when he migrated west.)

The next spring, while preparing the trees for planting, Gillett discovered that one had sprouted from the seedling rootstock below the bud union which, of course, meant that it would not produce a tree of the variety he had selected. He discarded the tree and gave it to his son, Alanson, who planted it in the corner of a field away from the family orchard on the banks of Ohio River.

Winning once more against the thousand-to-one odds which over the centuries had produced the comparatively few good varieties among the thousands of seedlings tried and discarded, this one produced such fine apples that it soon became a popular one for further propagation.

About the year 1832, a man by the name of George Walton named the apple *Rome Beauty*—for the Rome township in which the Gillett farm was located and Beauty because of its shape and attractive color. The original tree stood until about the year 1860 when it was washed away by the flood waters of the Ohio.

Like other major varieties, Rome Beauty has seen many more highly colored descendants which have been either mutations or hybridized crosses of Rome Beauty. *Gallia Beauty* is perhaps the best known bud or scion root sport of Rome Beauty. *Monroe*, a cross of Jonathan and Rome, *Ruby*, a cross of Gallia Beauty and Starking Delicious, are three of a number of the hybrid crosses with Rome Beauty parentage.

Rome Beauty is produced in very nearly all the apple producing states and provinces of the United States and Canada.

It became a popular commercial variety largely because of its long storage life and ease of handling without serious bruising, as well as for its attractive color and shape and large size.

Jonathan

A beautiful, brilliant red apple of excellent fragrance and flavor, the *Jonathan* variety was discovered at Woodstock, New York, in 1800. It was known locally as the Rick apple, after the name of the farmer, Philip Rick of Kingston, New York, who found it in his crchard.

It was later renamed Jonathan, not because of Johnny Appleseed, as some have surmised and who was at that time in the midst of his missionary and apple planting travels in the Ohio Valley country, but rather after a man named

Jonathan Hasbrouk, who, along with a Judge J. Buel of Albany, New York, first focused horticultural attention on this variety in 1826.

Jonathan is generally thought to have been a seedling of the popular old Esopus Spitzenburg variety, with the other parent unknown.

By 1845 this variety had received recognition by a number of eastern horticultural societies and was listed in a number of nursery catalogs.

In the first year of the Michigan Pomological Society, in 1870, Jonathan, already being grown extensively in Michigan, was extolled as a very choice apple, of excellent quality and a good keeper. Another major attribute of the Jonathan was that it was a very dependable annual producer.

In New York and in New England, the fruit tended to be small in size and the variety never became a major one for the area. In Michigan and the Ohio Valley area, in the Appalachian area and in the Northwest, it attains better size, color and finish. In the late 1800s and 1900s, it was the leading variety in Michigan and a major variety in a number of other states. Today, the important Jonathan states are Michigan, Ohio, Illinois, Missouri, Washington, Pennsylvania, the Virginias, Colorado and Idaho. Jonathan was the fourth ranking variety in the nation for a number of years and is still one of the top half dozen.

Jonathan has proved to be a great "parent" too, and modern plant breeding has developed a number of excellent new varieties using Jonathan as one of the crosses. A number of natural sports, also, have produced more highly colored fruits than the original tree found at Woodstock, New York.

It is one of the more difficult varieties to store, being susceptible to two or three postharvest conditions which limit its "keepability" in top quality and condition.

The advent of controlled atmosphere storage has been a boon for Jonathan, as it has for McIntosh, making both of these excellent varieties available for consumption during most of the year.

Winesap

Although it is one of our oldest and best known varieties and, for more than a century and a half, one of the most popular, probably less is known about the origin of *Winesap* than any of our other major varieties. Horticultural historians simply failed to record its origin. In 1817, William Coxe wrote that the Winesap was rapidly becoming "the most favorite cider fruit in West Jersey." This is the first early recorded reference to this variety. Because of this, the Winesap is generally believed to have originated in New Jersey prior to 1800.

The Winesap is a deep carmine red, moderately tart and rich in flavor. It is a late-season variety, a good keeper, and for many years was the major variety available from late winter into spring and early summer.

With the advent of controlled atmosphere storage, which has made it possible to store many varieties for longer periods of time, the Winesap has declined in popularity and in supply.

Over the years it has been grown and marketed in all apple-producing sections of the United States and Canada. Today it is produced mainly in Washington, Virginia and West Virginia, with limited production in other states, including New Jersey, Pennsylvania and Indiana.

York Imperial

A variety much in demand for commercial processing, the *York Imperial* is not often found in the fresh produce departments of food stores. Chances are good, however, that you have enjoyed it when eating apple pie or applesauce at your favorite restaurant, or purchasing these processed apple products for home consumption.

Red color sports of this green culinary variety have increased demand for it in the fresh market in recent years.

York Imperial was first discovered on a farm near York, Pennsylvania, about 1830. Children walking home from school in the early spring months discovered that "windfall" apples from a tree along the road, which had "hibernated" under snow and leaves all winter long, were mellow and crisp for eating.

Johnson, who owned the farm and tree, took samples of the fruit to a local nurseryman, Jonathan Jessup, who began propagating and marketing trees of this variety, calling it *Johnson's Fine Winter Apple*. Jessup found little demand for the trees, however, and so discarded his supply of young budded trees in a hollow along the road. Farmers, returning home from market, salvaged some of the trees and planted them on their farms in southern York County. Thus, in this rather unpretentious way, this variety became better known and appreciated for its excellent keeping qualities as well as its culinary attributes, and soon became a popular variety throughout Pennsylvania, Virginia, West Virginia, Maryland and elsewhere.

Charles Downing, horticulturist and writer in the early and mid 1800s, examined some of the fruit, looked into its origin and history, and suggested that it be called York Imperial because of its origin and its "imperial" keeping qualities.

An active apple export business with England in the early 1900s gave the York Imperial the market demand it needed to utilize its increasing production.

British import restrictions in the early 1930s sharply changed the markets for apples in the Appalachian area. York Imperial, being a green apple, found tough competition with the more favored red varieties in the domestic market. But once again good fortune interceded, and the commercial processing industry, starting first as a kind of salvage operation, utilizing the smaller sizes and poorer grades of apples, gradually grew and expanded at about the time of World War II. York Imperial then became a favored variety for processing.

The flesh of the York produces a much prized creamy yellow color in applesauce and canned sliced apples. It has excellent texture and holds its shape well when cooked. These qualifications, along with its good keeping characteristics, its small core and maximum yield of product, its firmness and resistance to bruising, all contributed to making it a top-rated variety for processing. In the early and mid 1930s several red color sports were discovered, which made it more competitive in the fresh market as well.

Stayman

This variety, grown throughout the Appalachian area, and to a lesser extent in the Midwest, originated as a seedling from the Winesap variety. The fruit is a less bright red than Winesap and is usually slightly russeted, particularly around the stem and blossom ends. It is marketed mainly in the Mid-east and Midwest and is not as universally available as some of our other varieties. The *Stayman* was discovered and named by a Dr. J. Stayman at Leavenworth, Kansas, in 1866 and bore its first fruit in 1875. It is often called *Stayman Winesap* or *Stayman's Winesap*.

The Stayman didn't attract a great deal of attention until about 1890 when its good qualities were publicized concurrently by Mr. R. J. Black of Breman, Ohio, and Mr. J. W. Kerr of Denton, Maryland, two horticulturists of the time. Soon after 1900, it was planted extensively in the East and Midwest. Today it is an important variety for the fresh market and for commercial processing in southern Pennsylvania, the Virginias and Maryland, and is produced in limited quantity in New Jersey, Ohio, Missouri, Michigan, Indiana and a few other states.

Newtown Pippin

While the exact date and place of the origin of *Newtown Pippin* is not positively known, the original seedling is believed to have stood near a swamp on the estate of Gersham Moore, in Newtown, Long Island, New York. It died in 1805, an old tree, from excessive cutting of bud and scion wood. Its origin is believed to have been in the early 1700s, though no exact record exists, nor is it known whether the original tree was a *Yellow Newtown* or *Green Newtown*.

The Yellow Newtown (which is really yellow-green when mature) was considered the better apple for export and was far more extensively planted than Green Newtown.

Both varieties, also called *Newtown Pippin* varied considerably depending on the soil and climate where grown. In the 1800s the Yellow Newtown was grown extensively throughout most apple-producing areas of the U.S., doing best in the middle latitude areas of the country. Today it is grown almost exclusively in California and Oregon, with a few still produced in Virginia where it is known as *Albemarle Pippin,* having been so named for Albemarle County where it grows to perfection and where for many years it was felt to be a variety distinct from Yellow Newtown. It was later proved to have been started from scion wood brought to Albemarle County from Philadelphia by Dr. Thomas Walker in 1755.

The Newtown Pippin was the first American variety to be exported in volume to Europe, and the first American variety to be planted extensively in England, in contrast to the many European varieties planted in America. Thomas Jefferson and George Washington both planted this variety and Benjamin Franklin extolled its virtues in Europe.

Andrew Stevenson, as Minister to the Court of St. James

in Queen Victoria's reign, had Albemarle Pippins shipped over from his farm in Albemarle County, Virginia, for his own use. He presented some of them to Queen Victoria, who was so delighted with them that she exempted this variety from a small tax which the Crown imposed on all imported apples. For many years thereafter the Albemarle Pippin, or Newtown Pippin, was by far the most popular apple exported from America to England. Today, nearly 200 years later, it continues to be one of our major export varieties; but now it is exported largely from Oregon rather than Virginia.

Cortland

Of the dozen or so major commercial apple varieties that account for most of our United States and Canadian production today, only the *Cortland* is the result of scientific plant breeding. All the others were chance seedlings or sports, selected and propagated from farm plantings or from untended trees in the wild because of local interest.

Cortland was selected from among a number of carefully cross-pollinated hybrids at the New York State Agricultural Experiment Station at Geneva, New York, and named and introduced for commercial planting in 1915. It is the result of a cross between the McIntosh and the Ben Davis.

Cortland lacks the bright red color and spritely aroma of McIntosh, but has an attractive deep purple-red color of its own, and a greater resistance to bruising acquired from Ben Davis.

It is a superb eating and salad apple, having a snow-white flesh that does not darken as quickly as most other varieties when sliced or diced for salads and fruit cups.

Today the Cortland is produced largely in the areas where McIntosh is grown.

Gravenstein

This red-striped, early fall variety is one of the few volume varieties in America introduced from Europe.

The origin of *Gravenstein* remains in doubt. Some say it originated in the Duke of Augustinberg's garden at Gravenstein, in Holstein, Germany, in the early to mid 1700s. Another account places its origin in the garden of the castle of

Grafenstein in Sleswick, Germany. Others attribute its origin to Italy and its introduction into Germany and Sweden from that country.

Its first introduction to American orchards is also somewhat vague. Early horticultural writers make no mention of it prior to 1822. In 1857 a Captain DeWolfe stated that he had imported Gravenstein apples from Denmark in 1826. In a letter dated October 11, 1829, published in the *New England Farmer* magazine, Judge Buel of Albany, a prominent horticulturist and writer of that period, called attention to Gravenstein and other German varieties and presented trees to members of the Massachusetts Horticultural Society. The variety is generally credited as having been introduced in the Albany, New York, area prior to 1826. After these early importations, it was gradually planted in many other areas of the United States, including mission orchards in parts of California.

The Russians planted Gravenstein and other varieties at Bodega, north of San Francisco, as early as 1820. Most early California plantings were begun about 1850. Thus the Gravenstein variety may have been planted in California before it was introduced to the eastern United States. Today, while grown in minor volume in a number of eastern states, most notably in New England and Delaware, the Gravenstein is largely a California product. In the Sebastopol area of California, it is the major variety for commercial processing into applesauce.

In Nova Scotia, Canada, Gravenstein and a red color sport of Gravenstein, called *Banks,* after a C. E. Banks of Kings County, Nova Scotia, who discovered it in 1880, are still grown quite extensively.

Rhode Island Greening

A highly rated culinary variety, the *Rhode Island Greening* is now produced largely in New York State and used mainly for commercial processing into canned and frozen apple slices and canned applesauce.

This variety is available in the fresh market at harvest time in the areas of production, but seldom marketed very widely.

The origin of the Rhode Island Greening is not known with certainty, but there is little reason to doubt early historical records, which place its origin in Rhode Island near a place known as Green's End in 1748. There a tavern keeper by the name of Green raised apple trees from seed and among the seedling trees he started was one that produced large green apples that were much in demand. Indeed history of the variety indicates that the original tree was ultimately killed from the extensive cutting of buds and scion wood!

The Rhode Island Greening was propagated in other New England states and New York in the mid 1700s. It was introduced into the old Plymouth Colony from Newport in 1765 and from there was carried to the state of Ohio in 1796 by General Putnam when he established a nursery at Marietta some years before Johnny Appleseed planted orchards in that frontier country.

Thus the Rhode Island Greening is one of our earliest known American varieties still being produced in commercial volume.

Northern Spy

The *Northern Spy*, or *Spy* as it is sometimes called, is a large, red, striped or blushed variety—tender, crisp and juicy, with a moderately tart, robust flavor. Highest in vitamin C of all our major American varieties, it is rated one of our finest dessert apples as well as a superb culinary variety. Apple pie made from Northern Spy is in a class by itself, while baked Northern Spy apples impart a flavor experience unequalled by any other variety.

The Northern Spy is produced mostly in New York, Michigan and Ontario, Canada, with small volumes in other northern states and provinces. In the areas of production it is available in late fall and early winter at roadside farm markets and to a limited extent in retail food stores; but the Spy today is utilized almost entirely for commercial processing where it is rated highly for frozen slices.

The Northern Spy originated as a seedling tree at East Bloomfield, New York, in an orchard planted in 1800 by Herman Chapin from seeds brought from Salisbury, Connecticut.

How it got its name is something of a mystery. Perhaps it was because it was discovered at the time when the "underground railroad," which secretly helped fugitive slaves escape to the northern states and to Canada in the years just preceding the Civil War, was in operation. One of the escape routes led through the area in the vicinity of Bloomfield to Sodus Point on Lake Ontario.

The original seedling tree died before bearing fruit, but suckers growing up from the base of the tree were transplanted by a Roswell Humphry, and he produced the first Northern Spy apples.

The Spy was propagated locally in western New York for many years before it attracted the attention of horticulturists in other areas. In about 1840, its qualities were more widely publicized. In 1852 the American Pomological Society listed it as a variety of considerable promise and worthy of general cultivation. By the turn of the century it was extensively planted in the more northern fruit areas of the Northeast, the Great Lakes States and Canada. Today, while it is an important variety in New York, Michigan and Northern Ontario, Canada, it has declined in most other areas.

The Spy has a strong tendency to bear crops only in alternate years and is a late starting variety, often taking seven to ten years to begin to bear crops. For these two major economic reasons, despite its premium quality as a dessert apple and as a processing apple, Northern Spy has declined in popularity and is not currently being extensively planted. It was not until the Delicious variety was discovered that growers and horticulturists began to look seriously for bud sports of all apple varieties. For nearly 100 years no sports of Northern Spy were reported. In the 1920s and thereafter a number were found and named, but none has ever really equalled or exceeded the quality of the original Northern Spy; and none to date has overcome the biennial bearing and slow starting characteristics of the original variety.

Northern Spy is one of the parents of a number of scientifically bred hybrids that are being planted and tested at the present time in the United States and Canada. It is too early to judge these latest introductions as yet; but, again, while Northern Spy transmits many excellent characteristics, it seems to keep its finest attributes—its flavor and crisp, juicy composition—to itself. It may be that, like fine wine, the long years to bearing age and the biennial bearing characteristics of Northern Spy are the price exacted for its excellent quality.

Baldwin

Soon after 1740 the *Baldwin* apple came up as a chance seedling on the farm of John Ball at Wilmington, near Lowell, Massachusetts. For almost 40 years the variety was known

A Basket of Early American Varieties: Lower tier (left to right): Black Gillflower, Fameuse (Snow), Pound Sweet, Winter Banana, Tolman Sweet, Roxbury Russet. Top tier (left to right): Roxbury Russet, Fameuse, Black Gillflower, Esopus Spitzenburg. Top: Winesap.

Lodi

Rambo

Summer Champion

Beacon

Note: The above illustrated single varieties (Lodi, Rambo, Summer Champion, Beacon) are but four of many summer and early fall apple varieties, old and new, available locally each year.

Delicious

Golden Delicious

McIntosh

Jonathan

Rome Beauty

York Imperial

Winesap

Stayman

Newtown Pippin

Gravenstein

Cortland

Northern Spy

R. I. Greening

Baldwin

Wealthy

Grimes Golden

Spartan

Idared

Note: Spartan and Idared are two of many new varieties which are increasing rapidly in popularity and production. Like the many summer and early fall varieties, so too there are many new fall and winter apple varieties that are available locally each fall but are not yet produced in sufficient volume for extensive distribution.

only locally. The Ball farm came into the possession of a man named Butters who gave the name "Woodpecker" to the variety because the tree was a haven for woodpeckers. The apple was known by this name, and as Butters' apple, for quite some time. A surveyor, Deacon Samuel Thompson, brought the variety to the attention of a Colonel Baldwin of Woburn, Massachusetts, who propagated it and publicized it. Because of this it ultimately became known as the Baldwin apple. Early horticultural writers made little mention of Baldwin until 1832 and after. By this time it was a popular and widely planted variety in Massachusetts. In 1852 Hovey published a description of Baldwin and cited it as the most popular variety in New England, much sought after for domestic culinary use as well as for extensive export to the East Indies. It was introduced into New York in about 1850, and for a number of years was the major variety produced in that state.

Today, the Baldwin is still grown in limited quantities in New England and in New York, and while declining rapidly in production after 1945, is still a major apple for commercial processing.

Like other varieties utilized largely for commercial processing, the Baldwin is not easily found in the fresh market. It can usually be purchased at retail farm markets in New England and in New York in the autumn months, but is no longer generally available as a fresh market variety.

Other Varieties

A number of newer varieties are gaining in popularity in the market today. Those who are fortunate enough to visit the many roadside or retail farm markets in the United States and Canada will have the opportunity to see and sample many of these long before they will be available in the metropolitan areas.

Unfortunately one of the less desirable requirements of modern-day mass food distribution is the need to limit the numbers of fresh produce items available in the food store to as few as possible and to those which are available in large enough volume to provide for uniform and consistent distribution to many stores. Thus a half dozen of our major volume apple varieties is about the maximum one can find in today's supermarket at any given time.

Many more varieties than those we have described and illustrated are also available in various sections of the country, in the areas of production. We urge you to try the many different varieties of apples offered in the area where you live. Each is a unique flavor experience and nearly all have fascinating histories.

APPETIZERS

The crisp, tart tang of apples makes them a perfect base for before-dinner appetizers. Wedges, slices or rings, edged with gold or scarlet, add color and appetite appeal to an hors d'oeuvres tray. Serve them with a spread or a dip. Let the calorie conscious nibble on apple alone!

APPLE ANTIPASTO

On each serving plate arrange thin, unpeeled apple slices, strips of green pepper, a mound of cole slaw, a pimiento, one or two sardines, pickled onions, black olives and stuffed olives. Serve olive oil and wine vinegar in cruets to accompany the antipasto.

APPLE ANTIPASTO PLATTER

Unpeeled slices red apples	Salami slices
Blue cheese spread	Cherry tomatoes or
Paprika	· tomato wedges
Maine sardines in oil	Celery
Canned tuna	Black and stuffed olives
Pimientos	

Dip apple slices in lemon juice; spread generously with blue cheese spread; dust with paprika. Arrange on platter with some or all of the other foods listed above. Serve with oil and vinegar. Accompany with thin slices of party rye bread.

APPLE PROSCIUTTO APPETIZER

Roll up tissue-thin slices of Italian prosciutto ham and serve with apple slices and white grapes for a different and delicious first course.

APPLE CANAPÉS

Core apples; do not peel; cut in crosswise ¼-inch-thick slices; then cut each slice in half. Spread with either of the following mixtures:

1. Mash ½ pound liverwurst; blend in 2 tablespoons mayonnaise and dash of Tabasco. Enough for 10 half slices.
2. Combine 1 jar (3 ounces) Smithfield deviled ham with ¼ cup dairy sour cream. Enough for 10 half slices.

APPLE CHEESE CANAPÉS

16 rounds fresh white bread
1 bar (6 ounces) chive cream cheese
16 thin, unpeeled apple rings
Lemon juice
1 jar (5 ounces) sharp Cheddar cheese spread
1 jar (5 ounces) olive-pimiento cheese spread
16 sprigs parsley

Spread bread rounds with chive cream cheese. Place an apple ring on each round. Brush with lemon juice. Blend cheese spreads together. Fill centers of apple rings with heaping spoonful of cheese spread mixture. Top each with a parsley sprig.

APPLE CHEESE DIP

2 jars (5 ounces each) relish cheese spread
½ cup mayonnaise
½ cup dairy sour cream
1 cup freshly grated tart apples
1 teaspoon sugar
Dash Tabasco
½ teaspoon Worcestershire sauce

Combine first 3 ingredients; whip until smooth. Stir in remaining ingredients; mix well. Use as a dip for raw vegetable relishes. Makes about 3 cups.

APPLE CRABMEAT APPETIZER

2 cans (6½ ounces each) crabmeat
6 pitted ripe olives, sliced
2 tablespoons very finely diced Cheddar cheese
1 tablespoon capers
1 teaspoon prepared horseradish
Mayonnaise
6 thick unpeeled apple rings

Flake crabmeat; combine with olives, cheese, capers, horseradish and enough mayonnaise to hold ingredients together.

Put one apple ring on each serving dish; cut into bite-size pieces while keeping in a circle. Place mound of crabmeat on each slice. Makes 6 servings.

APPLE DIP APPETIZER

Cut cored, unpeeled red apples into bite-size chunks; dip in lemon juice; spear on wooden picks; insert picks in whole red apples. Serve with a cheese dip.
Cheese Dip Suggestions:
1. Pineapple cheese spread blended with dairy sour cream.
2. Pimiento cheese spread blended with a little mayonnaise.
3. Cream cheese, softened with heavy cream plus crumbled blue cheese, whipped together to "dipping" consistency.

APPLE GINGER SPARKLE

3 apples	6 maraschino cherries
6 tangerines	Chilled ginger ale

Core and slice apples. Combine with tangerine sections in sherbet glasses. Top with maraschino cherries. Fill glasses with ice-cold ginger ale. Serve as a first course. Makes 6 servings.

APPLE RING SNACK

1 pound cottage cheese	Dash Tabasco
¼ pound blue cheese, crumbled	1 small onion, grated
	¼ cup whipping cream
1 teaspoon Worcestershire sauce	Salt and pepper
	6 red apples

Combine cottage cheese, blue cheese, Worcestershire sauce, Tabasco, onion and cream. Season to taste with salt and pepper. Beat until creamy. Core apples; do not pare; cut crosswise in thin slices. Spread with cottage cheese mixture.

APPLE SALAD APPETIZER

2 red apples	½ cup mayonnaise
2 small yellow onions	¼ cup chili sauce
1 cup diced celery	

Quarter and core apples (do not pare); slice thin; cut each slice in half. Slice onions; separate into rings. Combine apples, onion rings and celery. Combine mayonnaise and chili sauce; add to apple mixture; mix well. Makes 12 small servings.

APPLE SARDINE APPETIZER SALAD

On each plate arrange 1 or 2 romaine leaves, 2 thin slices Bermuda onion, and 3 sardines. Scatter with mixture of sliced celery, sliced sweet gherkins and chopped hard-cooked egg. Arrange unpeeled red apple slices at the side. Serve with tart French dressing or oil and vinegar.

APPLE SNACK TRAY

1 large package (8 ounces) cream cheese
⅓ cup milk
½ cup whipping cream
1 cup finely chopped tart apples
1 cup chopped walnut meats
½ cup finely cut pitted dates
Assorted crisp crackers

Soften cream cheese; whip with milk and cream; stir in apples, walnuts and dates. Makes about 3 cups. Serve with crisp crackers.

BLUE CHEESE DIP

½ pound cream cheese
¼ pound blue cheese
⅓ to ½ cup dairy sour cream*
1 teaspoon prepared horse-radish
¼ teaspoon Tabasco
¼ teaspoon Worcestershire sauce
1 teaspoon prepared mustard
½ teaspoon salt
Paprika

Blend cream cheese and blue cheese with a fork. Whip until light and fluffy. Beat in sour cream. Blend in remaining ingredients. Sprinkle with paprika. Serve with tart apples. Makes 8 servings.

* According to consistency desired.

CALIFORNIA DIP

½ pound cream cheese
3 medium-ripe avocados
2 tablespoons lemon juice
3 tablespoons grated onion
½ teaspoon salt

Soften cream cheese and whip with a fork or electric mixer until fluffy. Peel and stone avocados; mash; add to cream cheese with remaining ingredients. Serve on tray or lazy Susan with apple slices that have been dipped in diluted lemon juice.

CHEESE DIP

½ pound cream cheese
¼ pound blue cheese
Cream

1 teaspoon Worcestershire sauce
Few drops Tabasco
1 tablespoon finely cut chives

Beat cream cheese and blue cheese until well blended; mix in enough cream for good spreading consistency; add remaining ingredients; mix well. Serve with bite-size wedges of red apples skewered with wooden picks.

COTTAGE CHEESE CANAPÉS

½ cup creamed cottage cheese
½ cup finely chopped apples

½ teaspoon celery salt
¼ teaspoon curry powder
Crisp crackers

Combine cheese, apples and seasonings. Mound on crackers. Top each with small wedge of unpeeled red apple. Makes about 1 cup topping—enough for about 18 crackers.

DEVIL DIP

1 cup creamed cottage cheese
½ cup deviled ham
1 teaspoon grated onion

2 tablespoons chopped black olives
1 tablespoon minced pimiento
2 teaspoons dry sherry

Combine all ingredients; mix well. Makes about 1½ cups. Serve with wedges of unpeeled red apple. Provide cocktail picks.

DEVILED APPLE APPETIZER

Core large red apples; do not pare. Cut crosswise in half-inch slices. Spread cut surface with cream cheese. Cut into bite-size portions; arrange on salad greens. Combine 1 small can (2¼ ounces) deviled ham with 3 tablespoons cream cheese. Top apple slices with a spoonful of ham mixture and a slice of stuffed olive.

SNAPPY APPLE DIP

1 cup mayonnaise
½ cup ketchup
2 tablespoons lemon juice
1 tablespoon dry mustard
2 tablespoons prepared horseradish (drained)

2 tablespoons sugar (or to taste)
½ teaspoon Worcestershire sauce
¼ teaspoon pepper
½ teaspoon salt

Combine all ingredients; mix well. Chill. Makes 1½ cups. Serve as a dip for unpeeled red apple slices.

SAVORY CHEESE SPREAD

½ pound cream cheese
3 tablespoons bottled Italian salad dressing
¼ cup light cream
¼ teaspoon salt

2 tablespoons drained sweet pickle relish
2 tablespoons sliced small stuffed olives

Beat cream cheese until soft; add remaining ingredients; mix well. Spread on sliced raw apples. Makes about 1½ cups.

GUACAMOLE APPLE APPETIZER

1 ripe avocado
2 tablespoons lemon juice
½ cup mayonnaise
1 small onion, minced

½ teaspoon salt
⅛ teaspoon Tabasco
4 large red apples

Remove peel and pit from avocado; mash beat, or blend until smooth. Stir in lemon juice, mayonnaise, onion, salt and Tabasco. Chill until ready to serve. Core apples; do not peel; cut crosswise in 12 thick slices; dip in additional lemon juice.

Cut each slice in bite-size wedges; top with mound of avocado mixture. Makes 12 servings.

HERB BUTTER APPLE SNACK

½ pound butter or margarine	1 teaspoon basil
	¼ teaspoon rosemary
1 teaspoon parsley flakes	¼ teaspoon oregano

Whip butter until light and fluffy; stir in herbs. Chill. Serve crisp, cold apples with hot toast or oven-heated Melba toast spread with herb butter mixture.

DIP FOR APPLE CHUNKS

2 large packages (8 ounces each) cream cheese	1 small green pepper, minced
Cream	2 tablespoons grated onion
1 can (4½ ounces) pimientos, minced	2 tablespoons prepared horseradish

Mash cream cheese; beat until fluffy, adding a little cream if necessary. Stir in remaining ingredients. Chill. Makes about 2 cups.

SOUPS

Fruit soups are not well known in this country, but in Europe, especially among Scandinavians, they are an important item on the menu. And to many such soups the apple lends its distinctive flavor.

APPLE CHEESE SOUP

1 can (10½ ounces) condensed cream of chicken soup
1 soup can milk

1 cup grated sharp Cheddar cheese
2 tart apples, diced
1 teaspoon instant onion
1 teaspoon sugar

Combine all ingredients in saucepan; stir over low heat until cheese melts. Blend in electric blender or beat with electric mixer until smooth. Serve hot, garnished with dairy sour cream and additional grated cheese. Makes 3 servings.

CREAMY APPLE SOUP

¼ cup butter or margarine
¼ cup minced onion
2 pounds tart apples
2 cups hot water
4 instant chicken bouillon cubes

¼ teaspoon ginger
⅛ teaspoon nutmeg
2 tablespoons quick-cooking rice cereal
1 can (1 pound) pineapple juice

Melt butter or margarine in saucepan. Add onion; cook 2 minutes. Pare, core and cut up apples; add to saucepan with water, chicken bouillon cubes and spices. Cover; bring to boil; cook 10 minutes or until apples are soft. Add cereal. Put through food mill or sieve, or blend half at a time for ½ minute in electric blender. Return to saucepan. Add pineapple juice. Bring to boil; simmer 5 minutes, stirring frequently. Serve hot or chilled, with chopped parsley and croutons. Makes 6 servings.

CURRIED APPLE SOUP

2 large sweet onions, coarsely chopped
¼ cup butter or margarine
2 tablespoons curry powder
2 tablespoons cornstarch
¼ cup cold water
6 envelopes instant chicken broth mix
1 quart hot water
4 egg yolks, slightly beaten
1 cup whipping cream
2 apples, peeled, cored and chopped fine
Juice of 1 lemon
Salt and freshly ground black pepper
Thin slices unpeeled red apple

Cook onions in butter until soft but not brown. Stir in curry powder. Blend cornstarch and cold water; add. Dissolve instant broth mix in hot water; add. Stir over low heat until slightly thickened and clear. Add a little of the hot mixture to egg yolks; return to remaining hot mixture; cook and stir about 1 minute. Add cream. Remove from heat. Add diced apples. Put through electric blender or press through food mill or fine sieve. Add lemon juice. Season to taste with salt and pepper. Serve hot or chilled, garnished with thin slices of unpeeled red apple. Makes 8 servings.

DANISH APPLE SOUP

1 pound tart apples
5 cups water, divided
Grated peel of 1 small lemon
1 teaspoon cinnamon
½ teaspoon salt
3 tablespoons cornstarch
2 tablespoons sugar
½ cup white Tokay wine
Zwieback (optional)

Core apples; quarter; do not pare. Cook in 2½ cups of the water until soft. Add lemon peel and cinnamon. Put through food mill or sieve. Add remaining water and salt. Blend cornstarch with a little cold water; add to soup; cook, stirring, until slightly thickened and clear. Cook 10 minutes longer. Add sugar (amount depends on tartness of apples, but soup should not lose *all* its tart flavor). Add wine. Serve hot. If desired, pour over crushed Zwieback in soup plates. Makes 8 generous servings.

ONE-OF-A-KIND SOUP

1 medium potato
1 medium onion
1 cucumber
1 celery heart with leaves
1 tart apple
1 teaspoon salt
1 pint chicken stock

1 cup light cream
1 tablespoon butter or margarine
1 scant teaspoon curry powder
Few grains pepper
Chopped chives

Peel and chop vegetables and apple. Add salt to chicken stock; add chopped vegetables and fruit; simmer until tender. Put through food mill or fine sieve, or blend in electric blender, until smooth. Stir in cream, butter, curry powder and pepper. Chill thoroughly. Sprinkle with chopped chives. Makes 6 servings.

MAIN DISHES

In the realm of main dishes the apple can lend an epicurean touch. Add chopped apple to an everyday meat loaf for delightful new flavor. Roll fish fillets around a savory stuffing that contains crunchy bits of apple. Top pork chops with apple rings and bake them in a sweet-sour sauce. But there is no need to go on—read the recipes that follow and marvel at the apple's versatility.

APPLE MEAT LOAF

2½ pounds lean beef, ground
1½ cups packaged stuffing mix
2 cups finely chopped apples
3 eggs
2 teaspoons salt
2 tablespoons prepared mustard
1 large onion, minced
3 tablespoons prepared horseradish
¾ cup ketchup

Combine all ingredients; mix thoroughly. Pack into greased loaf pan 8" x 5" x 3". Bake at 350° for 1 hour and 15 minutes.

APPLESAUCE MEAT BALLS

¾ pound finely ground lean beef
¼ pound ground pork shoulder
½ cup fine soft bread crumbs
1 egg
1 cup unsweetened apple-sauce
2 tablespoons grated onion
1 teaspoon salt
⅛ teaspoon pepper
⅓ cup ketchup
¼ cup water

Combine all ingredients except ketchup and water; mix lightly. Form into 2-inch balls. Brown in hot vegetable oil. Place browned meat balls in baking dish. Combine ketchup

41

and water; pour over meat balls. Cover; bake at 350° for
1½ hours. Serve hot. Makes 4 servings.

MEAT BALLS GENEVA

2 pounds lean beef, ground
3 cups soft bread crumbs
2 eggs
1 can (1 pound) applesauce
¼ cup minced onion
2 teaspoons salt
⅔ cup ketchup
½ cup water

Combine all but last 2 ingredients; mix lightly. Shape into
balls about 2 inches in diameter. Brown on both sides in a
little hot fat or vegetable oil; transfer to baking dish. Combine ketchup and water; pour over meat balls. Cover; bake
at 350° for 1½ hours. Makes 6 to 8 servings.

APPLE CURRY

1 pound stewing lamb
3 tablespoons vegetable oil
1 onion, chopped fine
1 garlic clove, minced
1 tablespoon curry powder
1 teaspoon paprika
½ teaspoon powdered
  ginger
¼ teaspoon sugar
¼ teaspoon chili powder
1 can (6 ounces) tomato
  paste
2 cups chopped apple

Cut lamb in 1-inch pieces. Heat oil in skillet. Sauté onion
and garlic in oil until golden brown. Add curry powder,
paprika, ginger, sugar and chili powder; cook until brown.
Add lamb; brown on all sides. Add tomato paste and enough
boiling water to cover. Cover; cook 20 minutes. Add apples;
cook 10 minutes longer. Serve with rice. Serves about 5.

BOMBAY CURRY

1 pound stewing lamb
  (weight after boning)·
3 tablespoons vegetable oil
1 onion, chopped fine
1 garlic clove, minced
1 tart apple, chopped
1 tablespoon curry powder
1 teaspoon paprika
½ teaspoon powdered
  ginger
¼ teaspoon sugar
¼ teaspoon chili powder
1 can (6 ounces) tomato
  paste
1 cup boiling water (about)

Cut lamb in 1-inch pieces. Heat oil in skillet. Sauté onion,
garlic and apple in oil until golden brown. Add curry pow-

der, paprika, ginger, sugar and chili powder; cook till quite brown. Add lamb; brown on all sides. Add tomato paste and enough boiling water to cover. Cover; cook about 30 minutes. Meanwhile, prepare 1 package precooked rice according to directions, adding ¼ teaspoon powdered turmeric to the water to tint the rice deep yellow. Serve with curried lamb. Makes 4 servings.

EAST INDIAN LENTEN CURRY

1 large sweet onion, sliced thin	1 tablespoon sugar
	1 tablespoon vinegar
3 medium tart apples, chopped	2 cans (11¼ ounces each) condensed green pea soup
2 tablespoons butter or margarine	1 cup water
1 tablespoon curry powder	9 hard-cooked eggs, halved

Cook onion and apples in butter or margarine until soft but not brown. Combine curry powder, sugar and vinegar; stir into onion-apple mixture; cook 5 minutes. Combine soup and water; add. Simmer 15 minutes. Add eggs; heat through. Serve with parslied rice and curry accompaniments such as peanuts, chutney, coconut and raisins. Makes 6 servings.

ENGLISH LAMB CHOPS WITH APPLE CURRY SAUCE

2 tablespoons vegetable oil	2 tablespoons curry powder
1 large sweet onion, thinly sliced	2 cups chicken broth
	1 tablespoon lemon juice
2 cups chopped apples	½ cup flaked coconut
3 tablespoons flour	6 English lamb chops*
1 teaspoon salt	4 cups hot parslied rice
¼ teaspoon pepper	

Heat oil in frying pan. Cook onion and apples in oil over low heat until tender but not brown. Combine flour, salt, pepper and curry powder; blend in. Add broth and lemon juice. Cook and stir over low heat until slightly thickened. Cover; cook 20 minutes, stirring often. Add coconut. Meanwhile broil lamb chops to desired degree of doneness (15 to 20 minutes), turning once, with surface of meat 3 to 4 inches

* Have double lamb chops boned and rolled around lamb kidneys at your meat market.

below source of heat. Serve chops on hot parslied rice with curry sauce on the side. Makes 6 servings.

APPLE-CROWNED PORK CHOPS

6 loin pork chops
1 medium red onion
2 or 3 tart red apples
½ cup golden raisins
1 tablespoon brown sugar
1 teaspoon salt
Few grains pepper

¼ teaspoon nutmeg
½ teaspoon basil
⅛ teaspoon cloves
1 cup water
2 tablespoons red currant jelly

Brown pork chops on both sides in their own fat. Transfer to baking dish. Slice onion thin; core apples; cut in sixths (do not peel). Cover raisins with boiling water; let stand until plumped; drain. Cover chops with onion slices; arrange apples on onion. Scatter raisins over all. Combine brown sugar, salt, pepper, nutmeg, basil and cloves. Sprinkle over surface. Pour water into baking dish. Cover. Bake at 350° for 1½ hours. Remove cover during last half hour of baking time. Arrange chops and topping on serving platter. Stir currant jelly into sauce in pan; pour over all. Makes 6 servings.

APPLE PORK CHOP SUEY

1½ pounds lean boneless pork
4 tablespoons vegetable oil
3 medium onions, sliced
1½ cups water
1 can bean sprouts
1 teaspoon Ac'cent

2 cups slivered celery
2 apples, cored and thinly sliced
Soy sauce to taste
3 tablespoons cornstarch
¼ cup cold water

Cut pork in narrow strips about 2 inches long. Brown in hot oil, adding onions during last few minutes to brown lightly. Add water, liquid from bean sprouts and Ac'cent; cover; simmer until meat is thoroughly cooked, 20 to 30 minutes. Add celery and apples; continue cooking about 10 minutes. Add soy sauce. Blend cornstarch and cold water; add. Stir until thickened and clear. Add bean sprouts; bring to boiling point. Serve with rice. Makes 6 servings.

APPLE-SMOTHERED PORK CHOPS

6 loin pork chops, 1 inch thick
1/4 teaspoon salt
1/4 teaspoon sage
3 tart apples
3 tablespoons molasses

3 tablespoons flour
2 cups hot water
1 tablespoon vinegar
1/2 teaspoon salt
1/3 cup raisins

Sprinkle chops with 1/4 teaspoon salt and sage. Brown slowly in hot skillet. Place in large baking dish. Pare, core and slice apples in 1/4 inch slices or rings; arrange on chops. Pour molasses over apples. Add flour to fat in skillet; cook until brown, stirring constantly. Add water; stir until mixture boils. Add vinegar, salt and raisins. Pour over chops and apples. Cover and bake at 350° about 1 hour, or until apples are tender. Makes 6 servings.

APPLE-STUFFED SPARERIBS

1 package bread stuffing mix
1/2 cup chopped onions
2 cups chopped apples

1/8 teaspoon each powdered mace, sage, nutmeg and cloves
2 matching racks of spareribs

Prepare stuffing as directed on package, adding onions, apples and spices; mix well. Spread on rack of spareribs; top with second rack; tie together securely with white string. Put in roasting pan with 1/2 cup hot water; cover. Roast at 350° for about 3 hours or until done. Remove cover during last hour of roasting. Makes 8 generous servings.

BAKED PORK CHOPS NORMANDY

6 thick pork chops (about 3 to a pound)
Salt and pepper
Apple cider

1 can (20 ounces) pie-sliced apples
1/2 teaspoon cinnamon
1/8 teaspoon ground cloves
1/4 teaspoon nutmeg

Brown pork chops on both sides in their own fat. Place in baking dish; sprinkle with salt and pepper. Add enough apple

cider to cover chops. Cover pan; bake at 350° for 1 hour.
Top with drained apple slices; sprinkle with spices. Add syrup
from can. Return to oven, uncovered. Bake 20 minutes
longer. Makes 6 servings.

PORK AND APPLE LOAF

2 cups soft bread crumbs
½ cup evaporated milk
1 egg, beaten
3 cups ground leftover
   cooked pork
2 tart apples, pared and
   cored

1 medium onion
½ teaspoon salt
Few grains pepper
1 teaspoon Ac'cent
⅛ teaspoon rosemary

Combine bread crumbs, evaporated milk and egg; let stand
½ hour. Put pork, apples and onion through food chopper, using fine knife; add crumb mixture. Add seasonings; mix well.
Pack into 9" x 5" x 3" loaf pan. Bake at 350° about 45
minutes.

ROAST STUFFED SHOULDER OF PORK

1 medium onion, chopped
   fine
¼ cup butter or margarine
1 teaspoon salt
Few grains pepper
⅛ teaspoon thyme

2½ cups soft bread crumbs
1¾ cups chopped apple
½ cup boiling water
5 pounds boned pork
   shoulder with pocket

Cook onion in butter or margarine until golden brown. Add
salt, pepper, thyme, bread crumbs, apples and water; mix
thoroughly. Fill shoulder pocket with stuffing mixture; fasten
edges with skewers. Rub outside of meat with salt and pepper. Place on rack in open roaster. Bake at 350° for about
3 hours, or until tender.

STUFFED PORK CHOPS

6 pork chops, cut 1¼
   inches thick
Salt and pepper
¾ cup seedless raisins
½ cup chopped celery

½ cup chopped green
   pepper
2 tablespoons minced onion
1 cup chopped apple
1 cup apple cider

Slit chops through from sides to bone; sprinkle with salt and
pepper. Rinse raisins in hot water; drain. Combine raisins,

celery, green pepper, onion and apple. Fill slits in chops generously with this stuffing. Fasten with wooden picks. Brown chops on both sides. Place in casserole; sprinkle remaining stuffing over chops; add cider; cover. Bake at 350° for 1½ hours. Thicken gravy if desired. Makes 6 servings.

PORK AND APPLE SHEPHERD'S PIE

2 to 3 cups cubed leftover roast pork
2 tablespoons vegetable oil
2 cans (10½ ounces each) mushroom gravy
1 teaspoon salt
Few grains pepper
1 large onion, thinly sliced
¼ teaspoon rosemary
3 cups sliced tart apples
2 tablespoons lemon juice
3 tablespoons sugar
1 cup water
2 cups well-seasoned instant mashed potatoes
Melted butter or margarine

Brown pork cubes in the oil. Add mushroom gravy, salt, pepper, onion and rosemary. Simmer, uncovered, 15 minutes. Meanwhile, sprinkle apple slices with lemon juice; add sugar and 1 cup water. Add apple mixture to pork mixture. Simmer 15 minutes longer, or until onion and apples are tender. Thicken gravy, if desired. Turn into casserole. Prepare instant mashed potatoes as directed on package. Spoon around edge of casserole. Brush potatoes with melted butter or margarine. Bake at 425° for 12 to 15 minutes, or until potatoes are golden brown. Makes 4 to 6 servings.

SWEET AND PUNGENT PORK CHOPS

6 loin pork chops, 1 inch thick
½ teaspoon salt
3 large tart apples
5 tablespoons flour
3 tablespoons molasses
2 cups hot water
1 tablespoon cider vinegar
⅓ cup golden raisins
12 maraschino cherries

Score fat edges of chops; brown fat edges in frying pan, then brown chops on both sides. Arrange in shallow baking dish. Sprinkle with salt. Core apples; do not peel; cut into thick rings. Place on chops. Add flour to fat in frying pan; stir until browned. Combine molasses and water; add; stir over low heat until mixture thickens. Add vinegar and raisins;

pour over chops and apples. Cover; bake at 350° for 1 hour. Add maraschino cherries. Makes 6 servings.

APPLE-STUFFED SAUSAGE ROLL

2 cups finely chopped apples
⅓ cup finely chopped onion
1 cup soft bread crumbs

1 cup wheat germ
2 pounds bulk pork sausage

Combine apples, onion, bread crumbs and wheat germ; mix well. Pat sausage into oblong about ½ inch thick. Spread with apple stuffing. Roll up like jelly roll. Place in shallow pan. Bake at 350° for about 1 hour. Makes 8 to 10 servings.

ARMAGH PIE

1 pound pork sausage links
2 apples, sliced
2 onions, sliced
1 tablespoon flour

Salt and pepper to taste
1 cup stock or bouillon
2 to 3 cups hot mashed
    potatoes

Fry sausages slowly until golden brown; drain; put in 9-inch pie pan. Fry apples and onions in sausage fat; drain; place in pie pan with sausages. Leave 1 tablespoon fat in frying pan. Brown flour in fat; add seasonings and stock; stir until thickened. Pour over sausages, apples and onions. Mix lightly with fork. Top with mashed potatoes. Bake at 350° until potatoes are golden brown. Makes 4 or 5 servings.

BAKED APPLES WITH SAUSAGE STUFFING

½ pound pork sausage
    meat
1 cup diced celery
½ cup minced onion
6 cups small bread cubes
1 tablespoon flour

1 cup boiling water
1 tablespoon minced parsley
1 teaspoon poultry
    seasoning
6 large baking apples
6 teaspoons currant jelly

Combine sausage, celery and onion in frying pan. Cook over low heat until sausage is browned and celery is tender. Add sausage mixture to bread cubes; save drippings in pan. Blend flour with drippings; add boiling water gradually. Cook over low heat, stirring until smooth and thickened; pour over sausage-bread mixture. Add parsley and poultry seasoning. Core apples; pare about ¼ of the way down. Fill centers with some of the sausage mixture and top with currant jelly. Pile remaining stuffing in center of baking dish and arrange apples around it. Bake at 350° for 1 hour, or until apples are tender. Makes 6 servings.

GRILLED APPLES, PINEAPPLE AND SAUSAGE

2 large tart apples
16 pork sausages

Sugar
8 slices pineapple

Core apples; do not pare. Cut in 8 thick rings. Cook sausages; keep warm. Sprinkle apple rings with a little sugar; sauté in a little of the sausage fat until tender, turning to brown on both sides. Sauté pineapple slices in the same way, omitting sugar. Place apple rings on pineapple slices; top with sausages. Makes 8 servings.

KING-SIZE BREAKFAST

1 pound bulk pork sausage
3 or 4 tart apples

6 slices French toast

Form sausage meat into 12 patties. Cook slowly until brown, crisp and thoroughly done; drain on absorbent paper; keep warm. Core apples, do not pare; cut into ½-inch-thick rings. Cook in sausage fat until tender, turning to brown on both sides. Arrange 2 apple rings on each slice of French toast. Top each apple ring with sausage patty. Serve at once, with maple syrup if desired. Makes 6 servings.

SAUSAGE APPLE ROLL-UPS

1 pound pork sausage links
2¼ cups milk
1 egg, beaten
2 cups pancake mix

2 tablespoons melted butter
or margarine
1 cup grated raw apples

Place sausages in cold skillet; cook slowly over low heat, turning often, until brown and crisp. Meanwhile, add milk and egg to pancake mix; beat smooth. Stir in melted butter and grated apples. Pour batter on hot griddle, making pancakes about 4 inches in diameter. Cook until brown underneath and bubbly on top. Turn; brown other side. Drain sausages on absorbent paper. Roll each link in a pancake. Serve with maple syrup. Makes about 12 roll-ups.

HAM 'N' APPLES

6 large slices baked ham,
  ¼ inch thick
3 tablespoons prepared
  mustard
3 unpeeled red apples,
  sliced
3 tablespoons lemon juice

⅔ cup firmly packed brown
  sugar
1 tablespoon grated orange
  peel
3 tablespoons flour

Arrange 3 slices ham in shallow baking dish; spread with half the mustard. Top with half the apple slices. Sprinkle with half the lemon juice. Combine remaining ingredients; sprinkle half over apples. Repeat. Bake at 350° about 35 minutes or until apples are tender. Makes 4 to 6 servings.

HAM SLICE DIXIE

1 center slice ready-to-eat
  ham, 1½ inches thick
½ cup crunch-style peanut
  butter
4 red apples
¼ cup firmly packed brown
  sugar

½ teaspoon cinnamon
⅛ teaspoon ground cloves
¼ teaspoon nutmeg
⅛ teaspoon allspice
¼ cup golden raisins

Slash fat edges of ham; place in open roasting pan; spread with peanut butter. Core and slice apples (do not pare); set slices in one or two rows on ham slice and around ham. Combine brown sugar, spices and raisins; scatter over apples. Bake at 375° for 45 minutes. Makes 6 servings.

UPSIDE-DOWN HAM PATTIES

1 pound ground, cooked
  ham
½ cup soft bread crumbs
1 teaspoon prepared
  mustard
1 egg
2 tablespoons milk

1½ tablespoons butter or
  margarine
3 tablespoons maple syrup
4 cored, unpeeled apple
  rings
4 maraschino cherries
4 whole cloves

Combine ham, crumbs, mustard, egg and milk; mix well; form into 4 patties. Melt butter in small baking pan; add maple syrup; spread evenly over bottom of pan. Add apple rings; place cherry in center of each ring. Place ham patties on apple rings. Stick 1 whole clove in center of each patty. Bake at 375° for 35 to 40 minutes. Baste once during baking with syrup in pan. Remove cloves. Serve upside down. Makes 4 servings.

HAM SLICE WITH APPLES

1 slice ready-to-eat ham, 1 inch thick
Powdered cloves
Powdered cinnamon

1 can (20 ounces) pie-sliced apples or 3 cups fresh apple slices
½ cup firmly packed brown sugar*
½ cup water

Slash fat on ham slice at 1-inch intervals. Brown on both sides in hot frying pan. Springle lightly with spices. Drain apple slices; arrange on ham. Sprinkle with brown sugar. Add water to frying pan; cover. Simmer 15 minutes, if canned apples are used; 30 minutes for fresh apple slices. Makes 6 servings.

* If tart fresh apples are used, increase sugar to ¾ cup.

APPLE-CHICKEN STEW

3 chicken breasts (or 6 halves)
6 chicken legs
4 cups cold water
2 teaspoons salt
¼ teaspoon pepper

1 bunch carrots
3 medium apples
1 can (1 pound) boiled onions
¼ cup flour
½ cup cold water
1 green pepper, diced

Cover chicken pieces with 4 cups cold water. Bring to boil. Add salt and pepper. Lower heat to simmer. Scrape carrots; cut in 2-inch pieces; add. Simmer ½ hour. Core and peel apples; cut in eighths; add with drained onions; simmer ½ hour longer or until all ingredients are tender. Strain off broth; measure 3 cups. Blend flour and ½ cup cold water; add to broth; cook and stir over low heat until thickened.

Pour over chicken and vegetables; add green pepper. Reheat.
Makes 6 servings.

CHICKEN McINTOSH

2 cups diced leftover
  chicken
2 cans (10½ ounces each)
  chicken gravy
3 cups cooked buttered rice

¾ cup chopped peanuts
1 cup cubed, unpeeled red
  apples

Combine chicken and gravy; heat. Meanwhile, combine rice
and peanuts. Pour chicken into serving dishes; add apple
cubes. Serve with peanut rice. Makes 4 servings.

SHERRIED CHICKEN AND APPLES

2 or 3 large red apples
1 tablespoon lemon juice
¼ cup dry sherry
¼ cup firmly packed brown
  sugar

Flour
½ cup butter or margarine
Sugar and cinnamon

Core apples but do not pare; cut in sixths. Combine lemon
juice, sherry and brown sugar; pour over apple wedges and
let stand 1 hour. Drain apple wedges; dip in flour. Fry
slowly in butter, turning once, until golden brown and tender.
Sprinkle with sugar and cinnamon. Serve hot, with chicken.*
Makes 4 servings.

*Chicken:

½ cup flour, divided
1 teaspoon paprika
1 teaspoon salt
¼ teaspoon pepper

1 frying chicken (about 3½
  pounds, cut up)
¼ cup vegetable oil
½ cup apple cider
¼ cup dry sherry
2 cups light cream

Combine ¼ cup flour, paprika, salt and pepper; coat chicken
pieces with this mixture. Brown in hot oil. Add cider; cover;
simmer until tender (30 to 40 minutes). Add sherry; cook
2 minutes longer. Remove chicken to hot platter. Add remain-

ing flour to pan; blend with drippings. Add cream; stir over low heat until smooth and thickened; spoon over chicken. Makes 4 servings.

APPLE BREAD STUFFING

2 cups chopped tart apples	1 tablespoon lemon juice
5 cups soft bread crumbs	1 teaspoon grated lemon
½ cup raisins	peel
2 tablespoons melted butter	½ teaspoon cinnamon
or margarine	½ teaspoon salt
¼ cup sugar	¼ cup apple juice

Combine all ingredients. Mix well. Use to stuff pork shoulder or duck. Makes about 5 cups stuffing.

APPLE CORN BREAD STUFFING

¼ cup minced onion	1 cup diced, unpeeled red
⅓ cup melted fat	apples
(from duck or goose)	1 teaspoon poultry
4 cups crumbled corn bread	seasoning
	Few grains pepper
	½ cup hot giblet stock

Cook onion in fat until golden brown; combine with remaining ingredients; mix well. Makes enough stuffing for 5 or 6 pound duck. Double recipe for 10 to 12 pound goose.

ROAST DUCKLING WITH APPLE-SESAME STUFFING

2 ducklings (about 5 pounds	2 teaspoons poultry
each)	seasoning
2 packages stuffing mix	¼ teaspoon coarse black
½ cup diced celery	pepper
¼ cup dried parsley flakes	½ cup toasted* sesame
4 tart apples, chopped	seeds
1½ teaspoons salt	½ cup giblet stock
	1 tablespoon instant minced
	onion

Wash ducklings inside and out; pat dry. Cook giblets to make stock. Prepare stuffing mix as directed on package. Add next 7 ingredients; mix thoroughly. Pour hot stock on onion; let

* To toast sesame seeds: Spread seeds in shallow pan. Toast at 350° for 20 to 25 minutes.

stand 5 minutes; add; mix thoroughly. If stuffing is not moist enough, add a little more stock to taste. Stuff and truss ducklings; place on rack in large open roasting pan. Do not add water; do not cover. Roast in moderate oven, 350°, about 2½ hours, or until thoroughly done (25 to 30 minutes per pound). Makes 8 servings.

APPLE RAISIN STUFFING

½ cup minced onion
2 cups diced apples
4 cups lightly packed soft
  bread crumbs
½ cup raisins
¾ teaspoon salt

Few grains pepper
1 to 2 teaspoons poultry
  seasoning
2 tablespoons sugar
½ cup melted butter or
  margarine

Combine all ingredients; mix well. Makes enough to stuff a 6 to 7 pound capon or "apartment-size" turkey (8 to 10 pounds).

APPLE SWEET POTATO STUFFING

2 cups sliced, tart apples
4 cups sliced raw sweet
  potatoes
1 teaspoon poultry
  seasoning

1 teaspoon salt
Few grains pepper
½ cup dark corn syrup
Apple water

Cook apples and potato slices separately in a little water until just tender. Drain; save water that apples cooked in. Combine and mash. Add poultry seasoning, salt, pepper, corn syrup and enough apple water to give desired consistency. Use to stuff a 5 to 6 pound duck.

BRAZIL NUT APPLE STUFFING

½ package prepared
  stuffing mix
½ teaspoon cinnamon
¼ teaspoon ginger
¼ teaspoon nutmeg

¼ cup butter or margarine
½ cup chopped Brazil nuts
½ cup water
¼ cup raisins
¾ cup diced apple

Turn stuffing into bowl; add cinnamon, ginger and nutmeg; toss to distribute seasonings. Melt butter in a skillet; add Brazil nuts; cook until light brown—about 5 minutes. Add water and raisins; bring to boil. Pour over stuffing; stir in diced apple. Makes enough stuffing for one 4-lb chicken.

APPLE WHOLE WHEAT STUFFING

1½ cups chopped apples	1 tablespoon sugar
3½ cups whole wheat bread crumbs	1 teaspoon grated lemon peel
⅓ cup raisins	¼ teaspoon cinnamon
¼ cup melted butter or margarine	½ teaspoon salt
	¼ cup water

Combine all ingredients; mix well. Makes enough stuffing for 4 to 5 pound chicken. (Or stuffing may be baked separately in greased loaf pan at 375° for 30 minutes.)

APPLE CASSEROLE MEDLEY

1 package (8 ounces) elbow macaroni	cheese
3 cups well-seasoned medium white sauce	3 large or 4 medium apples
2 cups grated sharp Cheddar	8 frankfurters
	½ cup buttered crumbs

Cook and drain macaroni. Combine white sauce and cheese; stir until cheese melts. Core, pare and dice 2 large apples; add. Spoon half the mixture into large casserole. Slice 2 or 3 frankfurters; scatter on top. Add remaining macaroni mixture. Top with buttered crumbs; bake at 350° for 15 minutes. Cut remaining frankfurters in half; score. Arrange in a wheel on top of casserole with unpeeled apple wedges between. Bake 15 minutes longer. Makes 8 to 10 servings.

APPLE CHECKERBOARD CASSEROLE

6 tart apples	1 small onion, grated
1 can (1 pound) kernel corn, drained	¼ teaspoon Tabasco
2 cups medium white sauce	3 strips bacon
1 teaspoon Worcestershire sauce	Packaged sliced American cheese (about 2 slices)

Core and pare apples; cut in eighths. Arrange in shallow baking dish with corn. Combine white sauce, Worcestershire sauce, grated onion and Tabasco; pour over apples and corn, lifting with fork to let white sauce penetrate. Cut bacon strips in thirds; fry lightly; arrange on top of baking dish, alternating with squares of cheese of the same size. Bake at 350° for about 15 minutes, or until cheese melts slightly and is tinged with brown. Makes 6 servings.

APPLE-CRABMEAT RAMEKINS

6 tablespoons butter or margarine
1 medium onion, finely chopped
6 tablespoons flour
½ teaspoon salt
Few grains pepper
½ teaspoon paprika
2 cups milk
½ cup light cream

1 can (3 ounces) broiled sliced mushrooms
2 cans (6½ ounces each) crabmeat
1 can (20 ounces) pie-sliced apples
½ cup dry white wine
2 tablespoons snipped parsley
¾ cup buttered bread crumbs

Melt butter in frying pan; add onion; cook over low heat until onion is soft but not brown. Blend in flour, salt, pepper and paprika. Add milk and cream; stir over low heat until thickened. Drain mushrooms; add. Flake crabmeat, removing bits of cartilage; add apple slices, wine and parsley; mix well. Heat to serving temperature. Spoon into ramekins. Scatter buttered bread crumbs on top. Broil, with surface of food 4 inches below heat, until crumbs are brown. Makes 4 to 6 servings, depending on size of ramekins.

APPLE SEASHELL LENTEN CASSEROLE

2 cups cooked shell macaroni
2 cans (7 ounces each) chunk-style tuna
2 large red apples, diced
1 medium green pepper, diced
½ cup sliced, pitted black olives

2 cans (10½ ounces each) condensed cream of celery soup
1 cup milk
½ cup buttered bread crumbs
½ cup dairy sour cream

Combine first 5 ingredients; mix well. Turn into casserole. Combine soup and milk; pour over apple mixture; stir lightly

with fork. Top with buttered bread crumbs. Bake at 350°
for 5 minutes. Top with sour cream; serve at once. Makes
6 servings.

APPLE TUNA CASSEROLE

2 cans (6½ or 7 ounces
    each) tuna
½ cup chopped onion
1 cup sliced celery
1 can (10½ ounces)
    condensed cream of celery
    soup

¼ cup milk
¼ teaspoon marjoram
½ teaspoon Tabasco
1 can (20 ounces) pie-sliced
    apples
1 cup grated American
    cheese
½ cup buttered bread
    crumbs

Drain oil from tuna into 2-quart heatproof casserole; add
onion and celery. Cook until tender, but not brown. Remove
from heat; stir in soup, milk, marjoram, tuna, Tabasco and
drained apple slices.* Top with cheese. Sprinkle with bread
crumbs. Bake at 425° for about 25 minutes. Makes 4 to 6
servings.

* If desired, reserve enough apple slices to circle edge of casserole.

CORNISH CASSOULET

2 teaspoons instant minced
    onion
2 tablespoons water
2 tablespoons vegetable oil
½ pound sweet Italian
    sausage
2 Rock Cornish hens,
    split in half
½ teaspoon salt

3 tart apples, peeled and
    sliced
1 green pepper, cut in rings
1 can (1 pound 4 ounces)
    white kidney beans
    (Cannellini)
¼ teaspoon Tabasco
1 teaspoon Worcestershire
    sauce

Combine onion and water; let stand until water is absorbed.
Heat oil in large skillet. Cut sausages in chunks; brown in
oil; remove. Rub Cornish hens with salt; brown in same skillet; remove. Add apples and green pepper rings to skillet;
cook 5 minutes. Add beans, Tabasco, Worcestershire sauce
and onions; mix well. Spoon bean mixture into 4 individual

casseroles; place hens on top; cover. Bake at 350° for 45 to 60 minutes, or until hens are done. Makes 4 servings.

APPLE ZODIAC CASSEROLE

4 cups thinly sliced sweet potatoes
4 cups thinly sliced tart apples
2 teaspoons instant minced onion
2 teaspoons salt

¾ cup maple-blended syrup
¾ cup apple cider
½ cup melted butter or margarine
12 brown 'n' serve pork sausages

Arrange alternate layers of sweet potato and apple slices in greased 2-quart casserole, sprinkling each layer with instant minced onion and salt. Combine syrup, cider and melted butter; pour over all. Cover; bake at 350° for 1 hour. Arrange sausages on top; bake, uncovered, 15 to 20 minutes longer, or until sausages are brown and apples and sweet potatoes are tender. Makes 6 servings.

CHICKEN APPLE SCALLOP

2 cups cubed cooked or canned chicken
1 tablespoon prepared mustard
1 can (20 ounces) pie-sliced apples
1 tablespoon lemon juice
½ teaspoon salt

1 can (10½ ounces) condensed cream of mushroom soup
⅓ cup light cream
½ cup soft bread crumbs
2 tablespoons melted butter or margarine

Combine chicken and mustard; blend well; divide among 4 ramekins. Top with apple slices. Sprinkle with lemon juice and salt. Combine soup and cream; pour into ramekins. Top with buttered bread crumbs. Bake at 350° for 20 minutes, or until crumbs are brown. Makes 4 servings.

SATURDAY NIGHT CASSEROLE

4 large, tart apples
3 tablespoons bacon drippings
1 medium onion, finely chopped

2 jars (1 pound each) red cabbage
8 frankfurters
½ cup water

Pare, core and slice apples. Heat bacon fat in deep skillet; add apples and onion; cook over low heat 10 minutes. Spoon

1 jar of red cabbage into bottom of casserole. Add half the apple mixture; top with 4 frankfurters; repeat. Pour ½ cup water over all. Bake at 350° for 40 to 45 minutes, or until frankfurters are browned. (Frankfurters for top layer are more attractive if scored.) Makes 4 generous servings.

SCALLOPED APPLES AND CHEESE

1½ tablespoons vegetable oil	1½ cups milk
1½ tablespoons flour	¾ cup fine bread crumbs
½ teaspoon salt	4 apples, cored, pared and sliced crosswise
Few grains pepper	½ pound American cheese, grated
Dash paprika	2 tablespoons butter or margarine
1 teaspoon Worcestershire sauce	
Dash Tabasco	

Heat oil; blend in flour; add seasonings and milk. Cook over low heat, stirring constantly, until smooth and slightly thickened. Line a greased shallow baking dish with ¼ cup bread crumbs. Arrange alternate layers of apples and grated cheese in baking dish. Pour in sauce. Top with crumbs; dot with butter or margarine. Bake at 350° about 25 minutes or until apples are tender. Makes 6 servings.

SAUSAGE, APPLE AND YAM CASSEROLE

5 cups hot mashed seasoned yams	¼ cup melted butter or margarine
3 cups hot unsweetened applesauce	Milk
½ cup firmly packed brown sugar	1 pound pork sausage links, cooked

Combine yams, applesauce, brown sugar, butter and a little milk. Beat until fluffy. Pile in casserole. Top with cooked sausages. Bake at 350° for 20 minutes. Makes 6 servings.

FLUFFY APPLE FISH CAKES

1 cup (4-ounce package) shredded salt codfish	1 cup coarsely grated raw apples
2 cups hot dry mashed potatoes	1 egg
	⅛ teaspoon pepper

Freshen codfish in cold water to cover for 2 minutes. Drain; press dry. Combine codfish, mashed potatoes, apple, egg and pepper. Form into balls or cakes. Dust with flour. Fry in shallow vegetable oil (2 inches deep), heated to 375°, until golden brown. Drain on absorbent paper. Makes 12 to 16 cakes.

STUFFED FLOUNDER ROLL-UPS

6 strips bacon	1 cup chopped apples
½ cup fine Melba toast crumbs	½ pound sea scallops, chopped
8 to 10 scallions, minced	½ teaspoon poultry seasoning
2 tablespoons chopped parsley	6 flounder fillets
	Mushroom-Caper Sauce*

Fry bacon crisp; drain; reserve ¼ cup bacon drippings. Combine crumbs, scallions, parsley, apples, scallops, poultry seasoning and bacon drippings; mix well. Spread on fillets; roll up. Place close together in foil-lined baking dish. Bake at 375° for 30 minutes. Brush with melted butter; run under broiler to brown. Serve with Mushroom-Caper Sauce. Makes 6 roll-ups.

* Mushroom-Caper Sauce: Combine 1 can (10½ ounces) condensed mushroom soup, ⅓ cup milk or cream and 2 tablespoons capers. Heat. Makes 6 servings.

ARABIAN APPLES
(Fouja Djedjad)

4 or 5 large baking apples	½ teaspoon salt
1½ cups diced cooked chicken	¼ teaspoon powdered rosemary
1 can (10½ ounces) condensed cream of mushroom soup, undiluted	⅛ teaspoon powdered cloves
	½ cup buttered bread crumbs

Cut a thin slice from stem end of each apple. Do not peel. Core, being careful not to cut all the way through. Scoop out pulp, leaving shell about ½ inch thick. Chop pulp; combine with chicken, soup and seasonings. Fill apples with chicken mixture. Top with buttered bread crumbs. Set stuffed apples in large casserole or deep roasting pan. Add enough water to cover bottom of pan to a depth of about 1 inch. Bake at 350° for 40 to 45 minutes; or until apple shells are tender. Makes 4 to 5 servings.

APPLE, BANANA AND BACON GRILL

½ cup firmly packed brown sugar
½ teaspoon cinnamon
4 firm bananas
Lemon juice
4 bacon strips
8 apple rings

Combine sugar and cinnamon. Peel bananas; brush with lemon juice, then dip in sugar mixture. Wrap bacon strip around each banana; secure with wooden picks. Sprinkle apple rings with remaining sugar mixture. Place fruit on broiler rack with surface of food 3 inches below source of heat. Broil 8 to 10 minutes, turning bananas once. Makes 4 servings.

FRANKS WITH APPLE SAUERKRAUT

3 tart apples
1 can (1 pound) sauerkraut
1 tablespoon caraway seeds
3 tablespoons sugar
1 tablespoon vinegar
8 frankfurters

Pare, core and slice apples; combine with all remaining ingredients except frankfurters. Bring to a boil; reduce heat; simmer 15 to 20 minutes, or until apples are tender. Grill frankfurters; place on sauerkraut mixture. Makes 4 servings.

HASH-STUFFED BAKED APPLES

8 large baking apples
1 can (1 pound) corned beef hash
1 tablespoon minced onion
1 teaspoon Worcestershire sauce
Dash nutmeg
2 tablespoons ketchup
1 tablespoon prepared mustard
Salt and pepper to taste
½ cup grated sharp Cheddar cheese

Core apples; scoop out pulp, leaving shell ¼ inch thick. Chop pulp. Pare apples ⅓ down from stem end. Combine chopped pulp with hash, onion and seasonings; mix well. Fill hollows in apples with hash mixture. Set in baking pan. Add hot water to depth of ½ inch. Bake at 350° for about 35 minutes or until apples are tender. Top with cheese. Return to oven until cheese melts and browns. Serve at once. Makes 8 servings.

TAVERN BAKED APPLES

1 can (1 pound) corned beef
  hash
¼ cup flour

4 large apples
4 tablespoons chutney

Combine hash and flour; mix well. Divide hash into 4 equal portions and shape into balls. Core apples; do not pare; cut into sixths. Press wedges into hash balls. Set on rack in baking pan over hot water. Bake at 375° for about 40 minutes or until apples are tender. Top each with spoonful of chutney. Makes 4 servings.

HUNGARIAN STEW

4 tablespoons butter or
  margarine
½ cup light brown sugar
6 to 8 apple rings
½ cup minced onions
2½ cups leftover pork
  gravy (or canned
  mushroom gravy)

2 cans or jars (1 pound
  each) sauerkraut
½ teaspoon salt
2 teaspoons caraway seeds
Sliced leftover roast pork

Melt butter in skillet; stir in brown sugar; stir until sugar melts. Cook apple rings until brown and glazed on both sides; remove. Add onions to pan with gravy, 1 can sauerkraut, salt and caraway seeds. Bring to boil; simmer 5 minutes. Add pork slices; simmer 15 minutes longer. Meanwhile, simmer remaining sauerkraut separately for 15 minutes; arrange on serving platter. Top with pork-in-gravy and apple rings. Makes 4 generous servings.

SALADS
and SALAD DRESSINGS

Waldorf Salad, composed of diced apples, celery and walnuts, was probably the first apple salad to achieve national popularity. Today there are countless recipes that feature this beautiful fruit. First course salads, with a bow to California. Main dish salads that, with soup and dessert, make a satisfying luncheon or supper for family or guests. Salads that accompany or follow the main dinner course. And salads that serve as two courses in one—salad and dessert.

APPLE RELISH SALAD

2 avocados
4 red apples
1 cucumber

2 medium onions
½ cup diced celery
Yogurt Dressing*

Peel, stone and slice avocados; core and slice apples without paring them. Score and slice cucumber, without peeling it. Slice onions; separate into rings. Combine all ingredients except dressing. Serve as a first course, topped with dressing. Makes 8 servings.

*Yogurt Dressing:

½ pint Yogurt
¼ cup French dressing

1 teaspoon celery seed

Combine all ingredients. Garnish with additional celery seed if desired.

GOLDEN GATE SALAD

2 tart red apples
⅓ cup golden raisins
Lemon French dressing

⅓ cup slivered, toasted almonds
Heart leaves of lettuce

Core apples; do not pare; dice. Add raisins; marinate in lemon French dressing at least 1 hour in refrigerator. Drain; add almonds. Serve on heart leaves of lettuce with additional dressing as a first course. Makes 4 servings.

APPLE AVOCADO SALAD

2 tart red apples
2 tablespoons lemon juice
1 cup sliced celery
1/4 cup chopped pecans
1/2 cup seeded white grapes
1/2 cup miniature marshmallows
Salt and pepper
1/2 cup mayonnaise
2 or 3 avocados
Iceberg lettuce

Cube apples; sprinkle with lemon juice. Combine celery, pecans, grapes, marshmallows and drained apple cubes. Season; toss lightly with mayonnaise. Cut avocados in half; remove stones; fill with apple mixture. Serve on chipped ice, if desired, with crisp salad greens and extra mayonnaise served separately. Makes 4 to 6 servings.

APPLE CHEESE SALAD

2 cups diced unpeeled red apples
1 cup thinly sliced celery
3/4 cup pineapple tidbits, drained
1/2 cup cubed Cheddar cheese
1/2 cup Russian dressing

Combine all ingredients. Toss until well coated with dressing. Serve on lettuce, if desired. Makes 4 generous servings. Serve with soup and hot French bread for luncheon or supper.

APPLE CHICKEN SALAD

2 cups diced cooked or canned chicken*
1 cup sliced celery
1/2 cup sliced pitted black olives
3 red apples
1/2 cup mayonnaise
1/2 teaspoon rosemary
1/4 cup dairy sour cream
Salad greens

Combine chicken, celery and olives. Dice apples without peeling them. Combine mayonnaise, rosemary and sour cream;

* Or leftover turkey.

add apples and chicken mixture. Toss to coat evenly. Line individual salad bowls with salad greens. Heap apple mixture in center. Makes 4 to 6 servings.

APPLE FILBERT SALAD

3 large apples
½ cup sliced celery
¼ cup sliced ripe olives
½ cup diced cucumber
⅓ cup French dressing
Lettuce

2 cups creamed cottage cheese
½ cup chopped toasted filberts
Mayonnaise or salad dressing

Core and dice unpeeled apples; combine with celery, olives, cucumber and French dressing; toss until well mixed. Arrange lettuce leaves in 4 individual salad bowls. Add ½ cup cottage cheese to each. Top with apple mixture; sprinkle with filberts. Serve mayonnaise or dressing with the salad. Makes 4 generous servings.

APPLE HAM SALAD

4 red apples
1 tablespoon lemon juice
1 cup cold water
2 cups diced cooked ham

⅔ cup sliced celery
½ cup French dressing
½ cup crumbled blue cheese
Salad greens

Core apples, do not pare; cut in ½ inch cubes. Combine lemon juice and water; pour over apples; drain. Combine apples, ham, celery and French dressing; toss to mix. Add blue cheese; serve on crisp salad greens. Makes 6 servings.

APPLE LIMA SALAD

3 red apples
½ pound process American cheese
2 cups cooked dry lima beans

1 cup sliced celery
Salad greens
½ cup mayonnaise
½ cup dairy sour cream

Core apples; do not peel. Cut crosswise into rings, then into bite-size pieces. Cut cheese into "sticks" about 2 inches long and ¼ inch wide. Combine apples, cheese, lima beans and celery. Arrange in a salad bowl with crisp greens. Combine mayonnaise and sour cream; toss with salad ingredients or serve separately, as preferred. Makes 6 generous servings.

APPLE LOBSTER SALAD

1 Bermuda or Spanish onion
4 apples
1 cucumber
2 cans (5 ounces each) lobster meat
Crisp salad greens

1 cup mayonnaise
½ cup dairy sour cream
½ cup chili sauce
2 tablespoons chopped ripe olives
1 tablespoon pickle relish

Slice onion; separate each slice into rings. Core unpeeled apples; slice. Score unpeeled cucumber; slice thin. Combine onion rings, apple slices and cucumber slices. Cut lobster meat into chunks; add. Arrange on crisp salad greens. Combine remaining ingredients for dressing; serve separately. Makes 6 to 8 servings.

APPLE MEDLEY SALAD

2 cups thinly sliced cooked potatoes
6 slices crisp bacon, crumbled
1 cup diced cooked ham
1 cup diced Cheddar cheese

4 large red apples
½ cup bottled Italian salad dressing
3 anchovy fillets, minced
Mayonnaise
Salad greens

Combine potatoes, bacon, ham and cheese. Core apples; do not pare; slice thin. Combine salad dressing and anchovies; toss with apples; add to potato mixture. Toss to mix, with mayonnaise to taste. Serve on crisp salad greens. Makes 6 servings.

APPLE OASIS SALAD

4 red apples
1½ cups sliced pitted dates
2 cups diced dried figs
½ pound process Swiss cheese, diced

¼ cup chopped candied ginger
½ cup mayonnaise
½ cup dairy sour cream
Salad greens

Core apples; do not pare; slice thin. Combine with dates, figs, cheese and ginger. Combine mayonnaise and sour cream;

add to apple mixture; toss to mix. Serve on crisp salad greens.
Makes 8 to 10 servings.

APPLE MACARONI SALAD

2 tablespoons salt	2 medium onions, sliced and
4 to 6 quarts boiling water	separated into rings
4 cups elbow macaroni	2 cans (2 ounces each)
(1 pound)	anchovy fillets, drained
2 unpeeled red apples,	¼ cup French dressing
sliced very thin	1 cup dairy sour cream
½ cup sliced sweet gherkins	Romaine

Add salt to rapidly boiling water. Gradually add macaroni
so that water continues to boil. Cook uncovered, stirring occasionally, until tender. Drain in colander. Rinse with cold
water; drain again. Chill. Combine macaroni, apple slices,
gherkins, onion rings and half the anchovies; combine French
dressing and sour cream; add. Arrange on romaine; top with
remaining anchovies. Makes 8 servings.

APPLE PEANUT SALAD

3 red apples	¾ cup Southern Dressing*
1 cup sliced celery	Salad greens
½ cup salted peanuts	

Core and dice apples (do not peel). Combine with celery,
peanuts and dressing; toss well to mix. Serve on crisp salad
greens. Makes 4 to 6 servings.

*Southern Dressing:

½ cup orange juice	½ cup peanut butter
½ cup blended pineapple-	½ teaspoon salt
grapefruit juice	3 tablespoons sugar
¼ cup lemon juice	

Combine fruit juices; add slowly to peanut butter, blending
until smooth. Stir in salt and sugar; stir until sugar dissolves.

Store in covered container in refrigerator. Makes about 1½ cups.

APPLE MACARONI SALAD IN APPLE CUPS

4 large red apples
Juice of ½ lemon
1½ cups cooked elbow
   macaroni
1 small onion, finely
   chopped

2 tablespoons sweet pickle
   relish
¼ teaspoon salt
½ cup whipping cream
¼ cup mayonnaise

Cut slice from stem end of apple. Core, being careful not to cut through to bottom. Carefully scoop out pulp, leaving a shell ¼ inch thick. Cut a zigzag pattern around tops of the apples; sprinkle insides with lemon juice. Chop apple pulp; combine with macaroni, onion, pickle relish and salt. Whip cream; fold in mayonnaise; add to macaroni mixture. Fill apple shells, mounding tops. Chill before serving. Makes 4 servings.

APPLE SALAD NEPTUNE

¼ cup cider vinegar
½ cup vegetable oil
½ teaspoon salt
Few grains pepper
½ teaspoon sugar
4 tart apples

2 cups diced lobster meat,
   cooked or canned
1 pound jumbo shrimp,
   cooked, shelled and
   deveined
Salad greens
Mayonnaise

Combine first 5 ingredients; blend well. Core apples, slice thin (do not peel). Drop apple slices into oil mixture as they are sliced. Add lobster and shrimp; toss to coat with oil mixture. Drain off excess oil. Arrange on salad greens. Serve with mayonnaise. Makes 6 servings.

APPLE, SALMON AND VEGETABLE SALAD

1 can (1 pound) red salmon
½ cup thinly sliced celery
1 small onion, chopped
1 package (10 ounces)
   frozen lima beans, cooked
   and drained

1 cup thinly sliced uncooked
   zucchini squash
2 cups sliced apples
Bottled Italian salad dressing
Crisp salad greens

Drain salmon; remove bones and skin; break up in fairly large pieces. Combine with celery, onion, lima beans, zucchini and sliced apples. Toss with salad dressing and greens. Makes 6 servings.

APPLE POTATO SALAD

6 cups sliced cooked
   potatoes
1 cup diced celery
½ cup diced green pepper

2 cups thinly sliced
   unpeeled red apples
¼ cup minced onion
4 to 6 frankfurters
Sour Cream Dressing*

Combine potatoes, celery, green pepper, apples and onion. Cut frankfurters in 1-inch pieces; add. Add Sour Cream Dressing; mix well. Arrange on salad greens. Makes 8 servings.

*Sour Cream Dressing:

½ cup mayonnaise or
   salad dressing
½ cup dairy sour cream
1½ teaspoons salt

Few grains pepper
2 teaspoons prepared
   mustard
1 tablespoon minced parsley
¼ teaspoon paprika

Combine all ingredients; mix well. Add to apple-potato mixture.

APPLE SALMON SALAD BOWL

¼ cup lemon juice
½ cup vegetable oil
¼ teaspoon seasoned
   pepper
½ teaspoon salt
3 large red apples
1 large cucumber

1 can (1 pound) red salmon
Salad greens
2 tablespoons minced onion
6 stuffed olives, sliced
Avocado Dressing*

Combine lemon juice, oil, pepper and salt. Core apples; do not peel; slice thin. Drop immediately into lemon-juice marinade. Score unpeeled cucumber with tines of fork; slice thin; add to marinade. Break salmon into chunks, removing bones and skin; add to marinade. Chill. When ready to serve, arrange salad greens in a shallow bowl. Drain off marinade; arrange apple-salmon mixture in bowl. Scatter minced onion and sliced olives over apple mixture. Serve with a choice of oil and vinegar or Avocado Dressing. Makes 6 servings.

•Avocado Dressing:

1 large ripe avocado	¼ cup dairy sour cream
¼ cup mayonnaise	Salt and pepper to taste

Peel avocado; remove stone; mash avocado to smooth pulp. Fold in mayonnaise and sour cream. Season to taste. Makes about 1½ cups.

APPLE SHRIMP SALAD

2 cans (7 ounces each) deveined jumbo shrimp	Lettuce
2 medium onions	Water cress
2 red apples	Caper Mayonnaise*

Drain and rinse shrimp. Slice onions; separate into rings. Core apples; slice. Arrange salad greens on 4 serving plates. Place slices from ½ apple in center of each plate, peel side up. Arrange shrimp and onion rings around apples. Makes 4 servings.

•Caper Mayonnaise:

¾ cup mayonnaise	2 tablespoons capers

Combine and serve.

HARVEST HOME SALAD

4 red apples	2 packages (3 ounces each) cream cheese
Salad greens	
2 cups halved seeded grapes	½ cup mayonnaise
1 cup salted cashew nuts	¼ cup whipping cream
1 jar (5 ounces) sharp Cheddar cheese spread	Salt and pepper to taste

Core apples; do not peel; slice thin. Dip in water to which lemon juice has been added to prevent discoloration. Arrange crisp salad greens on individual plates. Add apple slices, grapes and cashew nuts. Form Cheddar spread into balls about ½ inch in diameter; add to salad. Mash cream cheese; add mayonnaise and cream; whip to spoonable consistency, adding more cream if desired. Season to taste with salt and pepper. Serve with salad. Makes 8 servings.

APPLE SALMON SLAW

1 can (1 pound) salmon
2 red apples, thinly sliced
4 cups shredded cabbage

Mayonnaise or salad dressing
Lettuce
Capers

Flake salmon into small pieces, removing skin and bones. Combine salmon, thinly sliced apples and cabbage; moisten with mayonnaise or salad dressing. Serve in cup-shaped leaves of lettuce; garnish with capers. Makes 6 servings.

APPLE SHRIMP SALAD BOWL

2 pounds large shrimp
1 large avocado
2 red apples
2 yellow apples
1 package (10 ounces)
  green lima beans, cooked
  and chilled

1 green pepper, cut in rings
1 cup bottled garlic French
  dressing
Salad greens

Cook, peel and devein shrimp; chill. Peel and stone avocado; slice. Slice unpeeled apples. Toss shrimp, avocado, apple slices, limas and green pepper in dressing. Serve on crisp salad greens. Makes 8 servings.

AUTUMN APPLE SALAD

1 pound elbow macaroni
½ cup broken walnuts
1 cup sliced celery
½ cup bottled Italian
  salad dressing

¾ cup mayonnaise
2 tablespoons minced onion
½ teaspoon oregano
2 red apples
Romaine

Cook elbow macaroni in boiling salted water until tender; drain; rinse with cold water; chill. Combine macaroni, walnuts and celery. Blend salad dressing and mayonnaise; add onion and oregano; mix well. Core apples; slice thin without peeling; add to mayonnaise mixture. Add to macaroni mixture; toss well. Line salad bowl with romaine. Add salad mixture. Makes 8 servings.

APPLE TUNA SALAD VIRGINIA

1 can (6½ or 7 ounces)
   tuna
2 red apples
½ cup sliced celery
½ cup halved seeded Tokay
   grapes
½ cup salted peanuts
Salad greens
⅓ cup mayonnaise
⅓ cup dairy sour cream

Drain tuna; flake. Core and dice apples; do not pare. Combine tuna, apples, celery, grapes and peanuts. Serve on crisp greens with dressing made with mayonnaise and sour cream. Makes 4 to 5 servings.

APPLE VEGETABLE SALAD BOWL

1 head iceberg lettuce
1 small cucumber
1 cup sliced celery
6 to 8 radishes, sliced
2 tablespoons cut chives
2 tablespoons snipped fresh
   dill
2 red apples
½ cup French dressing
Water cress

Cut lettuce into bite-size chunks. Score unpeeled cucumber with tines of fork; slice thin. Combine lettuce, cucumber, celery and radishes in salad bowl. Sprinkle with chives and dill. Core apples; do not peel. Cut in thin slices; add to salad bowl. Add French dressing; toss to mix. Garnish with sprays of water cress. Serve with French or Italian bread and sharp Cheddar cheese. Makes 6 servings.

APPLES ON THE HALF SHELL

2 cans (6½ ounces each)
   crabmeat
1½ cups diced unpeeled
   red apples
½ cup slivered toasted
   almonds
½ cup mayonnaise
⅓ cup dairy sour cream
3 to 4 large ripe avocados
Salad greens

Flake crabmeat; combine with apples and almonds. Combine mayonnaise and sour cream; add; toss to mix. Halve avocados; remove stones. Fill avocado halves heaping full with crabmeat mixture. Serve on salad greens with extra dressing, if desired. Makes 6 to 8 servings.

CUCUMBER BOAT SALAD

3 large cucumbers
1 cup diced cooked ham
1 cup diced American
  cheese

2 cups diced unpeeled red
  apples
Creamy Cheese Dressing*

Cut unpeeled cucumbers in half lengthwise; remove seedy portion. Scoop out pulp, leaving firm shells; chop pulp coarsely. Combine ham, cheese, apples and dressing. When ready to serve, add chopped cucumber; mix well; fill cucumber shells. Serve on salad greens. Makes 6 servings.

*Creamy Cheese Dressing:

½ cup dairy sour cream
2 ounces blue cheese,
  crumbled
3 tablespoons cream
1 tablespoon vegetable oil
¼ teaspoon Worcestershire
  sauce

2 tablespoons grated
  Parmesan cheese
⅛ teaspoon each garlic salt,
  onion salt and pepper
2 tablespoons light wine
  vinegar
1 tablespoon lemon juice

Combine all ingredients; mix well. Chill. Makes about 1¼ cups.

HOT APPLE POTATO SALAD, COUNTRY STYLE

1 cup boiling water
½ cup golden raisins
3 cups sliced cooked
  potatoes
1 cup sliced celery
2 tablespoons minced
  parsley
1 teaspoon salt
Few grains pepper

4 strips bacon
2 tablespoons cider vinegar
2 tablespoons tarragon
  vinegar
1 slice lemon
3 red apples

Pour boiling water over raisins; let stand 2 or 3 minutes; drain; cool. Combine potatoes, celery, parsley, salt and pepper in saucepan. Cut bacon in small pieces; fry until crisp; add vinegars and lemon to bacon and bacon fat. Heat; pour over potato mixture. Dice apples (do not peel). Add with raisins to potato mixture; mix well; heat to serving temperature. Serve hot. Makes 6 to 8 servings.

CHICKEN FRUIT SALAD

3 cups diced cooked or
canned chicken
1 cup diced unpared red
apples
1 cup pineapple tidbits,

drained
1 cup diced grapefruit
sections, drained
Mayonnaise
Water cress

Combine chicken with apples and well-drained pineapple tidbits and grapefruit. Mix well. Add enough mayonnaise to hold ingredients together. Serve on water cress with additional mayonnaise, if desired. Makes 8 servings.

DUTCH SALAD

1 cup (about) diced cooked
veal or beef
1 large sour pickle, minced
1 large apple, peeled and
diced

1 cup diced cooked potatoes
1 small onion, minced
1 tablespoon vegetable oil
1½ tablespoons vinegar
2 tablespoons mayonnaise

Combine first 5 ingredients. Mix oil, vinegar and mayonnaise; add to meat mixture; mix well. Garnish with mayonnaise, sliced hard-cooked egg and shredded pickled beets. Makes 4 servings.

MYSTERY MACARONI SALAD

1 tablespoon salt
3 quarts boiling water
2 cups (8 ounces) elbow
macaroni
2 medium-sized apples,
diced
¼ cup vinegar
1 jar (8 ounces) herring
fillets in cream, diced

⅓ cup sliced sweet gherkins
1 large sweet onion,
sliced thin
1 teaspoon salt
½ cup dairy sour cream
1 tablespoon chopped dill
Crisp salad greens

Add 1 tablespoon salt to rapidly boiling water. Gradually add macaroni so that water continues to boil. Cook uncovered, stirring occasionally, until tender. Drain in colander. Rinse with cold water; drain and chill. Meanwhile, combine apples, vinegar, herring, gherkins, onion, 1 teaspoon salt, sour cream and dill; mix well and chill. Combine apple mixture and macaroni; toss lightly but thoroughly. Serve on salad greens. Makes 6 to 8 servings.

FISHERMAN'S LUCK SALAD

2 cups cooked flaked fish
½ cup sliced stuffed olives
1 cup diced celery
⅓ cup tartar sauce

⅓ cup mayonnaise
2 red apples
Lettuce
Water cress

Combine fish, olives, celery, tartar sauce and mayonnaise. Core apples; do not peel; slice thin; add. Toss thoroughly to mix. Serve on lettuce and water cress. Makes 6 servings.

GALA FRUIT SALAD

3 red apples
1 cup halved, seeded Tokay grapes
¼ pound marshmallows, quartered

2 cups pineapple chunks
1 cup coarsely broken walnuts
Fruit Salad Dressing*
Salad greens

Core and quarter apples; do not pare. Cut in thin slices. Combine with grapes, marshmallows, pineapple and walnuts. Add Fruit Salad Dressing; mix well. Makes 6 to 8 servings.

*Fruit Salad Dressing:

1 tablespoon flour
⅓ cup sugar
1 egg
½ cup canned pineapple juice

Juice of ½ lemon
Juice of ½ large orange
½ cup of whipping cream

Mix flour and sugar. Beat egg until light; add. Strain fruit juices; add. Cook over hot water, stirring until thickened. Cool. Whip cream; fold in. Makes 6 to 8 servings.

LAST-OF-THE-TURKEY APPLE SALAD

3 red apples
1 small Bermuda or Spanish onion
4 stalks celery, sliced
2 cups diced leftover turkey

Bottled Italian salad dressing
Leftover stuffing
Mayonnaise
Iceberg lettuce

Core apples; do not pare; cut into cubes. Slice onion; separate into rings. Combine apples, onion, celery and turkey.

Add enough salad dressing to coat. Mix stuffing with enough mayonnaise to hold together; shape into small balls. Cut lettuce crosswise into 4 slices. Place lettuce slices on individual salad plates; top with salad mixture; garnish with stuffing balls. Makes 4 servings.

SAVORY APPLE POTATO SALAD

2 cups cubed cooked
  potatoes
3 cups sliced unpeeled red
  apples
1 tablespoon capers

1 can (2 ounces) anchovy
  fillets
3 tablespoons minced
  parsley
2 small onions, sliced
  Special Dressing*

Combine potatoes, apples, capers, anchovies, parsley and onions; toss well to mix. Add dressing; toss again. Makes 8 servings.

*Special Dressing:

½ cup mayonnaise
½ cup dairy sour cream
1 tablespoon wine vinegar
½ teaspoon salt
⅛ teaspoon coarsely
  ground black pepper

½ teaspoon paprika
1 teaspoon lemon juice
½ teaspoon curry powder
1 teaspoon sugar

Combine all ingredients; blend thoroughly. Makes about 1 cup.

SHRIMP ASPIC MOLD
WITH APPLE-POTATO-WALNUT SALAD

2 envelopes unflavored
  gelatin
½ cup cold water
3 cups boiling water
½ cup sugar
¾ teaspoon salt
½ cup lemon juice
Green food coloring
1½ pounds large shrimp,
  cooked and cleaned

1 container (1 pint) potato
  salad
½ cup sliced celery
¼ cup finely diced green
  pepper
1 cup diced unpeeled red
  apples
¼ cup broken walnuts

Sprinkle gelatin on cold water. Add boiling water; stir until gelatin dissolves. Add sugar, salt and lemon juice; stir until sugar dissolves. Tint sea green with food coloring. Arrange whole shrimp around edge of 5-cup ring mold. Carefully pour in enough gelatin to "anchor" the shrimp. Chill until set. Pour in remaining cooled gelatin mixture. Chill until set. Combine remaining ingredients, adding mayonnaise, if desired. Unmold shrimp ring on serving plate. Fill center with potato mixture. Garnish with remaining shrimp, thin slices of unpeeled red apple and water cress. Serve additional mayonnaise. Makes 6 servings.

SEABOARD APPLE SALAD

2 cups cooked flaked white fish (cod, haddock, halibut or flounder)
1 cup thinly sliced celery
½ cup diced green pepper

2 tablespoons pickle relish
Curry Dill Dressing*
2 red apples
Pimiento strips

Combine fish, celery, green pepper, pickle relish and half the dressing. Core apples; do not pare; slice thin. Add at once to fish mixture and toss to mix. Serve in individual salad bowls on crisp greens with remaining dressing. Garnish with pimiento strips. Makes 4 servings.

*Curry Dill Dressing:

1 cup vegetable oil
⅓ cup vinegar
1 teaspoon paprika
1 or 2 teaspoons curry powder

Few drops Tabasco
¼ teaspoon Worcestershire sauce
½ teaspoon ground dill seed
½ teaspoon sugar

Combine all ingredients; beat well with rotary egg beater just before serving.

TUNA, APPLE AND NUT SALAD

2 cans (6½ or 7 ounces each) tuna
2 cups chopped apples
1 cup chopped celery
2 cups shredded lettuce
⅓ cup coarsely chopped walnuts

⅓ cup sliced dates
Mayonnaise or salad dressing
Lettuce
Stuffed olives

Drain oil from tuna; flake. Combine tuna, apples, celery, lettuce, chopped walnuts and dates. Add enough mayonnaise or salad dressing to hold ingredients together. Arrange on lettuce. Garnish with stuffed olives. Makes 6 servings.

APPLE CRISP SALAD

1 envelope unflavored
  gelatin
½ cup cold water
1 cup hot apple juice
¼ cup lemon juice

3 tablespoons honey
½ teaspon salt
½ cup chopped celery
2 tart apples, diced
¼ cup chopped nuts

Soften gelatin in cold water; dissolve in hot apple juice. Add lemon juice, honey and salt. Stir until dissolved. Chill until syrupy; fold in remaining ingredients. Turn into 5-cup mold that has been rinsed in cold water. Chill. When firm, unmold on salad greens. Serve with any desired dressing. Makes 6 servings.

APPLE DESSERT SALAD MOLD

1 package orange-flavor
  gelatin
1½ cups diced unpared
  apples

1 cup halved seeded Tokay
  grapes
½ cup broken walnuts

Prepare gelatin according to directions on package; pour into mold to a depth of 1½ inches. Chill until firm. Meanwhile chill remaining gelatin until consistency of unbeaten egg white; fold in apples, grapes and walnuts. Spoon into mold on top of clear orange gelatin. Chill until firm. Unmold on heart leaves of lettuce. Serve with salad dressing and cottage cheese. Makes 6 to 8 servings.

APPLE CINNAMON GELATIN SALAD

1 package raspberry-flavor
  gelatin
1 cup hot water
¼ cup cinnamon "red hots"
½ cup boiling water

Cold water
1 cup diced tart apples
1 cup diced celery
½ cup chopped nuts

Dissolve gelatin in hot water. Add cinnamon candies to boiling water; stir until dissolved. Measure; add enough cold water to make 1 cup; add to gelatin. Chill until consistency of unbeaten egg whites; stir in remaining ingredients. Spoon into 5-cup mold. Chill until firm. Unmold. Garnish with salad greens. Serve with mayonnaise or salad dressing. Makes 6 servings.

TUNA APPLE SALAD

2 cans (6½ or 7 ounces each) tuna
1½ cups diced unpared red apples
½ cup diced celery

1 tablespoon grated onion
1 teaspoon capers
3 tablespoons French dressing
Mayonnaise
Black olives

Drain tuna; combine with apples, celery, onion, capers and French dressing. Arrange on salad greens. Top with mayonnaise. Garnish with black olives. Makes 6 servings.

WALDORF SALAD SUPREME

4 cups cubed unpeeled red apples
2 cups sliced celery
1 cup broken walnuts
1 cup dairy sour cream

½ cup mayonnaise
¼ pound blue cheese, coarsely crumbled
Crisp salad greens

Combine apples, celery and walnuts. Blend sour cream and mayonnaise; stir in blue cheese. Pour over apple mixture; toss until all ingredients are well mixed. Serve on crisp salad greens. Makes 8 servings.

APPLE LIME GELATIN DESSERT SALAD

1 package lime-flavor gelatin
1 cup hot water
1 cup ginger ale
2 apples

1 banana, sliced
¼ cup slivered toasted almonds
Water cress
Apple Cream Dressing*

Dissolve gelatin in hot water; add ginger ale. Quarter, core and slice 1 apple (do not pare). Rinse mold in cold water. Arrange apple slices around sides of mold in decorative pattern. Pour in enough gelatin to "anchor" slices. Chill until set. Meanwhile chill remaining gelatin until syrupy; dice the remaining apple, fold in with banana slices and almonds; pour

into mold. Chill until set. Unmold. Garnish with water cress.
Serve with Apple Cream Dressing. Makes 6 servings.

•Apple Cream Dressing:

3 tablespoons apple jelly
¼ cup mayonnaise
¼ cup whipping cream

3 tablespoons dairy sour
cream
½ teaspoon lime juice

Combine jelly and mayonnaise; beat with rotary beater until
blended. Whip cream; fold in with sour cream and lime juice.
Makes 6 servings.

APPLE LIME RING MOLD

2 packages lime-flavor
gelatin
1 quart apple juice
¼ cup lime juice
6 apples
½ cup diced celery

½ cup broken walnuts
½ cup mayonnaise
½ cup thick dairy sour
cream
Water cress

Prepare lime gelatin as directed on package, using hot apple
juice instead of water and adding lime juice. Pour into 5-cup
ring mold which has been rinsed in cold water. Chill until
firm. Pare, core and dice 5 apples; combine with celery,
walnuts, mayonnaise and sour cream. Unmold gelatin on
water cress; fill center with apple mixture. Garnish with thin
slices of remaining apple, unpared. Makes 8 servings.

COTTAGE CHEESE, WALDORF

4 cups cottage cheese
1½ teaspoons salt
1 tablespoon sugar
2 tablespoons lemon juice
1 cup light cream
2 envelopes unflavored
gelatin

½ cup cold water
Salad greens
4 or 5 tart red apples
1 cup diced celery
½ cup broken walnuts
Mayonnaise

Combine cottage cheese, salt, sugar, lemon juice and cream;
mix well. Sprinkle gelatin on cold water; dissolve over boiling water; stir into cheese mixture. Spoon into 5-cup ring
mold which has been rinsed in cold water. Chill until firm.
Unmold on salad greens. Dice unpeeled apples; combine

with celery and walnuts, add mayonnaise to taste; fill center of ring mold. Makes 8 servings.

APPLE MALLOW SALAD

1 package strawberry-flavor gelatin
1 cup hot water
8 marshmallows, diced
1 can (1 pound) applesauce
1/2 cup chopped walnuts
3 tablespoons mayonnaise or salad dressing

Dissolve gelatin in hot water. Add marshmallows; stir until partially dissolved. Add applesauce and walnuts; mix well. Blend in mayonnaise or salad dressing. Pour into 6 individual molds; chill until firm. Unmold on salad greens.

APPLE MELODY SALAD

1 package cherry-flavor gelatin
1 cup diced tart apples
1 cup drained crushed pineapple
1/2 cup chopped dates
1/2 cup chopped nuts
2 tablespoons mayonnaise
1/2 cup whipping cream
Water cress

Prepare gelatin according to package directions; chill until syrupy. Combine apples, pineapple, dates, nuts and mayonnaise; fold into gelatin. Whip cream; fold in. Turn into 5-cup mold; chill until firm. Unmold on water cress; garnish with additional mayonnaise. Makes 6 servings.

APPLE TUNA MOLD

1 package lemon-flavor gelatin
1 cup boiling water
1/4 teaspoon salt
Dash pepper
1 cup cold water
2 tablespoons lemon juice
1 can (6 1/2 or 7 ounces) tuna, flaked
1/2 cup chopped celery
1 cup diced unpeeled red apple
1/2 cup seedless white grapes

Dissolve gelatin in boiling water. Add salt, pepper, cold water and lemon juice. Chill until slightly thickened. Fold in tuna, celery, apple and grapes. Turn into 5-cup mold. Chill until firm. Unmold. Serve with mayonnaise or salad dressing. Makes 6 servings.

JELLIED APPLE SALMON SALAD

2 packages lime-flavor gelatin
4 cups hot water
1 can (1 pound) red salmon, boned and flaked
1½ cups diced unpeeled red apples

½ cup diced green pepper
½ cup thinly sliced celery
½ cup cooked or canned green peas
Salad greens
Fluted cucumber slices

Dissolve gelatin in hot water. Pour about ⅓ into a 6-cup mold; chill until set. Chill remaining gelatin until consistency of unbeaten egg white; fold in remaining ingredients; spoon on top of clear gelatin in mold. Chill until set. Serve on salad greens; garnish with fluted cucumber slices. Accompany with any preferred salad dressing. Makes 6 to 8 servings.

TROPICAL JELLIED APPLE SALAD

1 package lemon-flavor gelatin
2 cups hot cider
1 tablespoon lemon juice
1 cup diced unpeeled red apples

½ cup broken walnuts
½ cup sliced pitted dates
1 tablespoon coarsely grated orange peel

Dissolve gelatin in hot cider; add lemon juice. Chill until consistency of unbeaten egg white. Fold in remaining ingredients. Turn into quart mold; chill until firm. Unmold. Garnish with salad greens. Serve with Sour Cream Dressing.* Makes 6 servings.

*Sour Cream Dressing:

Combine equal amounts- dairy sour cream and mayonnaise. Sprinkle with coarsely grated orange peel.

APPLE BAVARIAN SLAW

1 Spanish onion
2 red apples
4 cups shredded red cabbage

½ cup cross-cut dill pickle slices
French dressing

Slice onion; separate into rings. Core apples; do not pare; cut in thin slices. Combine onion rings, apple slices, cabbage and pickle slices. Just before serving, toss with French dressing. Makes 6 servings.

MOLDED WINTER APPLE SALAD

1 package lemon-flavor
  gelatin
1 cup thinly sliced unpeeled
  apples
½ cup chopped dates

½ cup walnuts, coarsely
  chopped
2 tablespoons raisins
¼ cup diced celery
2 tablespoons mayonnaise
½ cup whipping cream

Prepare gelatin according to package directions. Arrange a few apple slices in bottom of a 6-cup mold. Spoon in enough gelatin to "anchor" apple slices; chill until set. Meanwhile, chill remaining gelatin until syrupy. Combine apples, dates, nuts, raisins, celery and mayonnaise. Whip cream; add to fruit mixture. Fold into gelatin; turn into mold on clear gelatin layer. Chill until set. Unmold; surround with salad greens. Makes 8 servings.

APPLE SOUR CREAM SLAW

1 cup dairy sour cream
2 tablespoons lemon juice
2 tablespoons cider vinegar
2 tablespoons sugar
1 teaspoon salt
¼ teaspoon coarsely
  ground black pepper
1 teaspoon dry mustard

1 cup sliced celery
2 cups shredded cabbage
1 cup shredded carrots
2 large red apples
⅓ cup raisins
⅓ cup chopped salted
  peanuts

Combine first 7 ingredients; beat until smooth. Combine remaining ingredients; add to first mixture, toss to mix. Makes 8 servings. (Excellent with all pork cuts.)

FRUIT SLAW

3 apples
2 bananas
½ cup French dressing

1 cup sliced celery
3 cups shredded cabbage

Core apples; do not pare; slice ⅛ inch thick. Slice bananas. Pour French dressing over apples and bananas; toss with a fork. Add celery and cabbage (red cabbage is especially good in this salad); mix well. Makes 6 servings.

APPLE GREEN GODDESS SALAD

1 head iceberg lettuce
1 garlic clove, cut in half
8 anchovy fillets
1 tablespoon vegetable oil
1 cup mayonnaise
2 tablespoons tarragon vinegar
¼ cup chopped chives
¼ cup chopped parsley
2 scallions or green onions, thinly sliced
½ teaspoon tarragon
3 or 4 red apples

Core lettuce; wash in cold water; drain well. Place in plastic bag or transparent plastic wrap; refrigerate. Rub salad bowl with garlic; discard garlic. Mash anchovies with oil in salad bowl. Blend in mayonnaise, vinegar, chives, parsley, scallions and tarragon. Let dressing stand at least 1 hour to develop flavor. Tear lettuce into bowl. Core apples; do not peel; slice thin; add to salad bowl. Add dressing. Toss lightly until lettuce and apples are well coated with dressing. Makes 8 servings.

FRUIT AND VEGETABLE SLAW

¼ cup dairy sour cream
¼ cup mayonnaise
1 envelope onion salad dressing mix
Juice of ½ lemon
¼ teaspoon salt
2 cups shredded cabbage
1 can (11 ounces) mandarin oranges, drained
1 large red apple, diced
2 raw carrots, shredded
3 tablespoons chopped dill pickle

Combine sour cream, mayonnaise, salad dressing mix, lemon juice and salt; blend well. Toss with remaining ingredients. Makes 4 to 6 servings.

JACKSTRAW SALAD

3 carrots uncooked
4 large stalks celery
2 large green peppers
2 large red apples
French dressing
Salad greens
Russian dressing

Scrape carrots; cut in thin sticks about 3 inches long. Cut celery and green pepper in matching sticks. Cut apples in

Two unusual dishes: Surprise your guests with a delicious soup of mysterious flavor—Curried Apple Soup, page 39. On another occasion serve Jellied Apple Salmon Salad, page 82.

Shrimp Aspic Mold (top right): Coral pink shrimp in a ring mold of shimmering green aspic make a perfect frame for the Apple Potato Walnut Salad in the center. Recipe, page 76.

Apple Salmon Salad Bowl (bottom right): The salad is as beautiful as the antique bowl that holds it! With the avocado dressing it is a symphony of color and flavor. Page 69.

Holiday Apple Pie (below): Glamorous is the word for this pie, all dressed up for the gala holiday season, with its decorated lattice top. You'll find the recipe on page 131.

Three wonderful ideas to spark your autumn menus: at the top, Candy Apple Pie, page 125; in the center, Baked Apples Supreme, page 115; below, Serve-Yourself Salad Platter, page 207.

A trio of delightful recipes: At the top, Apple Shrimp Salad Bowl, page 71, center left, Apple Scotch Cookies, page 159; at bottom of photograph, Baked Apples Marsala, page 114

Dessert sophistication (above): Beautiful apples, mellow cheese, and crisp, flavorful nuts—true flavor affinities. Here are six of the suggestions given on page 175.

Sweet and Pungent Pork Chops (below): Apple rings crown the chops and both are baked to perfection in a sweet-sour sauce. Bright cherries add a festive touch. Page 47.

Three beautiful apple pies: At the top, French, page 132, at left center, Sesame Crisscross, page 121, and at the bottom right, Streusel-Top, with neatly braided rim, page 136.

sticks, leaving red peel on ends. Combine; toss with enough French dressing to coat sticks evenly. Serve on crisp salad greens with Russian dressing. Makes 6 servings.

CRISP-TOP APPLE SALAD

1 large sweet onion, finely chopped
1 medium green pepper, diced
1 can water chestnuts, sliced
½ cup mayonnaise
½ cup dairy sour cream
1 teaspoon salt
Few grains pepper
2 teaspoons prepared mustard
1 tablespoon minced parsley
¼ teaspoon paprika
3 red apples, unpeeled, thinly sliced
Salad greens

Combine all ingredients except apples and salad greens. Place apples in center of large plate; surround with salad greens; top with first mixture. Makes 6 servings.

WINTER APPLE SALAD

1 cup golden raisins
Orange juice
2 cups diced celery
3 cups diced unpeeled red apples
½ cup seeded halved Tokay grapes
1 cup broken walnuts
1 cup mayonnaise
1 cup dairy sour cream

Place raisins in small bowl; add enough orange juice to barely cover. Let stand overnight, then drain off any remaining juice; combine raisins with celery, apples, grapes and walnuts. Blend mayonnaise and sour cream; add to fruit mixture; mix thoroughly. Serve on salad greens. Makes 10 to 12 servings.

APPLE BLOSSOM SALAD

3 red apples
2 grapefruit
4 large oranges
½ pound grapes
Water cress
Marsala Lime Dressing*

Core apples; do not pare; slice. Section grapefruit and oranges. Halve and seed grapes. Arrange alternate slices of fruits petal-wise on salad plates. Heap center with grapes. Garnish with water cress. Serve with Marsala Lime Dressing. Makes 6 servings.

•Marsala Lime Dressing:

Combine 1 cup vegetable oil, ½ cup sweet Marsala wine, the juice of 1 lime, and ¼ teaspoon salt. Beat until thoroughly blended. Serve at once, or beat again just before serving.

RED APPLE COLE SLAW

3 cups shredded red cabbage
2 cups sliced unpeeled red apples

½ cup golden raisins
½ cup mayonnaise
½ cup dairy sour cream

Combine cabbage, apples and raisins. Combine mayonnaise and sour cream; add to cabbage mixture. Toss until well blended. Makes 6 servings.

WALDORF SALAD

4 cups cubed, unpeeled red apples
2 cups chopped celery

⅔ cup chopped walnuts
Mayonnaise or salad dressing
Lettuce

Combine apples, celery and walnuts. Add enough mayonnaise or salad dressing to hold ingredients together. Serve on lettuce. Makes 6 servings.

APPLE GRAPE SALAD

4 apples
1 cup seedless white grapes
½ pint dairy sour cream

⅓ cup mayonnaise
½ cup chopped walnuts

Pare, core and dice apples; combine with grapes. Blend sour cream and mayonnaise; add half of this mixture to apples and grapes. Mix well; heap on water cress or other salad greens, top with remaining dressing and sprinkle with walnuts. Makes 6 servings.

APPLE MELON COUPE

4 small honey-ball melons
1 Persian melon or cantaloupe
4 red apples
½ cup French dressing
1 bunch water cress

2 packages (3 ounces each) cream cheese
⅓ cup finely chopped walnuts
8 sprigs fresh mint

Cut honey-ball melons in half, crosswise; remove seeds. Cut out pulp with small melon-ball cutter. Save shells. Cut balls from Persian melon or cantaloupe with larger cutter; combine the two kinds of melon balls. Core apples; do not pare; slice thin. Drop into French dressing to prevent darkening. Just before serving, drain apple slices. Arrange mixed fruits in honey-ball shells; surround with sprays of water cress; top each with a cream cheese ball rolled in chopped walnuts and a sprig of fresh mint. Serve with cream mayonnaise. Makes 8 servings.

APPLE PRUNE SALAD

8 large or 16 medium-size
　　raw prunes
1 package (3 ounces) cream
　　cheese
Cream
2 stalks celery, minced

¼ teaspoon salt
2 apples, peeled, cored and
　　sliced
Lettuce
Salad dressing

Soak prunes several hours or until quite soft. Dry, slit; remove pits. Soften cheese with fork, adding few drops of cream if necessary. Combine with celery and salt. Fill pitted prunes with cheese mixture, pressing prunes together around the cheese. Arrange apple slices on crisp lettuce. Place prunes between apple slices. Serve with mayonnaise or salad dressing. Makes 4 servings.

APPLE SALAD BOWL

2 cups diced unpared red
　　apples
1 cup diced pineapple
1 cup diced American
　　cheese
½ cup broken walnuts

⅓ cup mayonnaise
⅓ cup dairy sour cream
1 teaspoon lemon juice
1 teaspoon sugar
¼ teaspoon salt

Combine all ingredients; toss well to mix. Serve on crisp salad greens. Makes 6 servings.

APPLE RING SALAD

4 tart apples
3 packages (3 ounces each)
　　cream cheese
⅓ cup broken walnuts

½ cup drained, crushed
　　pineapple
¼ cup canned diced
　　candied orange peel

Core unpared, tart red apples. Cut in rings ½ inch thick. Mash cream cheese; blend in walnuts, pineapple and orange peel. Spread generously between apple rings, sandwich fashion. Cut through to make bite-size portions. Top with additional cheese mixture and garnish with small pieces of unpared apple. Surround with chicory. Serve with Honey Fruit Dressing.* Makes 4 servings.

*Honey Fruit Dressing:

2 tablespoons honey
2 tablespoons pineapple
 juice

2 tablespoons orange juice
⅔ cup mayonnaise

Combine honey and fruit juices; blend with mayonnaise. Makes 4 servings.

SWISS APPLE SALAD

2 cups diced, unpeeled red
 apples
½ cup bottled French
 dressing
4 ripe bananas

1 can (11 ounces)
 mandarin oranges
½ cup white seeded grapes
1 cup mayonnaise
½ cup dairy sour cream

Drop diced apples into French dressing. Cut a slit lengthwise in banana peel; remove banana carefully, leaving peel intact. Flute bananas with fork; slice into French dressing. Drain oranges; add with grapes. Toss to be sure fruits are well coated with dressing. Chill; drain; fill banana shells with fruits. Combine mayonnaise and sour cream; serve with salads. Makes 4 servings.

SUMMER APPLE SALAD

1 cup sugar
2 cups water
1 tablespoon lemon juice
Red food coloring
6 summer apples

3 ripe bananas
2 cups blueberries
Salad greens
Cream mayonnaise

Combine sugar and water in saucepan; bring to boil, stirring until sugar dissolves; boil 5 minutes. Add lemon juice; tint red with food coloring. Pare and core apples; cut in halves. Simmer halves in syrup until just tender; chill in syrup; drain. Arrange 2 halves on salad greens on each of 6 individual salad plates. Peel bananas; score with tines of fork; slice. Arrange on salad plate with blueberries. Serve with cream mayonnaise made by combining equal parts of whipped cream and mayonnaise. Makes 6 servings.

APPLE WHIRL DESSERT SALAD

3 packages (3 ounces each)
   cream cheese
Whipping cream
½ cup chopped pecans

Heart leaves of lettuce
3 tart juicy apples
Cherry preserves
Apricot preserves

Mash cream cheese with a little cream. Form into small balls; roll in chopped pecans. Place heart leaves of lettuce on 6 salad plates, at one side. Place 3 cheese balls on lettuce on each plate. Dip apple slices in lemon juice and arrange on other side of plates. Pass preserves to be spooned on apple slices. Makes 6 servings.

SUMMER FRUIT SALAD

1 cup seedless white grapes
1 cup sliced bananas
1 cup cashew nuts

2 cups thinly sliced
   unpeeled red apples
Honey Cream Dressing*

Combine fruits and nuts with a little of the dressing; arrange in bowl on salad greens. Serve remaining dressing separately. Makes 6 servings.

*Honey Cream Dressing:

¼ cup dairy sour cream
1 cup fine-curd creamed
   cottage cheese
1 cup mayonnaise

¼ cup honey
2 teaspoons lime juice
2 teaspoons minced parsley

Combine sour cream, cottage cheese and mayonnaise; mix well. Blend in honey and lime juice. Stir in parsley. Makes about 2½ cups.

TRIPLE-A SALAD

4 apples
2 avocados
½ cup grapefruit juice

¼ lb. salted almonds
1 bunch water cress
French dressing

Core apples; do not pare. Slice ⅛ inch thick. Pare avocados; halve; remove stones. Slice ⅛ inch thick. Cover apple and avocado slices with grapefruit juice to prevent discoloration. Just before serving, drain; add almonds and toss with French dressing. Serve on water cress. Makes 6 servings.

CRANBERRY WALDORF SALAD

2 cups diced apples
1 cup chopped celery
½ cup broken walnuts
Mayonnaise

1 can (1 pound) jellied
cranberry sauce
Water cress

Combine apples, celery and walnuts with enough mayonnaise to hold ingredients together. Cut cranberry sauce into 6 slices; top each slice with apple salad mixture. Garnish with water cress. Serve with additional mayonnaise or salad dressing. Makes 6 servings.

APPLE SALAD JULIENNE

3 red apples
2 medium green peppers
2 cups celery sticks

½ cup slivered blanched
almonds
Salad greens
Chutney Dressing*

Do not peel apples. Cut into very thin sticks with red peel at either end. Drop at once into water to which lemon juice or ascorbic-citric acid powder has been added. Cut green peppers and celery into very thin sticks. Drain apples thoroughly; combine with green pepper sticks, celery sticks and almonds; toss to mix. Place in a salad bowl lined with crisp salad greens. Serve with Chutney Dressing. Makes 8 servings.

*Chutney Dressing:

Combine 1 cup mayonnaise, ½ cup dairy sour cream and ½ cup drained, chopped chutney. Mix well.

SANDWICHES

A new role in the apple culinary repertoire! Not long ago a recipe for an apple sandwich won first prize in a national sandwich recipe contest for professional chefs. This was a main dish sandwich and our version of it—"Open-Face Apple Sandwich"—is in this chapter, on page 93. You'll like the other sandwich ideas, too.

APPLE CHEESE SANDWICH SPREAD

1 tablespoon butter or margarine
½ cup slivered roasted almonds
1 cup coarsely chopped apple
1 cup grated sharp Cheddar cheese
½ cup raisins
Mayonnaise

Melt butter or margarine; add almonds. Stir over low heat until golden brown; drain on absorbent paper. Combine almonds, apple, cheese and raisins with enough mayonnaise to hold ingredients together. Use as a filling for canned brown bread sandwiches. Makes about 2½ cups.

FRENCH TOAST SANDWICHES CALEDONIA

1 jar (6 ounces) crunch-style peanut butter
⅔ cup canned applesauce
8 slices white bread
3 eggs
½ teaspoon salt
1 tablespoon sugar
1 cup milk
Butter or margarine
Maple-flavored syrup

Blend peanut butter and applesauce; spread mixture on 4 slices bread. Top with remaining bread slices. Beat eggs slightly; add salt, sugar and milk; mix well. Dip sandwiches in egg mixture; fry in butter or margarine until golden brown on both sides. Cut each sandwich in half; serve hot with maple-flavored syrup. Makes 4 servings.

APPLE TEA SANDWICHES

1 package (8 ounces) cream cheese
¼ cup red currant jelly
¼ cup finely chopped walnuts
1 large tart apple
Thin-sliced white bread

Beat cheese until light and fluffy. Beat in jelly. Stir in walnuts. Peel and core apples; chop fine; add; mix well. Spread between thin slices of white bread; cut in fancy shapes. Makes about 2 dozen small tea sandwiches.

APPLE CURRY "SANDWICHES"

½ pound cream cheese
½ teaspoon curry powder
Few drops Tabasco
1 teaspoon prepared horse-radish
1 tablespoon pickle relish
1 tablespoon chopped stuffed olives
¼ cup chopped peanuts
2 or 3 tart red apples
Lemon juice
Paprika

Mash cream cheese; whip until soft. Blend in next 6 ingredients; mix well. Core apples; do not pare; cut in crosswise slices about ¼ inch thick. Put 2 slices together, with filling between. Brush with lemon juice; sprinkle with paprika. Serve at once. Makes 7 or 8 "sandwiches."

GRILLED APPLE SANDWICHES

1 package (8 ounces) cream cheese
2 tablespoons mayonnaise
1 cup finely chopped tart apples
6 slices bacon, cooked and crumbled
16 slices white bread
Melted butter or margarine

Mash cream cheese; add mayonnaise; beat until fluffy. Stir in apples and bacon. Spread between bread slices. Brush both sides of sandwiches generously with melted butter or margarine; grill until golden brown. Serve with soup as a beverage. (Green pea soup is especially good as a flavor companion.) Makes 8 sandwiches.

GRILLED APPLESAUCE SANDWICHES

18 pork sausage links
6 slices bread
1½ cups applesauce

6 thin slices American
Cheddar cheese

Cook sausages until crisp and brown. Meanwhile toast bread slices on both sides. Spread toast slices generously with applesauce. Place 3 sausage links on each slice; top with cheese. Broil 5 minutes, or until cheese melts. Serve at once.

OPEN-FACE APPLE SANDWICH

6 slices white sandwich
bread
Mayonnaise
Mustard
6 slices cooked ham

3 to 4 apples
12 slices (1 ounce each)
process American cheese

Spread bread slices with mayonnaise, then with mustard. Top with ham slices. Core apples; do not peel; slice crosswise about ⅛ inch thick to make 18 slices. Place 3 apple slices on each sandwich. Top each sandwich with 2 cheese slices. Broil under medium heat until cheese melts and browns slightly. Serve at once. Makes 6 open-face sandwiches.

TEATIME TREAT

24 slices raisin bread
½ pound cream cheese
¾ cup orange marmalade
2 red apples

3 bananas
Mayonnaise
1 can or package flaked
coconut

Spread half the bread slices with cream cheese, then with marmalade. Core apples; do not peel; cut in thin slices. Arrange apple slices on marmalade; top with remaining bread slices. Trim off crusts; cut sandwiches in half, on the diagonal. Peel bananas; cut in half crosswise, then cut each half in half again, lengthwise. "Paint" banana pieces with mayonnaise; coat generously with coconut; serve as an accompaniment to the sandwiches. Makes 12 servings.

PATIO SANDWICHES

8 slices white bread
8 slices American Cheddar
   cheese

1 can (1 pound) applesauce,
   heated
16 strips (about 1 pound)
   crisply cooked bacon

Toast bread on one side. Place cheese slices on untoasted side. Broil until cheese melts and browns. Top with hot applesauce and bacon strips. Serve at once. Makes 8 servings.

GRILLED APPLE-CHEESE SANDWICHES

1 cup grated sharp Cheddar
   cheese
1 cup finely chopped apples
⅓ cup minced stuffed olives

Mayonnaise
8 thin slices white bread
Melted butter or margarine

Combine cheese, apples and olives with enough mayonnaise to hold ingredients together. Spread between slices of bread. Brush outside of sandwiches generously with melted butter; grill until golden brown on both sides. Serve hot. Makes 4 sandwiches.

BREADS

Apple breads, made with baking powder or yeast, are among the most delicious of all breads. Bake Apple Batter Coffee Cake for the winter holidays. Make lunchbox sandwiches with Autumn Apple Bread. Serve apple griddlecakes, waffles or muffins for a lazy Sunday brunch. And there are other good recipes in this section that you won't want to miss.

APPLE GRIDDLECAKES

1½ cups sifted all-purpose flour
1¼ teaspoons baking powder
¾ teaspoon salt
½ teaspoon cinnamon
¼ cup sugar

1 egg, well beaten
1 cup milk, at room temperature
¼ cup butter or margarine melted
1 cup finely chopped apples

Mix and sift flour, baking powder, salt, cinnamon and sugar; sift again. Combine egg, milk, butter and apples. Add gradually to the flour mixture, stirring only until dry ingredients are moistened. Bake on hot greased griddle. Makes 14 to 16 griddlecakes.

APPLE BATTER COFFEE CAKE

½ cup shortening
1½ cups applesauce, divided
½ cup sugar
¼ cup warm water (105° to 115°)
1 tablespoon sugar
1 package active dry yeast
2 eggs, beaten
3 cups sifted all-purpose flour
1½ teaspoons salt

1 cup quick-cooking rolled oats
2 tablespoons butter or margarine
¼ cup firmly packed brown sugar
½ cup flaked coconut
½ cup chopped walnuts
1 teaspoon cinnamon
½ teaspoon nutmeg
3 glacé cherries, sliced

Melt shortening; stir in 1 cup of the applesauce and ½ cup sugar. Combine warm water, 1 tablespoon sugar and yeast;

stir until yeast dissolves. Combine beaten eggs, applesauce mixture, yeast mixture, flour and salt. Beat 2 minutes on medium speed of electric mixer, or 300 vigorous strokes by hand. Stir in rolled oats; mix well. Cover; let rise in warm place (85°) until double in bulk. Stir down batter by beating about 25 strokes. Spread batter evenly in two greased square pans, 8″ x 8″ x 2″. Mix butter and brown sugar until crumbly; add remaining applesauce and coconut; spread on each loaf evenly. Sprinkle with walnuts, cinnamon, nutmeg and sliced cherries. Cover; let rise in warm place until double in bulk. Bake at 375° for 40 to 45 minutes.

TROPICAL APPLE DATE BREAD

3 cups sifted all-purpose flour	1½ cups milk
1 cup sugar	1 egg, beaten
1 tablespoon baking powder	1 teaspoon vanilla
1½ teaspoons salt	1 cup packaged California diced dates
1 cup flaked coconut, toasted *	1 cup finely chopped apples

Mix and sift flour, sugar, baking powder and salt. Stir in coconut. Combine milk, egg and vanilla; stir in; blend well. Stir in dates and apples. Spoon into greased and floured loaf pan 9″ x 5″ x 3″. Bake at 350° for 1 hour and 15 minutes. Cool on rack.

* To toast coconut: spread flaked coconut in shallow pan. Place in 375° oven for 8 to 10 minutes, stirring often for even toasting. Cool.

APPLE CHEESE MUFFINS

½ cup shortening	1 cup finely chopped apples
½ cup sugar	⅔ cup coarsely grated sharp Cheddar cheese
2 eggs	½ cup chopped pecans
1½ cups sifted all-purpose flour	¾ cup milk
1 teaspoon baking powder	12 to 15 thin slices unpeeled red apple
1 teaspoon baking soda	Melted butter or margarine
½ teaspoon salt	Cinnamon-sugar
¾ cup quick-cooking rolled oats	

Cream shortening and sugar. Add eggs, one at a time, beating well after each addition. Mix and sift flour, baking powder, baking soda and salt; stir into shortening mixture. Stir in oats, apples, cheese and pecans; mix well. Add milk gradually, stirring only to moisten other ingredients. Fill well-greased muffins pans ⅔ full. Dip apple slices first in melted butter, then in cinnamon-sugar. Press 1 slice into batter in each muffin cup. Sprinkle lightly with cinnamon-sugar. Bake at 400° for 25 minutes. Makes 12 to 15 muffins.

APPLE FILBERT GRIDDLECAKES

2 cups sifted all-purpose
  flour
1 teaspoon baking soda
½ teaspoon salt
2 tablespoons sugar
2 eggs, well beaten
2 cups buttermilk

2 tablespoons shortening,
  melted
1½ cups very finely
  chopped apples
½ cup chopped filberts

Mix and sift flour, baking soda, salt and sugar. Combine eggs, buttermilk and melted shortening; add gradually to dry ingredients; stir until smooth. Fold in apples and nuts. Drop by spoonfuls on hot griddle. Bake until surface is covered with bubbles that do not break. Turn and brown on other side. Makes about 20 griddlecakes.

APPLE SPIRAL LOAF

Dough:
1 package active dry yeast
¼ cup warm water
  (105°–115°)
1½ cups milk, scalded
½ cup sugar
2 teaspoons salt
⅓ cup shortening
5½ to 6 cups sifted all-
  purpose flour

2 eggs, beaten
1½ cups rolled oats (quick
  or old-fashioned,
  uncooked)
Filling:
3 tablespoons melted butter
  or margarine
⅓ cup sugar
2 teaspoons cinnamon
1 cup chopped apples

Sprinkle yeast over warm water; stir to dissolve. Pour milk over sugar, salt and shortening. Stir occasionally until shortening is melted; cool to lukewarm. Stir in 1 cup flour and eggs; add softened yeast and oats. Stir in enough additional flour to make a soft dough. Turn out on lightly floured board or canvas; knead until satiny, about 10 minutes. Round dough into ball; place in greased bowl; turn to bring greased side up. Cover; let rise in warm place (85°) until double in size, about 1 hour. Punch down; cover; let rest 10 minutes. Roll half the dough to form a 15" x 8" rectangle. Brush with melted butter; sprinkle with sugar, cinnamon and apple mixture. Roll up dough as for jelly roll, starting at short end. Place in greased 9" x 5" x 3" loaf pan. Repeat with other half of dough. Cover; let rise in warm place until nearly double in size, about 45 minutes. Bake at 375° for 45 to 50 minutes. Remove from pans; brush tops with additional melted butter. Cool. Makes 2 loaves.

APPLE JOLLY BOYS

½ package (1¾ cups) buckwheat ready-mix for pancakes	1 teaspoon cinnamon
	1 egg, well beaten
	3 tablespoons molasses
1 package (2 cups) corn muffin mix	1 cup cold water
2 tablespoons sugar	1 cup diced canned pie-sliced apples

Combine mixes with sugar and cinnamon; blend well. Combine egg, molasses and water; stir in gradually. Stir in diced apples. Drop by heaping tablespoonfuls on hot greased griddle; flatten with back of spoon. Cook slowly, turning often, until well browned on both sides and cooked through. Set finished cakes in 300° oven to keep warm while remainder are cooked. Serve with butter and syrup or jam.

APPLE YEAST BRAID

1 package active dry yeast	1½ teaspoons salt
¼ cup warm water (105° to 115°)	4 to 4½ cups sifted all-purpose flour
1 cup milk, scalded	1 egg
½ cup butter or margarine, melted	1 cup enriched corn meal
⅓ cup sugar	1 can (1 pound 6 ounces) apple pie filling

Sprinkle yeast on warm water. Stir to dissolve. Pour milk and butter over sugar and salt. Stir until sugar dissolves. Cool to lukewarm. Beat in 1 cup flour and egg; add softened yeast and corn meal. Stir in enough additional flour to make a soft dough. Turn out on a lightly floured board or canvas; knead until smooth and satiny, about 10 minutes. Round dough into ball; place in greased bowl; brush lightly with melted shortening. Cover; let rise in warm place (85°) until double

in size, about 1 hour. Punch down; cover; let rest 10 minutes.
Roll half the dough to form a 14" x 9" rectangle. Place
on greased cookie sheet. Spread half the filling down center
third of dough, covering space about 3 inches wide. On each
side of filling, make 2-inch cuts in dough at 1-inch intervals.
Take a strip on each side and cross them at center over filling.
Pull strips down, keeping ends inside. Continue to lace opposite strips of dough over filling, tucking under last ends.
Repeat with other half of dough. Cover; let rise until nearly
double in size, about 45 minutes. Bake at 350° about 30
minutes or until golden brown. While warm, drizzle with
confectioners' sugar frosting. Makes 2 braids.

APPLE RAISIN PINWHEELS

2½ cups biscuit mix
2 tablespoons melted butter
3 apples, pared and cored,
  chopped fine
½ cup chopped peanuts

½ cup seedless raisins,
  chopped
1 tablespoon sugar
¼ teaspoon cinnamon
6 tablespoons molasses,
  divided

Make baking powder biscuit dough according to package
directions. Knead on floured board for about half a minute.
Roll out ½ inch thick in oblong shape. Spread with butter.
Combine apples, peanuts, raisins, sugar and cinnamon; mix
well; spread on dough. Pour 2 tablespoons molasses over all.
Roll up like a jelly roll; cut in 12 1-inch slices; place in
greased baking pan about ½ inch apart. Pour 1 teaspoon
molasses on each pinwheel. Bake at 400° for 18 to 20 minutes,
or until golden brown. Makes 12 pinwheels.

APPLE WALNUT BREAD

1½ cups sifted all-purpose
  flour
2 teaspoons baking powder
½ teaspoon baking soda
1 teaspoon salt
1 teaspoon cinnamon
¼ teaspoon nutmeg
⅛ teaspoon allspice

1½ cups crushed ready-to-
  serve wheat cereal flakes
1 cup broken walnuts
¾ cup chopped apple
1 egg, slightly beaten
¾ cup firmly packed brown
  sugar
1½ cups buttermilk
2 tablespoons vegetable oil

Mix and sift flour, baking powder, baking soda, salt and
spices. Stir in cereal flakes, walnuts and apple. Combine egg,

brown sugar, buttermilk and oil; add; mix just enough to moisten dry ingredients. Do not beat. Turn into well-greased loaf pan 9" x 5" x 3". Bake at 350° for 1 hour.

APPLE-TOPPED MUFFINS

1 can pie-sliced apples
¼ cup sugar
½ teaspoon cinnamon
1 package muffin mix

Drain apple slices; coat with mixed sugar and cinnamon. Prepare muffin mix as directed on package; fill muffin pans ⅔ full. Arrange 2 or 3 apple slices on top of each muffin, inserting edges in batter. Bake at 425° for 20 minutes or until brown. Makes 12 small muffins.

APPLE WAFFLES

2 cups milk
2 eggs
2 cups pancake mix
⅓ cup melted butter or margarine
1 cup finely chopped apples

Place milk, eggs, pancake mix and melted butter in bowl. Beat with rotary beater until batter is fairly smooth. Stir in apples. Bake in hot waffle baker until steaming stops. Serve with butter and cinnamon sugar. Makes 6 servings.

CINNAMON APPLE COFFEE CAKE

1 egg
⅓ cup sugar
1 cup sifted all-purpose flour
1 tablespoon baking powder
½ teaspoon salt
½ cup milk
1 cup rolled oats (quick or old-fashioned, uncooked)
¼ cup shortening, melted

2 large cooking apples, peeled and sliced
Topping:
¼ cup sugar
½ teaspoon cinnamon
¼ teaspoon nutmeg
2 tablespoons melted butter or margarine

Beat egg and sugar together until creamy. Mix and sift flour, baking powder and salt; add alternately with milk to egg mixture. Stir in oats and shortening. Spread half the batter in greased 9-inch round baking pan. Arrange apple slices over batter. Spread remaining batter over apple slices. Combine sugar, cinnamon and nutmeg. Add melted butter, mixing well. Sprinkle over batter. Bake at 375° for 25 to 30 minutes. Serve hot.

APPLE WALNUT GRIDDLECAKES

2 cups pancake mix
1 tablespoon sugar
½ teaspoon cinnamon

1 cup finely chopped apples
½ cup chopped walnuts
1¾ cups milk

Combine pancake mix, sugar and cinnamon. Stir in apples and walnuts. Add milk gradually. Bake on a hot griddle, turning when underside is golden brown and bubbles on top have "set." Makes 12 large griddlecakes.

APPLESAUCE RAISIN BREAD

1½ cups sifted all-purpose
  flour
1 teaspoon baking powder
1 teaspoon baking soda
1 teaspoon salt
1 teaspoon cinnamon
½ teaspoon nutmeg
½ cup firmly packed brown
  sugar

1 cup seedless raisins
1 cup rolled oats (quick or
  old-fashioned, uncooked)
2 eggs, beaten
⅓ cup vegetable oil
1 cup sweetened canned
  applesauce

Mix and sift flour, baking powder, baking soda, salt and spices. Stir in sugar, raisins and oats. Add remaining ingredients; stir only until dry ingredients are moistened. Pour into greased 9″ x 5″ x 3″ loaf pan. Bake at 350° about 1 hour. Remove from pan immediately; cool. Wrap cooled bread and store one day for ease in slicing.

AUTUMN APPLE BREAD

¼ cup shortening
⅔ cup sugar
2 eggs, well beaten
2 cups sifted all-purpose
  flour
1 teaspoon baking powder
1 teaspoon baking soda

1 teaspoon salt
2 cups coarsely grated raw
  apples
1 tablespoon grated lemon
  peel
⅔ cup chopped walnuts

Cream shortening and sugar until light and fluffy; beat in eggs. Mix and sift flour, baking powder, baking soda and salt; add alternately with the grated apple to egg mixture. Stir in lemon peel and walnuts (batter will be stiff). Bake in greased and floured loaf pan, 8" x 5" x 3", at 350° for 50 or 60 minutes. Do not slice until cold.

MOLASSES APPLE GEMS

1 cup yellow corn meal	1 cup milk
1½ cups sifted all-purpose flour	1 egg, beaten
3 tablespoons sugar	4 tart apples, pared, cored and chopped fine
½ teaspoon salt	2 tablespoons molasses
3 teaspoons baking powder	

Mix and sift corn meal, flour, sugar, salt and baking powder. Combine milk and egg; add; mix well. Add chopped apples and molasses. Fill hot, greased muffin or gem pans ⅔ full. Bake at 400° for 20 to 25 minutes. Makes about 1 dozen gems.

SPICY APPLE BREAD

3 cups sifted all-purpose flour	1⅛ cups firmly packed light brown sugar (1 cup plus 2 tablespoons)
1½ teaspoons baking soda	3 eggs
1½ teaspoons salt	1½ teaspoons vanilla
1½ teaspoons cinnamon	1½ cups grated raw apples
¾ teaspoon nutmeg	3 tablespoons cider vinegar plus water to make ¾ cup
½ teaspoon allspice	¾ cup chopped walnuts
¼ teaspoon ground cloves	
¾ cup shortening	

Mix and sift flour, baking soda, salt and spices. Cream shortening and sugar. Add eggs 1 at a time, beating well after each addition. Add vanilla. Stir in flour mixture, alternating with grated apples and liquid. Stir in walnuts. Turn into greased loaf pan, 11¼" x 4½" x 2½", or 2 small loaf pans. Bake at 350° for 1¼ hours, or until done. Cool on wire rack.

BEVERAGES

When apples are transformed into cider, apple juice, or even applesauce, they become a source of delight as a base for tall drinks, hot mulled drinks or punch. In England a hot drink called Lamb's Wool is always served on Twelfth Night. The English use ale with apples in this beverage, but we like the cider version on this page.

APPLE BLOSSOM ICE CREAM SODA

2 cups apple juice
1 pint peach ice cream

Dry ginger ale

Pour ½ cup apple juice in each of 4 tall glasses. Divide ice cream equally among glasses. Fill glasses with ice-cold ginger ale. Stir gently to mix.

APPLE COOLER

1 quart apple juice or cider
2 cups apricot nectar

Juice of 6 limes
Club soda

Combine apple juice, apricot nectar and lime juice. Pour over ice into 6 tall glasses. Fill glasses with club soda.

LAMB'S WOOL°

8 large baking apples
2 quarts apple cider
1 cup firmly packed brown sugar

2 tablespoons mixed pickling spices

Wrap each apple in double thickness of heavy aluminum foil; place in baking pan. Roast at 450° until soft (about 1½ hours). Remove foil. Put apples through food mill or sieve (there should be from 5 to 6 cups of pulp). Meanwhile com-

* Traditional in certain parts of England as a wassail bowl on Twelfth Night.

bine cider, brown sugar and spices in kettle. Stir over low heat until sugar dissolves; bring to boil. Lower heat; simmer ½ hour; strain. Add hot cider mixture to apple pulp; serve hot in sturdy mugs. Makes about 3½ quarts.

CONCORD APPLEADE

1 quart apple juice or cider   ¼ cup lime juice
2 cups grape juice

Combine apple juice, grape juice and lime juice. Pour over ice in 6 tall glasses.

FRUITED MOCHA FOAM

2 apples, peeled and diced   3 tablespoons sugar
1 ripe banana, cut in chunks   ⅔ cup non-fat dry milk
2 teaspoons instant coffee   1⅔ cups ice water
2 tablespoons instant cocoa   1 teaspoon vanilla

Combine all ingredients in an electric blender. Operate on low speed until fruit is liquefied. Beat on high speed until foamy. Makes 2 or 3 servings.

PARTY PUNCH

1 cup orange juice   1 cup pineapple juice
¼ cup lemon juice   1 pint apple cider
1 pint cranberry juice   2 quarts chilled ginger ale
    cocktail

Combine all ingredients except ginger ale; mix well. Just before serving, pour over ice in punch bowl; add ginger ale. Makes about 30 punch-cup servings.

TRURO APPLE FOAM

1 quart apple juice   1 egg white
1 cup canned cranberry   2 tablespoons sugar
    juice cocktail   Nutmeg

Combine ice-cold apple juice and cranberry juice; mix well. Divide among 4 tall glasses. Beat egg white stiff, adding sugar while beating. Top each glass with spoonful of sweetened egg white. Sprinkle with nutmeg.

MULLED APPLE PUNCH

3 pounds cooking apples
2 teaspoons cinnamon
½ teaspoon cloves
1 teaspoon nutmeg

3 cans frozen lemonade
   concentrate
1 red apple
Whole cloves
1 gallon apple cider

Wash apples; do not peel or core; cut into eighths. Cook in small amount of water until very soft. Put through food mill or sieve. Stir in spices. Add frozen concentrate; heat gently until lemonade is thawed. Stud red apple with whole cloves; place in heatproof punch bowl; add spiced apple mixture. Heat cider (do not boil). Pour into punch bowl. Serve in mugs. Makes about 20 1-cup servings.

ROSY GLOW

Apple juice "ice" cubes with
   mint
1 quart chilled apple juice
2 cups chilled Apple Red
Hawaiian punch

2 tablespoons lemon juice
Chilled carbonated lemon-
   lime beverage

Place a mint sprig in each section of ice cube tray; fill with apple juice; freeze solid. Combine 1 quart apple juice, Hawaiian punch and lemon juice; pour over apple juice "ice" cubes in tall glasses, filling ⅔ full. Fill to top with carbonated lemon-lime beverage. Stir gently to mix. Makes 12 servings.

ACCOMPANIMENTS

Applesauce has always been the traditional accompaniment for pork. There is sound reasoning behind this, because apples speed and aid digestion. However, apples prepared in other ways make delicious meat accompaniments, too, as you will find when you go through this chapter.

APPLE SOODLE

8 cooking apples
2 tablespoons flour
⅔ cup sugar
¼ teaspoon salt

2 cups warm water
Red food coloring
Nutmeg

Pare and core apples; cut in quarters. Place in layers in casserole, rounded side up. Combine flour, sugar and salt. Add water; stir smooth. Tint deep pink with food coloring. Pour over apples. Sprinkle generously with nutmeg and additional sugar. Bake at 350° for 35 to 40 minutes, or until apples are tender but have not lost shape. Serve warm as a meat accompaniment. Makes 6 to 8 servings.

APPLE-STUFFED ACORN SQUASH

2 acorn squash
3 tart red apples
1 cup broken cashew nuts

½ cup maple syrup
¼ cup melted butter or
   margarine

Cut acorn squash in half lengthwise; scoop out seeds and stringy substance. Core and dice unpeeled apples; combine with remaining ingredients. Fill squash with apple mixture. Brush surfaces of squash with additional melted butter or margarine. Set in baking pan. Pour hot water in pan to depth of ½ inch. Cover pan with foil. Bake at 400° for 45 minutes. Serve with ham or fresh pork. Makes 4 servings.

BAKED APPLE SLICES

2 large tart red apples
⅓ cup firmly packed brown sugar

4 teaspoons prepared mustard
Whole cloves

Wash and core apples; do not pare. Slice crosswise ½ inch thick. Combine brown sugar and prepared mustard; spread on apple slices. Stud with whole cloves. Lay slices in shallow baking pan; pour small amount of boiling water in bottom of pan. Bake at 350° for 15 minutes. Serve as garnish for roast pork.

CURRIED APPLE HALVES

3 tart apples
¾ cup sugar
¾ cup water
1½ tablespoons curry powder

1 tablespoon minced onion
½ teaspoon salt
⅓ cup finely chopped chutney

Wash, core and pare apples; cut in half crosswise. Combine sugar, water, curry powder, onion and salt in saucepan; bring to a boil, stirring until sugar dissolves. Add apples; cover; simmer 3 to 5 minutes. Turn apples carefully; cover; cook 2 to 3 minutes longer or until apples are easily pierced with a fork but still hold their shape. Remove apples to shallow pan. Continue cooking sugar mixture until it forms a thick syrup. Add chutney. Pour over apples; broil until apples are well glazed, basting several times with syrup. Serve as a meat accompaniment. Makes 6 servings.

JELLIED SPICED APPLESAUCE

1 envelope (1 tablespoon) unflavored gelatin
¼ cup cold water
2½ cups sweetened applesauce

2 tablespoons lime juice
⅛ teaspoon salt
¼ teaspoon nutmeg
½ teaspoon cinnamon

Soften gelatin in cold water; dissolve over hot water. Combine applesauce, lime juice, salt, spices and dissolved gelatin; stir thoroughly. Pour into individual molds that have been rinsed in cold water; chill until firm. Unmold. Serve as a meat garnish. Makes 6 to 8 servings.

CAPE COD RELISH

2 red apples
½ lemon
¼ cup orange marmalade

1 can (1 pound) whole berry cranberry sauce

Core apples; do not pare; put through food chopper with seeded lemon, using fine knife. Combine with marmalade and cranberry sauce; chill. Serve with meat course.

PUCHIDEE RELISH

6 large, tart apples
1 medium onion
½ green pepper
½ sweet red pepper

¼ cup dairy sour cream
½ teaspoon salt
Few grains pepper

Pare, core and dice apples. Mince onion and peppers; add to apples. Add sour cream, salt and pepper; mix well. Chill 1 hour. Makes 8 servings.

QUICK APPLE CRANBERRY CONSERVE

1 cup whole berry cranberry sauce

1 cup pared diced eating apples
⅓ cup broken pecans

Combine all ingredients; chill. Serve with cream cheese and crackers for dessert. Makes 6 servings.

RAW APPLE RELISH

2 large red apples
Juice of 1 lemon
1 medium onion, chopped
¼ cup sliced sweet gherkins

1 tablespoon capers
¼ cup sliced ripe olives
½ cup French dressing

Core apples; do not peel. Cut crosswise into ½-inch slices, then into ½-inch chunks. Sprinkle with lemon juice. Add remaining ingredients; toss to mix well. Makes 6 servings.

A fine accompaniment for roast pork, pork chops, baked ham, ham slice, smoked pork butt—indeed, any kind of pork, fresh or cured.

RED CABBAGE AND APPLES

4 large tart apples
1 large onion
¼ cup bacon fat
1 medium-size red cabbage, shredded

Water
½ cup dark corn syrup
⅓ cup vinegar
2 tablespoons butter or margarine

Pare, core and chop apples. Chop onion; add. Melt bacon fat in deep skillet or Dutch oven; add apple mixture; cook over low heat for 10 minutes. Add cabbage and ½ cup water. Cook 20 minutes, adding more water if necessary. Add corn syrup and vinegar; cook 5 minutes longer. Just before serving, add butter or margarine. Season to taste with salt and pepper. Serve with grilled frankfurters. Makes 8 servings.

RUBY BAKED APPLES
Garnish Accompaniment for Roast Duckling

6 firm, tart red apples
1 cup canned (whole berry) cranberry sauce
¼ cup slivered blanched almonds
⅓ cup minced candied ginger
¼ cup light corn syrup

2 tablespoons sugar
2 tablespoons water
2 teaspoons lemon juice
Few drops red food coloring
3 tablespoons butter or margarine

Core apples from stem end almost through to blossom end. Pare about ⅓ of the way down from stem end. Combine cranberry sauce, almonds and ginger; fill centers of apples heaping full. Combine all remaining ingredients except butter in small saucepan; simmer 5 minutes. Brush pared surfaces lavishly with this syrup. Set each apple on a generous double thickness of heavy-duty aluminum foil; top each apple with ½ tablespoon butter; bring ends of foil up and around apples, and twist. Place on baking sheet. Bake at 400° about 40 minutes or until apples feel soft. Remove foil. If desired, brush with any remaining syrup; run under broiler a few seconds to glaze. Makes 6 servings.

SAUERKRAUT APPLES

6 large cooking apples
4 cups sauerkraut

2 teaspoons caraway seeds
2 tablespoons lemon juice

Core apples, cut slice from top of each; scoop out pulp, leaving thin shells. Dice pulp; combine with drained sauerkraut, caraway seeds and lemon juice. Fill apple shells with sauerkraut mixture. Place in shallow baking dish containing ¼ inch of water. Bake at 350° for 50 to 60 minutes, or until apples are tender. Serve on platter with roast pork.

YAMS WITH APPLES

6 cooked yams, cubed
4 apples, cored, pared and
    diced

¼ cup butter or margarine
½ cup maple syrup
¼ cup water

Arrange alternate layers of yams and apples in a baking dish, dotting each layer with butter or margarine. Combine maple syrup and water; pour over all. Cover; bake at 350° for 30 minutes, or until apples are tender. Serve with pork. Makes 6 servings.

DESSERTS

We have followed the apple through the menu, finding that it can take its place in any course with delightful results. But in the field of desserts this fruit really takes over. There is no limit, save imagination, to the desserts that can be based on apples—pies, cakes, puddings, cookies, and a host of others that defy classification. Read on!

AFTER-CHRISTMAS BAKED APPLES

10 large tart apples
⅔ cup crumbled fruit cake
1 cup finely chopped raw
   cranberries
⅔ cup sugar
⅔ cup crushed peppermint
   candy
¾ teaspoon cinnamon

Core apples, being careful not to cut all the way through. Peel ⅓ of the way down from stem end. Combine remaining ingredients; fill apples, rounding mixture on top. Set in large baking pan. Pour hot water into pan to a depth of ½ inch. Cover; bake at 350° for 40 minutes to 1 hour, or until apples are tender. Sprinkle peeled portions generously with granulated sugar; run under broiler to glaze. Serve warm or cold with plain or whipped cream. Garnish with whole peppermint candies, if desired. Makes 8 to 10 servings.

BAKED APPLE MERINGUE GLACÉ

6 large baking apples
Canned whole cranberry
   sauce
Light corn syrup
Nutmeg
1 egg white
4 tablespoons sugar

Core apples, being careful not to cut all the way through. Pare about ⅓ of the way down from stem end. Fill cored section with cranberry sauce. Brush pared surfaces with light corn syrup; dust with nutmeg. Beat egg white to soft peaks; beat in sugar; continue beating until very stiff. Place a small mound of this meringue on each apple. Set apple in baking pan.

111

Add hot water to depth of about ½ inch. Bake at 325° for 50 to 60 minutes, or until apples are tender and meringues golden brown. Serve with vanilla ice cream. Makes 6 servings.

BAKED APPLE ALASKA

4 large baking apples	2 egg whites
1 jar marrons in syrup	¼ cup sugar

Core apples; do not pare. Fill centers with marrons and syrup. Bake at 350° for 30 to 35 minutes, or until apples are tender. Chill. Beat egg whites stiff but not dry; add sugar gradually, beating constantly. Swirl high on apples. Bake at 450° for 3 to 5 minutes, or until meringue is golden brown. Serve at once. Makes 4 servings.

• BAKED APPLES CANTON

6 large baking apples	1 cup light corn syrup
1 cup coarsely chopped walnuts	1 teaspoon powdered ginger
½ cup chopped pitted dates	Red food coloring
⅓ cup chopped candied ginger	Sugar

Core apples almost through. Pare about ⅓ of the way down from stem end. Combine walnuts, dates and candied ginger. Fill centers of apples. Combine corn syrup and powdered ginger. Tint red with food coloring; simmer 5 minutes. Brush apples thickly with this mixture. Place in baking dish; add enough boiling water to cover bottom of baking dish. Bake at 350° about 40 minutes, or until tender, basting frequently with syrup. Remove from oven. Sprinkle with sugar. Broil, with surface of apples 4 inches below source of heat, basting with remaining syrup and sprinkling with additional sugar, until glazed—about 15 minutes. Makes 6 servings.

BAKED APPLES FLORIDA

6 large baking apples	6 tablespoons dark corn syrup
Prepared mincemeat	1 cup orange juice

Core apples, being careful not to cut completely through. Hollow out, leaving shell about ⅓ inch thick. Chop the pulp; combine with equal amount of mincemeat and corn syrup.

Fill apple shells with this mixture. Place in baking pan. Pour orange juice into pan. Bake at 350° for 45 minutes, basting frequently with the orange juice in the pan. Makes 6 servings.

BAKED APPLES GRENADA

4 large baking apples
Grenadine syrup
½ cup whipping cream

2 tablespoons orange marmalade
Nutmeg

Core apples, being careful not to cut through blossom end. Pare about ⅓ of the way from stem to blossom end. Fill centers with grenadine syrup, and brush cut surface with this syrup also. Place in baking dish; add hot water to a depth of ½ inch; cover. Bake at 350° about 45 minutes, or until apples are tender, brushing cut surfaces once or twice with grenadine during this time. Chill. When ready to serve, whip cream; fold in orange marmalade. Fill centers of apples; sprinkle lightly with nutmeg. Makes 4 servings.

BAKED APPLES IN FOIL

6 large baking apples
1 teaspoon cinnamon
½ cup sugar
¼ cup light corn syrup

Red food coloring
3 tablespoons butter or margarine

Core apples; pare ⅓ of the way down from the stem end. Place each apple on double thickness of heavy-duty aluminum foil. Combine cinnamon and sugar; mix well; fill centers of apples. Tint light corn syrup deep pink with food coloring; brush generously over peeled surface. Top each apple with 1½ teaspoons butter or margarine. Bring foil up around apples and twist top of each foil-wrapped package. Set in shallow baking pan lined with foil. Bake at 400° for 50 to 60 minutes or until apples are tender.

BAKED APPLES WITH APPLEJACK SAUCE

6 large baking apples
⅓ cup sugar

1 tablespoon cinnamon
Applejack Sauce*

Core apples but do not cut through to blossom end. Pare about ⅓ of the way down from stem end. Combine sugar and cinnamon; fill center of apples. Wrap each apple in heavy-duty foil. Place on rack in baking pan. Pour hot water into pan to depth of about ½ inch. Bake at 350° for 45 minutes. Remove foil; chill. Serve with Applejack Sauce. Makes 6 servings.

° Applejack Sauce:

Combine 1 pint dairy sour cream, ½ cup confectioners' sugar, ¼ teaspoon nutmeg, ¼ cup finely chopped mixed diced candied fruits and peels, and ½ cup applejack. Mix well. Chill.

BAKED APPLES MARASCHINO

6 large baking apples
¼ cup quartered maraschino cherries
1 cup drained, crushed pineapple
½ cup slivered blanched almonds
⅓ cup light corn syrup
⅓ cup maraschino syrup
Red food coloring
Sugar

Core apples almost through. Pare about ⅓ of the way down from stem end. Combine cherries, pineapple and almonds. Fill centers of apples. Combine corn syrup and maraschino syrup. Tint deep red with food coloring. Brush apples with this mixture. Place in baking dish; add enough boiling water to cover bottom of baking dish. Bake at 350° about 40 minutes, or until tender. Remove from oven. Sprinkle with sugar; broil, with surface of apples 4 inches below source of heat, basting often with remaining syrup and sprinkling with additional sugar, until glazed—about 15 minutes. Makes 6 servings.

BAKED APPLES MARSALA

8 large dried apricots
3 tablespoons sugar
¼ cup finely chopped walnuts
4 large baking apples
8 teaspoons Marsala wine
¼ cup firmly packed brown sugar
Dairy sour cream

Soak apricots in warm water until soft. Drain; chop fine. Combine chopped apricots, sugar and walnuts; blend well. Core apples; pare about ⅓ of the way down. Fill apple centers with apricot mixture. Pour 2 teaspoons Marsala wine over filling in each apple. Pour 1 cup water into baking dish; stir

in brown sugar; put apples in baking dish. Bake at 350°
about 45 minutes or until apples are tender, basting occasionally with liquid in pan. Chill. Serve with dairy sour
cream. Makes 4 servings.

BAKED APPLES SUPREME

6 large baking apples
½ cup sugar
1 teaspoon cinnamon
⅓ cup light corn syrup
Red food coloring

3 tablespoons butter or
  margarine
1 jar (14 ounces) cranberry
  orange relish

Core apples, being careful not to cut all the way through;
pare about ⅓ of the way down from stem end. Place each
apple on large square of doubled heavy-duty aluminum foil.
Combine sugar and cinnamon; fill centers with this mixture.
Tint corn syrup deep pink with food coloring; brush over
peeled surface of apples. Dot each apple with butter or margarine. Bring foil up around apples and twist top of each
foil-wrapped package. Set in shallow baking pan. Bake at
400° for 50 to 60 minutes, or until apples are tender. Remove from foil; chill. To serve, top generously with cranberry orange relish. May be used as a garnish for turkey or
other poultry, or as dessert, accompanied by plain cream or
whipped cream if desired. Makes 6 servings.

BAKED STUFFED APPLES

6 large baking apples
¾ cup light corn syrup
6 whole cloves
Cinnamon
2 packages (3 ounces each)
  cream cheese

2 tablespoons light cream
2 tablespoons honey
⅓ cup raisins
⅓ cup chopped walnuts

Core apples, being careful not to break all the way through.
Do not peel. Set in baking pan. Into cavity of each apple
pour 2 tablespoons light corn syrup, 1 whole clove and a
dash of cinnamon. Cover bottom of pan with hot water. Bake
at 350° about 30 minutes, or until apples are tender, basting occasionally. Chill. Remove cloves. Place in dishes surrounded by syrup. Whip cream cheese with cream and honey
until soft and fluffy. Add raisins and walnuts; mix well. Fill

apple cavities with cream cheese mixture, heaping generously on top. Makes 6 servings.

BAKED APPLES WITH RASPBERRY FLUFF

6 large baking apples
1 cup marshmallow fluff
⅓ cup broken pecans

⅓ cup flaked coconut
⅓ cup raspberry jam

Core apples almost through to blossom end. Pare about ⅓ of the way down from stem end. Place in baking pan; add enough boiling water to cover bottom of pan. Cover; bake at 350° about 20 minutes. Remove cover. Sprinkle tops lightly with sugar. Bake 15 to 20 minutes longer or until apples are tender. Remove from pan; cool. Combine remaining ingredients; serve as a sauce with apples. Makes 6 servings.

CANDIED BAKED APPLES

4 large baking apples
½ cup well-drained crushed
  pineapple
2 tablespoons broken
  walnuts
4 maraschino cherries,
  chopped

½ cup light corn syrup
¼ cup sugar
¼ cup water
1 tablespoon lemon juice
Red food coloring

Core apples, being careful not to cut through blossom end. Pare ⅓ of the way down from stem end. Combine pineapple, walnuts and cherries; fill cavities in apples. Place in large casserole. Cover. Bake at 400° for 20 minutes. Combine corn syrup, sugar, water and lemon juice; tint red with food coloring; boil slowly until thickened (about 10 minutes); spoon over apples. Continue baking, uncovered, 10 minutes or until apples are tender. Serve with Hard Sauce "Apples" (page 207). Makes 4 servings.

CAPE COD BAKED APPLES

1 can (1 pound) whole berry
  cranberry sauce
6 large baking apples

½ cup miniature marsh-
  mallows
⅓ cup finely chopped
  pecans

Spread half the cranberry sauce in shallow baking pan. Add enough water to fill to a depth of ½ inch. Core apples; peel about ⅓ of the way down from stem end; place cut side down on cranberry sauce in pan. Bake at 350° about 30 minutes. Turn apples peeled side up. Combine remaining cranberry sauce, marshmallows and pecans. Fill apples heaping full. Return to oven; bake 15 minutes longer or until apples are tender. Makes 6 servings.

GOLD COAST BAKED APPLES

6 baking apples	½ cup sugar
¼ cup seedless raisins	½ cup water
¼ cup canned slivered blanched almonds	1 teaspoon grated orange peel
1 tablespoon orange marmalade	¼ cup orange juice
	1 tablespoon butter

Core apples, being careful not to cut all the way through. Peel about ⅓ of the way down from stem end. Combine raisins, almonds and marmalade; fill apple centers with this mixture. Combine remaining ingredients in saucepan; stir over low heat until sugar dissolves; simmer 5 minutes. Place apples in baking pan; pour syrup over them. Cover; bake at 350° for 45 minutes to 1 hour, basting frequently with syrup in pan. When tender, baste once more and run under broiler to glaze. Serve with whipped cream.

HONEY BAKED APPLES

6 large tart apples	Sugar
6 tablespoons honey	Nutmeg
¼ cup orange juice	

Core apples, being careful not to cut all the way through. Peel about ⅓ of the way down from stem end. Combine honey and orange juice; pour into centers of apples. Set in baking dish. Pour a little hot water in bottom of pan. Bake at 400° for 50 to 60 minutes or until apples are tender. Sprinkle tops with a little sugar and nutmeg. Run under broiler to glaze.

HONEY MERINGUE BAKED APPLES

6 large baking apples	¼ teaspoon mace
¾ cup light corn syrup	1 egg white
6 small pieces stick cinnamon	3 tablespoons honey

Core apples, being careful not to cut all the way through; do not peel. Set in baking dish. Pour 2 tablespoons light corn syrup into each apple; place stick cinnamon in each apple. Pour ½ cup hot water into pan. Bake at 350° for 30 to 40 minutes, or until apples are tender, basting occasionally. Chill. Add mace to egg white; beat until stiff. Add honey, a little at a time, while continuing to beat. Top apples with a spoonful of this mixture. Makes 6 servings.

SNOWY BAKED APPLES

6 large baking apples
½ cup water
¾ cup firmly packed dark brown sugar
¼ cup prepared mincemeat
1 cup flaked coconut, divided
2 egg whites
4 tablespoons sugar

Core apples; remove about 1 inch of peel from stem ends. Place apples cut side down in shallow baking dish. Add water. Sprinkle water with brown sugar. Cover; bake at 375° for 30 minutes. Uncover; turn apples cut side up; baste with liquid in dish. Combine mincemeat and half the coconut; fill apple centers. Bake 15 minutes longer, or until apples are just tender. Meanwhile, beat egg whites until foamy. Add sugar, 1 tablespoon at a time, continuing to beat until meringue stands in stiff peaks. Spoon on top of apples; sprinkle with remaining coconut; return to oven for about 10 minutes, or until meringue is golden brown. Makes 6 servings.

STREUSEL-TOPPED BAKED APPLES

5 or 6 large baking apples
⅔ cup (packed) pie crust mix
½ cup firmly packed light brown sugar
⅛ teaspoon nutmeg
1 teaspoon cinnamon

Core apples, being careful not to cut all the way through. Pare ⅓ of the way down from stem end. Combine remaining ingredients, mixing with fork or fingertips until crumbly. Fill centers of apples with some of the streusel mixture. Set apples in baking pan. Pour in enough hot water to cover bottom of pan to a depth of ¼ inch. Cover pan (if fitted cover is not available, use aluminum foil). Bake at 350° for 40 to 45 minutes. Remove cover; heap remaining streusel mixture on apples; run under broiler just long enough to brown topping. Serve with hot maple syrup.

TROPICAL BAKED APPLES À LA MODE

4 large baking apples
1¼ cups light corn syrup, divided
1½ cups water, divided
Red food coloring
¼ cup sugar

1 package (8 ounces) fresh California pitted dates
Few grains salt
½ cup chopped pecans
1 pint coffee ice cream

Core apples; pare ⅓ of the way down from stem end. Combine ¾ cup corn syrup, 1 cup water and enough food coloring to tint deep pink; pour into baking pan. Place apples in baking pan, cut side down. Bake at 350° for 35 to 45 minutes or until tender. Turn cut side up; spoon syrup in pan over pared surfaces; sprinkle with sugar. Chill. Snip dates into small pieces; add salt and remaining ½ cup water. Heat to boiling. Stir in remaining ½ cup corn syrup and pecans. Chill. Serve apples topped with date sauce and ice cream.

APPLE ALASKA PIE

Pastry for 1-crust pie
6 medium apples
¾ cup sugar
1½ teaspoons flour
¼ teaspoon nutmeg
½ teaspoon cinnamon

1½ tablespoons butter or margarine
3 egg whites
½ cup sugar
1 quart butter pecan ice cream

Line 9-inch pie pan with pastry; trim edge; press edge down with tines of fork. Core, pare and slice apples. Combine ¾ cup sugar, flour and spices; rub a little of this mixture into pastry, then make alternate layers of apple slices and spice mixture; dot with butter or margarine. Bake at 425° for 30 minutes or until apples are tender. Remove from oven, let cool thoroughly. Beat egg whites stiff but not dry; add ½ cup sugar 1 tablespoon at a time, beating well after each addition. Spoon ice cream evenly on top of pie to within ½ inch of rim. Cover entire surface of pie with meringue. Bake at 500° for 2 minutes.

APPLE COBBLESTONE PIE

6 to 8 large tart apples
Pastry for 1-crust pie
1 cup sugar
3 tablespoons butter

1 tablespoon lemon juice
¼ teaspoon nutmeg
½ teaspoon cinnamon

Wash apples; pare; cut in quarters. Remove cores. Line 9-inch pie pan with pastry; trim edge; flute. Cut enough thin slices of apple from quarters to cover bottom of pie pan. Place remaining quartered apples on top, close together, to look like cobblestones. Add sugar; dot with butter or margarine; sprinkle with lemon juice, nutmeg and cinnamon. Bake at 425° for 15 minutes. Reduce heat to 325°; bake 20 minutes longer, or until apples are tender.

APPLE ORANGE PIE

5 tart apples
3 navel oranges
½ cup sugar
¼ cup flour
¾ cup firmly packed
  brown sugar
½ teaspoon nutmeg

½ teaspoon cinnamon
¼ teaspoon allspice
Grated peel of 1 orange
Grated peel of 1 lemon
Pastry for 2-crust 10-inch pie
3 tablespoons butter or
  margarine

Pare, core and slice apples. Peel oranges, removing all white membrane; remove sections carefully. Combine sugar, flour, brown sugar, spices and grated peels. Line 10-inch pie pan with pastry. Alternate layers of apple slices and orange sections in pan, sprinkling each layer with sugar mixture. Dot with butter. Adjust top crust. Cut slits in center. If desired, brush with slightly beaten egg white and sprinkle with a little sugar. Seal and flute edges. Bake at 425° for 15 minutes; lower heat to 400°; bake 30 minutes longer.

APPLE JAM PIE

6 large tart apples
½ cup peach or apricot jam
Pastry for 2-crust pie

¼ teaspoon nutmeg
1 cup dairy sour cream

Pare, core and slice apples. Add jam; stir with a fork until well mixed. Arrange in 9-inch pie pan lined with pastry. Sprinkle with nutmeg. Spoon sour cream over apples. Top with pastry. Press edges together with tines of fork. Cut slits in center. Bake at 425° for 40 to 45 minutes, or until apples are tender.

APPLE SESAME CRISSCROSS PIE

6 to 8 large tart apples
1 cup sugar
1 tablespoon flour
½ teaspoon cinnamon
¼ teaspoon nutmeg

2 tablespoons toasted sesame seeds,* divided
Pastry for 2-crust 9-inch pie
2 tablespoons butter or margarine

Core and pare apples; slice thin. Combine sugar, flour and spices; add to apples; mix well. Add 1 tablespoon sesame seeds to half the pastry; roll out; fit into 9-inch pie pan. Fill pan with apple mixture; dot with butter; sprinkle with remaining sesame seeds. Roll out remaining pastry; cut in strips about ½ inch wide. Arrange lattice fashion on pie. Trim edges; flute. If desired, brush pastry strips with slightly beaten egg yolk mixed with a little water. Bake at 425° for 40 to 45 minutes.

* To toast sesame seeds: spread in shallow pan; set in 350° oven until golden brown, stirring often.

APPLE RIBBON PIE
(illustrated on back cover)

6 to 8 large tart apples
Pastry for 2-crust pie
1 cup sugar
1 tablespoon flour
¼ teaspoon nutmeg
½ teaspoon cinnamon

2 tablespoons butter or margarine
¼ cup grated sharp Cheddar cheese
1½ teaspoons poppy seeds

Pare and core apples; slice thin. Line 9-inch pie pan with pastry. Combine sugar, flour and spices; rub a little of this mixture into pastry in pie pan. Fill pie pan with sliced apples; add remaining sugar mixture. Dot with butter or margarine. Divide remaining pastry in two equal portions. Roll out 1 portion ⅛ inch thick; top with grated cheese; fold over in 3 layers; roll out again. Cut into 5 strips 10 inches long by ¾ inch wide. Repeat with remaining portion of pastry, using poppy seeds instead of cheese. Weave strips, lattice fashion, on pie, alternating cheese strips and poppy seed strips; trim and flute edges. Bake at 425° for 40 to 45 minutes, or until apples are tender.

APPLE PECAN CRUMB-TOP PIE

¼ cup chopped pecans
1 unbaked 9-inch pie shell
1 cup sugar
2 teaspoons flour
¼ teaspoon nutmeg
½ teaspoon cinnamon

6 cups thinly sliced tart apples
2 tablespoons butter or margarine
Crumb Topping*

Sprinkle pecans on bottom of pie shell. Mix sugar, flour and spices; mix through apples. Heap apples in pie shell. Dot with butter or margarine. Top with Crumb Topping. Bake at 425° for 40 to 45 minutes or until apples are tender.

* Crumb Topping:

½ cup firmly packed brown sugar
¼ cup butter or margarine

⅓ cup sifted all-purpose flour
¼ teaspoon cinnamon
¼ cup chopped pecans

Blend first 4 ingredients with fork until butter is size of peas. Stir in pecans.

APPLE SNOW PIE

1½ envelopes unflavored gelatin
2 cups cold water, divided
1¼ cups sugar
½ teaspoon salt

1 tablespoon grated lemon peel
⅓ cup lemon juice
3 egg whites, unbeaten
1½ cups grated tart apples
10-inch baked pastry shell

Soften gelatin in ½ cup cold water in top of double boiler. Set over boiling water; stir until gelatin is dissolved. Remove from heat. Add sugar, salt, lemon peel, lemon juice and remaining cold water; stir until sugar is dissolved. Chill until mixture is the consistency of unbeaten egg white, stirring frequently. Add egg whites; beat with electric or rotary beater until mixture begins to hold its shape. Fold in grated apples. Turn into pie shell; chill until firm. Top with whipped cream and chopped walnuts, if desired.

APPLE CRANBERRY PIE

½ cup sugar	½ cup honey
2 tablespoons flour	1 tablespoon butter or
¼ teaspoon cinnamon	margarine
¼ teaspoon salt	3 cups fresh cranberries
1 teaspoon grated orange	2 cups diced peeled apples
peel	Pastry for 2-crust pie

Combine sugar, flour, cinnamon, salt, orange peel, honey and butter or margarine. Cook 2 minutes, stirring until sugar dissolves. Add cranberries and apples; boil 5 minutes, or until cranberries burst. Cool. Pour into pastry-lined 9-inch pie pan. Arrange strips of pastry lattice fashion over filling. Trim edges; flute. Bake at 425° for 35 to 40 minutes.

APPLE PIE PROVENÇAL

Pastry for 2-crust pie	½ teaspoon cinnamon
½ cup red currant jelly, divided	5 cups thinly sliced tart apples
1 cup sugar	2 tablespoons butter or
2 tablespoons flour	margarine
¼ teaspoon nutmeg	

Line 9-inch pie pan with pastry. Spread with ¼ cup currant jelly. Combine sugar, flour and spices; mix gently with apples; heap in pie pan. Dot with butter or margarine. Top with remaining jelly. Roll out remaining pastry; cut in strips about ½ inch wide; arrange on pie lattice fashion; trim edges; flute. Bake at 425° for 45 minutes, or until apples are tender.

APPLESAUCE MINCE PIE

1 package pie crust mix	1½ cups prepared mince-
2½ cups sweetened applesauce	meat
	2 tablespoons melted butter or margarine

Line 9-inch pie pan with pastry Combine applesauce, mince-meat and melted butter or margarine; fill pie pan. Top with remaining pastry, rolled thin and slashed in the center; trim; press edges together. Bake at 425° for 35 minutes.

APPLE, RAISIN AND WALNUT PIE

½ cup raisins
1½ cups apple cider
1½ cups water, divided
¾ cup sugar
2 cups finely chopped tart apples
¾ teaspoon salt
1 tablespoon lemon juice
½ teaspoon grated lemon peel
2 tablespoons butter or margarine
1 teaspoon cinnamon
4 tablespoons cornstarch
1 cup broken walnuts
Pastry for two 8-inch pies

Rinse and drain raisins. Combine with cider, 1 cup water, sugar, apples, salt, lemon juice and peel, butter and cinnamon. Heat to boiling. Blend cornstarch with remaining ½ cup cold water; add; boil 3 to 4 minutes longer, or until thick. Stir in walnuts. Spoon into 2 pastry-lined 8-inch pie pans; top with strips of pastry arranged lattice fashion. Trim edges; flute. Bake at 400° for about 45 minutes.

COCONUT DUTCH APPLE PIE

Pastry for 1-crust pie
2 tablespoons flour
¾ cup sugar, divided
⅛ teaspoon salt
1 teaspoon cinnamon
5 cups tart apple slices, cut ¼ inch thick
1 tablespoon lemon juice
5 tablespoons butter or margarine, divided
½ cup flour
¾ cup flaked coconut

Line 9-inch pie pan with pastry; flute edge. Combine 2 tablespoons flour, ½ cup sugar, salt and cinnamon. Place a layer of apple slices in pie shell; sprinkle part of flour-sugar mixture over apples. Add remaining apples in layers alternately with flour-sugar mixture. Sprinkle lemon juice over top of pie; dot with 1 tablespoon butter or margarine. Bake at 425° for 45 minutes, or until apples are tender. Combine remaining sugar and flour. Melt remaining butter or margarine; add; mix well until crumbly. Add coconut. Sprinkle this mixture over top of baked pie. Return to oven; bake about 7 minutes longer, or until topping is browned.

COCONUT STREUSEL APPLE PIE

1½ tablespoons quick-cooking tapioca	5 cups peeled sliced apples
½ cup sugar	1 tablespoon lemon juice
⅛ teaspoon salt	Pastry for 1-crust pie
¾ teaspoon cinnamon	Crumb Topping*
¼ teaspoon nutmeg	½ cup flaked coconut

Combine tapioca, sugar, salt, cinnamon and nutmeg; add to apple slices with lemon juice. Mix well. Line 9-inch pie pan with pastry; flute edges. Fill pan with apple mixture; bake at 425° about 25 minutes, or until apples are tender. Sprinkle Crumb Topping over surface of pie; sprinkle coconut evenly over topping. Bake 5 to 10 minutes longer, or until syrup boils with heavy bubbles that do not burst.

* **Crumb Topping:** Combine ⅓ cup firmly packed brown sugar, ⅓ cup fine graham cracker crumbs, ¼ cup slightly soft butter or margarine; mix until crumbs are the size of peas.

CANDY APPLE PIE

1½ cups sugar	Pastry for 2-crust pie
1 teaspoon cinnamon	2 tablespoons butter or margarine
¼ teaspoon nutmeg	
¼ teaspoon ground cloves	1 egg yolk
1 cup water	1 tablespoon water
1 tablespoon lemon juice	1 tablespoon sugar
5 cups thinly sliced apples	

Combine 1½ cups sugar, spices and water in saucepan; stir over low heat until sugar dissolves; boil 10 minutes. Stir in lemon juice. Add apple slices; cover; simmer gently until apples are tender. Line 9-inch pie pan with pastry; fill pan with apples and syrup; dot with butter. Cut remaining pastry in long strips; arrange, lattice fashion, over apples; trim edges; flute. Beat egg yolk slightly; add water; blend; brush over pastry strips; sprinkle with 1 tablespoon sugar. Bake at 425°

for 20 to 25 minutes, or until golden brown. Serve warm. If pie is served a second time, reheat.

BROWN SUGAR APPLE PIE

7 tart apples
1 cup firmly packed brown sugar
2 tablespoons flour
1/8 teaspoon salt
1 1/2 teaspoons cinnamon
1/4 teaspoon nutmeg
1/4 teaspoon mace
1 tablespoon grated lemon peel
Pastry for 2-crust pie
2 tablespoons butter or margarine

Pare and core apples; slice thin. Combine with sugar, flour, salt, spices and lemon peel; mix with apple slices. Line 9-inch pie pan with pastry. Fill heaping full with apple mixture. Dot with butter or margarine. Adjust top crust; cut slits in crust to allow steam to escape. Seal edges; crimp or flute. Bake at 450° for 10 minutes; lower heat to 350°, bake 40 minutes longer. Serve hot.

CRANBERRY-GLAZED APPLE PIE

6 to 8 large tart apples
1 cup sugar
1 tablespoon flour
1/2 teaspoon nutmeg
1/2 teaspoon cinnamon
1 unbaked 9-inch pie shell
2 tablespoons butter or margarine
Cranberry Glaze*

Pare and core apples; slice thin. Combine sugar, flour and spices. Line pie pan with pastry. Rub a little of the sugar mixture into pastry in pan. Arrange apple slices in pan; sprinkle remaining sugar mixture evenly over apples. Dot with butter or margarine. Cut 9-inch circle from aluminum foil; place on top. Bake at 425° for 40 to 45 minutes, or until apples are tender. Remove foil. Spoon warm Cranberry Glaze over surface. Chill until glaze sets.

* Cranberry Glaze:

1/2 cup water
1/2 cup sugar
1/2 cup fresh cranberries
4 teaspoons cornstarch
2 tablespoons cold water

Combine water and sugar in small saucepan; stir over medium heat until sugar dissolves. Add cranberries; cook until cranberries begin to "pop." Blend cornstarch and cold water; add; stir over low heat until thickened and clear.

CIDER EGGNOG PIE

1 envelope unflavored gelatin
¼ cup orange juice
¾ cup hot water
1 tablespoon grated lemon peel
1 tablespoon lemon juice
¼ cup sugar
¼ teaspoon salt
3 eggs, well beaten
1⅓ cups apple cider
Sherry flavoring
1 9-inch baked pie shell
1 cup whipping cream
½ cup broken walnuts

Soften gelatin in orange juice; dissolve in hot water. Add lemon peel, lemon juice, sugar and salt; stir until sugar dissolves. Beat in eggs. Cook over hot water until mixture thickens, stirring constantly. Remove from heat; add cider; cool. Add sherry flavoring to taste. Chill until consistency of unbeaten egg white; beat with rotary beater until very light and fluffy. Spoon into pie shell. Top with whipped cream and walnuts.

CORNUCOPIA APPLE PIE

Pastry for 2-crust 9-inch pie
¾ cup sugar
¼ teaspoon nutmeg
½ teaspoon cinnamon
⅛ teaspoon salt
4 cups sliced tart apples
1 cup golden raisins
½ cup flaked coconut
2 teaspoons lemon juice
1 teaspoon grated lemon peel
1 tablespoon butter or margarine
6 slices American cheese
6 maraschino cherries

Line 9-inch pie pan with pastry. Combine sugar, spices and salt. Combine apple slices, raisins and coconut. Arrange half the apple mixture in pie pan. Add half the sugar mixture. Sprinkle with half the lemon juice and peel. Repeat. Dot with butter or margarine. Top with pastry; flute edges; cut slits in center. Brush top with a little milk; sprinkle with sugar. Bake at 425° for 45 to 50 minutes, or until apples are tender. Let cheese come to room temperature. Roll each slice into a cornucopia. Arrange on pie. Put maraschino cherry in each cornucopia.

CHEESE CRUST APPLE PIE

1 package pie crust mix
¾ cup sugar
½ teaspoon cinnamon
½ teaspoon nutmeg
6 cups sliced apples

4 tablespoons butter or
margarine, divided
½ cup grated sharp Cheddar cheese

Prepare pie crust mix as directed on package. Line 9-inch pie pan with half the pastry, rolled thin. Combine sugar and spices; add to apples; mix lightly. Pour into pastry-lined pie pan. Dot with 2 tablespoons butter or margarine. Roll out remaining pastry; sprinkle with cheese; dot with remaining butter. Roll up like jelly roll; fold ends to center; fold again to center; fold again in middle; roll out thin. Place cheese pastry over apples; trim edges; press together with fork, or flute. Cut gashes in top to allow steam to escape. Bake at 400° for 50 to 60 minutes, or until apples are tender.

GLAZED APPLE CRISSCROSS PIE

6 to 8 large tart apples
⅓ cup sugar
½ teaspoon cinnamon
¼ teaspoon nutmeg
1 package pie crust mix
1 tablespoon sugar

2 tablespoons sesame seeds
1 tablespoon butter or
margarine
1 egg white
Juice of ½ lemon
1 cup confectioners' sugar

Core and pare apples; slice thin; add ⅓ cup sugar and spices; mix well. Mix pastry according to package directions; divide in half. Combine 1 tablespoon sugar and 1 tablespoon sesame seeds with half of pastry; roll out. Line 9-inch pie pan; trim edge, leaving ½-inch overhang. Fill pie pan with apple mixture; dot with butter or margarine. Roll out remaining pastry, cut in strips about ½ inch wide; arrange in crisscross fashion on apples. Bring undercrust rim up and over end of strips; flute. Sprinkle remaining sesame seeds over surface of pie. Combine unbeaten egg white, lemon juice and confectioners' sugar to make a thick soft frosting; pour over top of pie. Bake at 425° for 40 to 45 minutes, or until apples are tender.

CHINA CLIPPER APPLE PIE
(illustrated on back cover)

Pastry for 2-crust pie
1 cup sugar
½ teaspoon ginger
1 teaspoon cinnamon
¼ teaspoon nutmeg
¼ teaspoon salt
2 tablespoons flour
3 tablespoons strong tea
1 tablespoon lemon juice
4 cups sliced tart apples
2 tablespoons butter or margarine

Line 9-inch pie pan with half of pastry. Combine sugar, spices, salt, flour, tea and lemon juice. Alternate layers of sliced apples and sugar mixture until pan is filled, heaping slightly in center. Dot with butter or margarine. Roll out top crust; cut slits for escaping steam; place over apples. Trim pastry; press edges together with tines of fork. Brush with cream. Bake at 425° for 40 to 45 minutes.

HONEY CREAM APPLE PIE

½ cup dairy sour cream
¾ cup honey
¼ teaspoon salt
1 teaspoon cinnamon
½ teaspoon nutmeg
6 large tart apples, sliced thin
Pastry for 2-crust pie

Combine sour cream, honey, salt and spices; add sliced apples; mix well. Line 9-inch pie pan with pastry; add apple mixture, heaping in center. Top with remaining pastry; seal; flute edge. Prick top with fork to outline wedges for serving. Bake at 425° for 40 to 45 minutes, or until apples are tender.

CUSTARD APPLESAUCE PIE

1 package pie crust mix
2 cups thick, unsweetened applesauce
⅛ teaspoon nutmeg
½ cup sugar*
4 eggs, slightly beaten
3 cups milk, scalded
Few grains salt
1 teaspoon vanilla

Make pastry according to package directions. Line two 8-

* If canned applesauce is used, less sugar may be used.

inch pie pans (or 1 deep 10-inch pie pan); flute edges. Combine applesauce and nutmeg. Add sugar to eggs; add scalded milk slowly while stirring. Add salt and vanilla; pour slowly into applesauce mixture, blending well. Taste for sweetness; if necessary, add more sugar. Pour into pie shells. Sprinkle with additional nutmeg. Bake at 425° for 30 to 40 minutes, or until knife inserted near rim of pie comes out clean. Cool. Garnish with a ruffle of whipped cream, if desired.

CRUMBLE-TOP APPLE CREAM PIE

6 large tart apples
Pastry for 1-crust 9-inch pie
1 cup sugar
1 tablespoon flour
1/4 teaspoon nutmeg
1/2 teaspoon cinnamon
Topping:
2 tablespoons brown sugar

2 tablespoons sugar
1/8 teaspoon each nutmeg, cinnamon and salt
3 tablespoons flour
2 tablespoons butter or margarine

Pare and core apples; slice thin. Line 9-inch pie pan with pastry. Combine next 4 ingredients; rub a little of this sugar mixture into pastry. Arrange overlapping apple slices in pastry-lined pie pan. Add remaining sugar mixture. Combine topping ingredients; mix with fingertips until crumbly; sprinkle over surface. Bake at 425° for 40 to 45 minutes, or until apples are tender. Remove from oven. Carefully and slowly pour 1/2 cup whipping cream over apples. Let stand 15 minutes. Serve warm.

CRUMBLE-TOP APPLE PIE

1 package pie crust mix, divided
1/2 cup firmly packed brown sugar
1 teaspoon cinnamon
1/4 teaspoon allspice
1/8 teaspoon cloves

2 tablespoons butter or margarine
1 cup grated sharp Cheddar cheese
1/2 cup sugar
1 tablespoon flour
4 cups thinly sliced apples

Combine 1/2 cup pie crust mix, brown sugar, cinnamon, allspice and cloves; cut in butter or margarine until mixture is crumbly. Stir in cheese; set aside. Add enough cold water (about 3 tablespoons) to remaining pie crust mix to form pastry dough. Roll out ⅛ inch thick; line 9-inch pie pan; make cutouts with any remaining pastry. Wet rim of pie shell; place cutouts around rim. Combine sugar and flour. Arrange apples in pie pan, sprinkling evenly with sugar-flour mixture. Top with reserved crumb mixture. Bake at 375° about 45 minutes, or until apples are tender.

DEEP-DISH APPLE DATE PIE

6 tart apples
1 cup pitted dates, sliced
½ cup sugar
½ cup firmly packed brown sugar
½ teaspoon nutmeg
Grated peel of 1 lemon
Grated peel of 1 orange
3 tablespoons butter or margarine
Pastry for 1-crust pie

Pare and core apples; cut into eighths. Arrange half the apple slices in baking dish; top with half the dates; repeat. Combine sugars, nutmeg and grated peels; sprinkle over top. Dot with butter. Top with thin sheet of pastry. Cut slits in pastry to allow steam to escape. Bake at 425° for 45 minutes, or until apples are soft. Serve warm with plain cream. Makes 6 servings.

HOLIDAY APPLE PIE

6 to 8 large tart apples
Pastry for 2-crust 9-inch pie
½ cup granulated sugar
½ cup firmly packed brown sugar
1 tablespoon flour
½ teaspoon nutmeg
Grated peel of 1 lemon
Grated peel of 1 orange
2 tablespoons orange juice
3 tablespoons butter or margarine

Pare and core apples; cut in quarters; slice thin. Line 9-inch pie pan with pastry. Combine sugars, flour and nutmeg; rub a little of this mixture into pastry. Add fruit peels to remaining sugar mixture. Arrange apples in pie pan, sprinkling each layer with some of the sugar mixture. Sprinkle with orange juice; dot with butter or margarine. Cut remaining pastry into strips 10 inches long and ½ inch wide. Weave, lattice fashion, over pie filling. Trim and crimp edges. Bake at 425° for 40 to 45 minutes, or until apples are tender. Let cool. For a special occasion, brush top with thin confectioners' sugar icing; decorate with chopped candied orange peel and chopped glacé cherries. Makes 6 servings.

FRENCH APPLE PIE

1½ tablespoons quick-cooking tapioca
¾ cup sugar
⅛ teaspoon salt
¾ teaspoon cinnamon
¼ teaspoon nutmeg
5 cups thinly sliced tart apples
Pastry for 2-crust 8-inch pie
2 tablespoons butter or margarine

Mix tapioca, sugar, salt, cinnamon, nutmeg and apples. Line 8-inch pie pan with pastry rolled ⅛ inch thick. Fill with apple mixture; dot with butter or margarine. Moisten edge of pastry. Cut slits in top crust to permit escape of steam, and adjust on pie, opening slits with knife. Bake at 425° for 55 minutes, or until syrup boils with heavy bubbles that do not burst. Cool. Frost top with thin confectioners' sugar icing. Sprinkle with chopped walnuts.

RUBY APPLESAUCE PIE

1 can (1 pound) applesauce or 2 cups fresh applesauce
2 cups whole berry cranberry sauce
3 tablespoons cornstarch
¼ cup cold water
½ teaspoon nutmeg
1 teaspoon cinnamon
1 9-inch baked pie shell

Combine applesauce and cranberry sauce. Dissolve cornstarch in cold water; add to applesauce mixture with spices. Cook over low heat, stirring constantly, until thickened; cool. Pour into baked pie shell. Chill.

GRANDMA'S APPLE PIE

6 to 8 large tart apples
Pastry for 2-crust pie
½ cup sugar
½ cup firmly packed dark brown sugar
2 teaspoons flour
½ teaspoon nutmeg
¼ teaspoon cinnamon
¼ teaspoon allspice
1 tablespoon grated lemon peel
2 tablespoons butter or margarine

Core and pare apples; cut in quarters, then slice thin. Line 9-inch pie pan with pastry. Mix sugars, flour and spices. Rub

Holiday Apple Pudding: A steamed pudding with a difference, made with chocolate and walnuts, fruited with bits of apple, surrounded with jaunty hard sauce snowmen. Page 148.

Applesauce Bowl Cake (above): A perfectly scrumptious dessert, so easy to make you'll never believe how delicious it is unless you actually try it. Just read the recipe on page 152.

Stuffed Flounder Roll-Ups (below): Guaranteed to convert non-fish lovers! Tender fillets with a savory apple-scallop stuffing and creamy caper sauce. Recipe on page 60.

Apple Raisin Pastry Strip: This is one of our most popular recipes. Flaky pastry with scalloped edges partly encloses a luscious apple-raisin filling. Recipe, page 140.

Apple Ricotta Refrigerator Cake: Unusual, delicious, easy to make. Based on an Italian original as to flavor. The recipe, page 176.

English Apple Flan: First a pie shell in a pizza pan, then a layer of thick homemade applesauce topped with concentric circles of apple slices and apricot glaze. Recipe is on page 141.

Molded Winter Apple Salad (above): A handsome affair, with a clear layer atop a creamy layer, the latter holding apples, dates, walnuts and raisins. The recipe, page 83.

Coconut Streusel Apple Pie (below): A wonderful idea! Crunchy streusel topping over apple filling, snowy coconut scattered over all, to toast in the oven. Recipe, page 125.

Tropical Baked Apples à la Mode: Luscious baked apples with a rich topping of dates and nuts, crowned with a scoop of coffee ice cream. The recipe for this dessert is on page 119.

a little sugar mixture into pastry in pan. Arrange apple slices
in pan, heaping slightly in center. Sprinkle evenly with remaining sugar mixture. Scatter lemon peel over surface. Dot
with butter or margarine. Adjust top crust; trim edges, flute.
Cut slits in center to allow steam to escape. Bake at 425°
for 40 to 45 minutes, or until apples are tender and pastry
golden brown.

INDIVIDUAL DEEP-DISH APPLE PIES

6 large tart apples	2 tablespoons grated orange
½ cup sugar	peel
½ cup firmly packed brown	3 tablespoons butter or
sugar	margarine
½ teaspoon nutmeg	Pastry for 1-crust pie
1 tablespoon grated lemon	
peel	

Pare, core and slice apples. Combine sugars, nutmeg and
peels. Add to apple slices; toss to mix. Fill 6 deep individual
ramekins with apple mixture. Dot each with ½ tablespoon
butter or margarine. Top with pastry cut in rounds or apple
shapes. Bake at 425° for 40 to 45 minutes, or until apples are
tender.

LITTLE BROWN SUGAR APPLE PIES

2 packages pie crust mix	1 tablespoon grated lemon
6 large tart cooking apples	peel
1 cup firmly packed brown	2 tablespoons grated orange
sugar	peel
½ teaspoon nutmeg	3 tablespoons butter or
	margarine

Prepare pie crust mix as directed on package. Roll out thin,
half at a time, on lightly floured board. Cut out 4 circles to
fit 6-inch pie pans; fit into pans, leaving ½-inch overhang.
Repeat for top crusts. Pare, core and slice apples. Combine
sugar, nutmeg and peels; add to apple slices; mix well. Heap
in pie pans. Dot with butter or margarine. Adjust top crusts;
bring overhang up over edge of top crusts; flute. Cut gashes

in tops of pies. Bake at 425° for 40 to 45 minutes. Serve hot with blue cheese.

MONTPELIER CRISSCROSS APPLE PIE

Pastry for 2-crust 9-inch pie
4 cups thinly sliced apples
1 cup maple syrup
2 tablespoons quick-cooking tapioca
¼ teaspoon nutmeg
½ teaspoon cinnamon
½ cup chopped walnuts

Line pie pan with pastry for bottom crust. Combine remaining ingredients; mix well; arrange in pie pan. Cut remaining pastry in long strips; arrange, lattice fashion, over apples; trim edges; flute. Brush strips with beaten egg white; sprinkle with a mixture of sugar and cinnamon, if desired. Bake at 425° for 45 minutes, or until syrup boils with thick bubbles that do not burst.

OLD-FASHIONED APPLE PIE

6 to 8 large tart apples
Pastry for 2-crust pie
1 cup sugar
2 teaspoons flour
¼ teaspoon nutmeg
½ teaspoon cinnamon
2 tablespoons butter or margarine

Pare apples, cut in quarters. Remove cores; slice thin. Line 9-inch pie pan with pastry. Mix sugar, flour and spices; rub a little sugar mixture into pastry. Arrange sliced apples overlapping in pan. Add remaining sugar mixture. Dot with butter or margarine. Cut slits in top crust; moisten edge of lower crust. Place top crust over apples; press edges together; trim. Bake at 425° for 40 to 45 minutes, or until apples are tender.

OLD-TIME APPLE CUSTARD PIE

1 package pie crust mix
3 eggs, slightly beaten
½ cup sugar
¼ teaspoon salt
3 cups milk
1 teaspoon vanilla
2 cups grated apples
Nutmeg

Make pastry according to package directions; line two 8-inch pie pans (or 1 *deep* 10-inch pie pan), making fluted edges. Combine eggs, sugar and salt. Add milk gradually; mix well. Add vanilla. Stir in grated apple. Pour carefully into unbaked pie shells. Sprinkle with nutmeg. Bake at 425° for 40 minutes, or until knife inserted near rim of pie comes out clean. Cool. Garnish with a ruffle of whipped cream, if desired.

OLD VIRGINIA APPLE CRUMB PIE

3 cups thinly sliced tart apples or 1 can (20 ounces) pie-sliced apples, well drained*
1 8-inch unbaked pie shell
1 tablespoon lemon juice
⅓ cup sugar
4 tablespoons crunch-type peanut butter

2 tablespoons butter or margarine
½ cup flour
½ cup firmly packed brown sugar
½ teaspoon cinnamon
¼ teaspoon nutmeg
1 tablespoon grated lemon peel

Arrange apple slices in pie shell. Sprinkle with lemon juice and sugar. Cut peanut butter and butter into mixture of flour, brown sugar, spices and lemon peel. Spread over surface of pie. Bake at 400° for 45 to 50 minutes, or until apples are tender.

* If canned apples are used, reduce sugar to ¼ cup and increase lemon juice to 2 tablespoons. Baking time will be 35 to 40 minutes.

OZARK PIE

½ cup sifted all-purpose flour
2 teaspoons baking powder
½ teaspoon salt
2 eggs
1 cup firmly packed brown sugar

1 tablespoon vanilla
1 cup chopped walnuts
1 cup finely chopped apples
1 unbaked 9-inch pie shell

Mix and sift flour, baking powder and salt. Beat eggs until light and lemon colored. Beat in sugar gradually, continuing to beat until creamy. Stir in flour mixture, vanilla, nuts and apples; mix well. Spoon filling mixture into pie shell. Bake at 450° for 15 minutes; lower heat to 350°; bake 15 minutes longer, or until filling is set. Cool. Garnish with ice cream or whipped cream and chopped nuts.

STREUSEL-TOP APPLE PIE

1 package pie crust mix	½ teaspoon cinnamon
5 cups thinly sliced apples	1 tablespoon grated orange
⅓ cup orange juice	peel
½ cup firmly packed brown sugar	¼ teaspoon salt
	¾ cup sifted all-purpose
½ cup sugar	flour
½ teaspoon nutmeg	½ cup butter or margarine

Line 9-inch pie pan with pastry; trim edge. Arrange apples in pan; sprinkle with orange juice. Combine sugars, spices, orange peel, salt and flour. Cut in butter. Spread evenly over apples. Roll remaining pastry ⅛ inch thick; cut in long strips about ¼ inch wide. Braid 3 strips together, joining when necessary, to make a braid long enough to go around rim of pie. Moisten edge of lower crust; place braid on moistened edge loosely, to allow for shrinkage during baking. Bake at 400° for 45 to 50 minutes. Serve warm with whipped cream or ice cream.

TOPSY-TURVY APPLE PECAN PIE

¼ cup softened butter or margarine	2 tablespoons lemon juice
	1 tablespoon flour
½ cup pecan halves	½ cup sugar
⅔ cup firmly packed brown sugar	½ teaspoon cinnamon
	½ teaspoon nutmeg
Pastry for 2-crust pie	¼ teaspoon salt
6 cups sliced apples	

Spread softened butter evenly on bottom and sides of 9-inch pie pan. Press pecan halves, rounded side down, into butter. Pat brown sugar evenly over pecans. Roll out enough pastry for 1 crust; place in pie pan over sugar; trim, leaving ½-inch overhang. Combine apples, lemon juice, flour, sugar, spices and salt; pour into pie pan, keeping top level. Top with remaining pastry; trim even with bottom crust; fold edges together, flush with rim, and flute. Prick top of pie with fork. Bake at 450° for 10 minutes; reduce heat to 350°; bake for 30 to 45 minutes longer, or until apples are tender. Remove from oven. When syrup in pan stops bubbling, place serving plate over pie and invert. Carefully remove pie pan. Serve hot.

SPICY APPLE CHIFFON PIE

1 envelope unflavored gelatin
¼ cup cold water
3 eggs, separated
½ cup molasses
½ teaspoon salt

1 teaspoon grated lemon peel
2 tablespoons lemon juice
1½ cups unsweetened spiced applesauce
1 9-inch baked pie shell or crumb crust

Sprinkle gelatin on cold water. Beat egg yolks slightly; combine with molasses, salt, lemon peel and juice. Cook over hot water, stirring constantly, until thickened. Add softened gelatin; stir until dissolved. Add applesauce. Chill until mixture begins to thicken. Beat egg whites stiff; fold in. Turn into pie shell. Chill until firm.

APPLE CRANBERRY TARTS

2 cups fresh cranberries
1½ cups diced unpeeled red apples
¾ cup drained canned pineapple tidbits
1½ cups sugar

Few grains salt
2 bananas, sliced
6 baked tart shells
½ cup whipping cream, whipped

Chop cranberries; combine with apples, pineapple, sugar and salt. Let stand 2 to 3 hours. Just before serving, add bananas. Fill tart shells with fruit mixture, top with whipped cream. Makes 6 servings.

STRAWBERRY FESTIVAL PIE

1 package vanilla pudding and pie filling mix
2 cups milk
1 package strawberry-flavor gelatin

1 cup hot water
⅓ cup cold water
2 cups applesauce
2 baked 8-inch pie shells

Combine pudding mix and milk in saucepan. Cook and stir over medium heat until mixture comes to full boil. Remove from heat. Pour into bowl. (To avoid surface film, place

Saran wrap directly on surface of hot pudding.) Chill. Dissolve strawberry-flavor gelatin in hot water. Add cold water and applesauce. Chill until slightly thickened. Whip until fluffy and thick. Add chilled pudding gradually to fluffy gelatin, beating after each addition until well blended. Pour into pie shells. Chill until firm (about 1 hour). Top with whipped cream.

Variation: Make 1 pie, then pour remainder of filling into lady-finger lined parfait or sherbet glasses. Chill until firm. Before serving, garnish with whipped cream. Makes 4 to 5 servings, depending on size of dessert glasses.

STATE OF MAINE APPLE PIE

1 package pie crust mix
¼ cup flour
¼ cup sugar
¼ teaspoon nutmeg
½ teaspoon cinnamon

6 to 8 tart apples, cored, pared and sliced thin
½ cup molasses
2 tablespoons butter or margarine

Prepare pie crust mix as directed on package; roll out thin, half at a time. Line 9-inch pie pan with pastry. Combine flour, sugar and spices; pat a little of this mixture into pastry in pie pan. Add some of the apple slices; sprinkle with some of remaining spice mixture; continue until pan is full, heaping apples slightly in center. Pour molasses over all. Dot with butter or margarine. Top with remaining pastry; trim and flute edges. Bake at 425° for 40 to 45 minutes, or until apples are tender.

VERMONT APPLE PIE

5 to 8 large tart apples
1 package pie crust mix
1 cup firmly packed maple sugar
2 teaspoons flour

¼ teaspoon nutmeg
½ teaspoon cinnamon
2 tablespoons butter or margarine

Pare, core and slice apples. Line 9-inch pie pan with pastry. Combine sugar, flour and spices. Rub a little of the sugar mixture into pastry in pan. Arrange sliced apples in pan. Add remaining sugar mixture. Dot with butter or margarine. Roll out top crust; place over apples. Cut slits in top; flute edges. Brush top with egg yolk. Bake at 435° for 40 to 45 minutes, or until apples are tender.

APPLE BANBURY TARTS

2 apples, cored, pared and chopped
1 cup raisins
Juice and grated peel of 1 lemon

¾ cup sugar
1 egg, beaten
2 packages pie crust mix

Combine first five ingredients; bring to boil; lower heat; simmer 15 minutes. Cool. Prepare the pie crust mix. Roll out, ¼ at a time, to ⅛ inch thickness. Cut in 4-inch circles. Place 1 tablespoon apple mixture in each circle; fold over; press edges together with floured tines of fork. Bake at 425° about 20 minutes, or until golden brown. Makes 3½ to 4 dozen tarts.

APPLE COCONUT PASTRIES

1 package pie crust mix
7 to 8 large apples, cored, pared and sliced thin
½ cup firmly packed brown sugar
½ teaspoon cinnamon

2 tablespoons butter or margarine
1 can flaked coconut
½ cup sugar
Few grains salt
1 egg, beaten
¼ cup whipping cream

Line jelly roll pan (15" x 10" x 1") with pastry. Place apple slices in rows on pastry. Combine brown sugar and cinnamon; sprinkle over apples. Dot with butter or margarine. Bake at 425° for 25 minutes. Combine coconut, sugar, salt, egg and cream. Spread over apples. Lower heat to 350°; bake 15 minutes longer. When cool, cut into 12 pieces.

FRIED APPLE PASTRIES

1 package pie crust mix
4 tablespoons butter or margarine

3 tart cooking apples
½ cup sugar
1 teaspoon cinnamon

Prepare pie crust as directed on package. Roll out into oblong ⅛ inch thick. Dot surface with 2 tablespoons butter or margarine. Roll up like jelly roll. Roll out again in oblong. Dot with remaining butter or margarine. Fold from long side to make 3 layers, then again from narrow side to make 3 layers. Wrap in waxed paper; chill thoroughly. Roll into rectangle ⅛ inch thick and 10 inches wide. Cut crosswise into 1-inch strips (about 18 strips). Pare and core apples; cut each into 6 wedges. Wrap each wedge in a strip of pastry, winding it so that edges overlap. Pinch edges together at both ends. Fry in shallow fat or oil heated to 375° about 10 minutes, or until golden brown. Drain on absorbent paper. Roll in sugar and cinnamon, mixed.

APPLE PASTRY ROLLS

1 can (20 ounces) pie-sliced apples	⅓ cup chopped walnuts
1 teaspoon lemon juice	⅓ cup flaked coconut
⅓ cup sugar	2 packages pie crust mix
¼ teaspoon grated nutmeg	2 tablespoons butter or margarine
½ teaspoon ground cinnamon	1 egg yolk, slightly beaten
⅛ teaspoon salt	Cinnamon-sugar

Combine first 8 ingredients. Set aside. Roll pastry ⅛ inch thick on lightly floured surface. Cut into 5-inch squares. Put 2 measuring tablespoons apple mixture in center of each square; dot with butter or margarine. Fold one end of pastry square up and over filling. Fold sides up and over. Bring remaining end of pastry up and over. Place, seam side down, on baking sheet. Make 3 or 4 gashes in top of each roll. Brush with egg yolk; sprinkle with cinnamon-sugar. Bake at 425° for about 18 minutes, or until deep golden brown. Makes 12 to 14 rolls.

APPLE RAISIN PASTRY STRIP

½ cup apple cider	1 cup raisins
¼ cup sherry	1 can (20 ounces) pie-sliced apples
1 tablespoon lemon juice	Pastry for 1-crust pie
½ teaspoon cinnamon	
¼ teaspoon nutmeg	1 tablespoon butter or margarine
⅛ teaspoon salt	Pecans
2 tablespoons sugar	

Combine first 7 ingredients; bring to boil; boil 5 minutes to reduce liquid. Lower heat; add raisins; simmer about 5 minutes longer. Add drained apple slices. Roll pastry into oblong, about 13″ x 9″. Scallop long edges, if desired. Spoon filling down center of pastry strip; dot with butter or margarine. Bring scalloped sides of pastry up and over filling toward center of filling, leaving a center strip exposed. Turn narrow ends up and over. Brush pastry with milk. Bake at 425° for 25 to 30 minutes. Garnish with whole pecans, if desired. Slice crosswise to serve. Makes 6 servings.

APPLE BINDLES

Core, pare and quarter large baking apples. Place each quarter apple on 6-inch-square pastry, hollow side up. Top with a spoonful of Pineapple Filling.* Bring pastry up around apple and twist. Pull out corners. Bake at 425° for 25 to 30 minutes, or until apples are tender. Serve warm with cream.

*Pineapple Filling:

1 cup drained crushed pineapple	¼ cup firmly packed brown sugar
½ cup golden raisins	½ teaspoon ginger

Combine all ingredients. Makes enough for 8 to 10 bindles.

ENGLISH APPLE FLAN

1 package pie crust mix	4 or 5 large tart apples
3 cups thick homemade applesauce, spiced and sweetened	⅔ cup apricot jam
	⅓ cup cold water

Roll pastry ⅛ inch thick; place in 12-inch pizza pan; flute edge. Spoon applesauce into pastry-lined pan. Pare and core apples; slice thin. Place on applesauce in concentric circles. Combine apricot jam and water; heat and stir until well blended. Spread over apple slices. Bake at 425° about 30 minutes, or until apple slices are tender. Serve warm with whipped cream. Makes 12 servings.

APPLE KNAPSACKS

6 cups coarsely chopped apples	Few grains salt
¾ cup sugar	2 packages pie crust mix
1 teaspoon cinnamon	2 tablespoons butter or margarine
¼ teaspoon nutmeg	

Combine apples, sugar, spices and salt. Prepare pie crust mix as directed on package. Roll out ⅛ inch thick. Cut in eight

7-inch squares. Place a generous amount of apple mixture in center of each square. Dot with butter or margarine. Fold corners of pastry to center. Prick top surface with fork. Roll out remaining scraps of pastry, cut in 1-inch strips, prick with a fork and twist to form a "tie" for the top of each knapsack. Place on cookie sheet. Bake at 450° for 30 to 35 minutes, or until pastry is golden brown and apples tender.

OLD-FASHIONED APPLE DUMPLINGS

1 package pie crust mix
4 medium tart apples
⅓ cup sugar
¾ teaspoon cinnamon
1 tablespoon butter or
  margarine
Syrup*

Roll pastry ⅛ inch thick; cut into four 7-inch squares. Pare and core apples (save peels for syrup). Place apple in center of each square; combine sugar and cinnamon; fill centers of apples; dot with butter. Bring opposite ends up to top of apple; fold over. Seal with tines of fork. Prick top with fork. Place in baking dish. Chill while making syrup. Pour syrup into baking dish around apples. Brush dumplings with slightly beaten egg white; sprinkle with sugar. Bake at 375° for 40 minutes, or until apples are tender. Serve warm with hard sauce.

●Syrup:

1¼ cups boiling water
Apple peels
2 tablespoons sugar
3 tablespoons butter or
  margarine
¼ teaspoon cinnamon
3 tablespoons lemon juice
1 tablespoon grated lemon
  peel

Pour boiling water on apple peels; simmer, covered, 20 minutes; drain, discarding peels. Combine hot liquid with remaining ingredients; stir to dissolve sugar.

VERMONT APPLE FLAN

1 package pie crust mix
4 apples
2 cups maple syrup
1 tablespoon butter

Line a 9" x 9" x 1" baking pan within ½ inch of top with pastry rolled to ⅛ inch thickness. If desired, make a rolled "rope" edge of the pastry around top of pan. Pare and core apples; cut in thick slices. Heat syrup to boiling point. Add ¼ of the apple slices; cook until apples are tender and transparent, but not mushy. Repeat until all apples are cooked. Arrange in rows on pastry so that slices overlap slightly. Pour remaining syrup over apples; dot with butter. Bake at 425° for 35 minutes, or until pastry is lightly browned. Cut in 3-inch squares. Serve with whipped cream or vanilla ice cream. Makes 9 servings.

BAKED APPLE DUMPLINGS

1 package pie crust mix
4 small baking apples
½ cup firmly packed brown sugar
1 teaspoon cinnamon
¼ cup chopped walnuts
1 tablespoon lime juice
1 tablespoon butter or margarine

Prepare pie crust mix as directed on package; roll out in thin sheet on lightly floured board. Cut in four 6- to 7-inch squares. Pare and core apples; place each on a pastry square. Combine brown sugar, cinnamon and nuts; fill apple centers with this mixture. Sprinkle with lime juice; dot with butter or margarine. Bring opposite corners of pastry together on top of apples. Moisten edges of sides; seal. Prick pastry with tines of fork. Bake at 375° for 35 to 40 minutes, or until apples are tender. Serve with Danish blue cheese and Lemon-Nutmeg Sauce.*

*Lemon-Nutmeg Sauce:

1 tablespoon cornstarch
½ cup sugar
1 teaspoon grated lemon peel
1 cup water
2 tablespoons lemon juice
2 tablespoons butter or margarine
⅛ teaspoon salt
¼ teaspoon nutmeg

Combine cornstarch, sugar and lemon peel in top of double boiler. Blend in water. Stir over low heat until thickened. Cook over hot water 10 minutes, stirring occasionally. Remove from heat; add remaining ingredients. Stir until butter melts. Makes 4 servings.

APPLE PUDDING SOUFFLÉ

2 cups bread cubes
3 tablespoons butter or
   margarine
1½ cups milk, scalded
¼ cup finely chopped
   candied orange peel
½ cup blanched slivered
   almonds

½ cup packaged diced
   dates
½ cup sugar
Grated peel of 1 lemon
1 can (20 ounces) pie-sliced
   apples
3 eggs, separated
½ teaspoon vanilla

Sauté bread cubes in butter or margarine until golden brown; add milk. Combine orange peel, almonds, dates, sugar and lemon peel. Chop apples; add; mix well. Beat egg yolks slightly; add with milk and bread cubes; add vanilla. Beat egg whites stiff; fold in. Spoon into 1½-quart baking dish. Sprinkle with nutmeg. Set baking dish in shallow pan of hot water; bake at 350° for 45 minutes. Makes 6 to 8 servings.

APPLE BREAD PUDDING

6 slices whole wheat bread
Melted butter or margarine
½ cup sugar
½ teaspoon cinnamon

1 can (1 pound) applesauce
⅓ cup golden raisins
¼ cup maple-blended syrup

Cut crusts from bread slices; cut each trimmed slice into 3 strips. Roll strips in melted butter or margarine, then in mixed sugar and cinnamon. Line bottom of baking dish with bread strips; add half the applesauce; sprinkle with raisins. Repeat, ending with bread strips. Pour syrup over all. Bake at 350° about 30 minutes, or until top is golden brown. Serve warm with plain cream. Makes 6 servings.

APPLE-DATE RICE PUDDING

2 medium tart apples
2 cups cooked rice
½ cup milk
2 eggs, separated
¾ cup sugar

2 tablespoons melted butter
½ cup chopped pitted dates
1 teaspoon vanilla
½ cup whipping cream

Pare, core and chop apples fine. Combine apples, rice, milk. Beat in egg yolks, sugar, butter, dates and vanilla. Beat egg whites stiff; fold in. Pour into greased casserole; set in pan of hot water. Bake at 350° for 45 minutes, or until knife blade inserted at outer edge of pudding comes out clean. Chill. Top each serving with whipped cream. Garnish with toasted coconut. Makes 6 servings.

BUTTERSCOTCH APPLE PUDDING

2 cans (20 ounces each) pie-sliced apples
3 tablespoons lemon juice
1 teaspoon cinnamon
1 cup firmly packed brown sugar
½ cup finely chopped walnuts
½ cup flour
¼ cup butter or margarine

Drain apples. Put slices from 1 can into greased 1½-quart casserole. Sprinkle with half the lemon juice. Mix cinnamon and brown sugar together; sprinkle half over apples. Cover with remaining apples. Sprinkle with remaining lemon juice. Mix together remaining brown sugar, walnuts and flour; work in butter with a fork. Spread mixture over top layer of apples, pressing down firmly. Bake uncovered at 350° for 25 minutes. Serve warm with cream. Makes 8 servings.

CHOCOLATE APPLE PUDDING

2¼ cups sifted all-purpose flour
2 cups sugar, divided
2 teaspoons baking powder
1 teaspoon baking soda
½ teaspoon salt
1 teaspoon cinnamon
¾ teaspoon nutmeg
½ cup butter or margarine
2 squares (1 ounce each) unsweetened chocolate, melted
1½ cups hot water
4 cups chopped apples

Mix and sift flour, 1 cup sugar, baking powder, baking soda, salt, cinnamon and nutmeg. Cut in butter until mixture is like coarse meal. Blend chocolate and remaining 1 cup sugar. Stir in hot water. Alternate layers of flour mixture, apples and chocolate mixture in greased shallow 2½-quart casserole, beginning and ending with flour mixture. Stir gently 2 or 3 times with fork to moisten all of flour mixture. Bake at 350° for 45 to 50 minutes. Serve warm with ice cream, whipped cream or plain cream. Pudding may be baked ahead and

reheated, covered with foil, at 350° for 15 to 20 minutes.
Makes 8 to 10 servings.

APPLE INDIAN PUDDING

⅓ cup corn meal
⅓ cup cold water
1 quart milk
½ teaspoon salt
¼ cup sugar

½ teaspoon ginger
½ teaspoon cinnamon
¼ teaspoon nutmeg
½ cup molasses
2 cups thinly sliced apples

Combine corn meal and water. Scald milk; add corn meal;
stir over low heat until thickened. Cover; cook over hot water
20 minutes. Remove from heat; stir in salt, sugar, ginger,
cinnamon, nutmeg, molasses and apples. Pour into greased
1½-quart casserole. Bake at 325° for 2 hours. Serve warm
or chilled, with cream, ice cream or hard sauce. Makes 6
servings.

FRENCH APPLE PUDDING

4 eggs, separated
Grated peel and juice of
1 lemon

2 cups sweetened apple-
sauce
¼ teaspoon salt
½ cup sugar

Beat egg yolks until thick and lemon colored. Add grated
lemon peel and juice; stir into applesauce. Beat egg whites stiff;
add salt and sugar while continuing to beat. Fold egg whites
into applesauce mixture. Turn into casserole; set in pan of
water; bake at 350° about 45 minutes, or until set. Cool.
Serve with unsweetened whipped cream. Makes 6 to 8 servings.

STEAMED APPLE PUDDING

¼ cup butter or margarine
½ cup firmly packed brown
sugar
1 egg
½ cup light molasses
1 tablespoon grated lemon
peel
1½ cups sifted all-purpose
flour

½ teaspoon baking soda
1 teaspoon baking powder
½ teaspoon each ginger,
cinnamon, allspice and
mace
½ cup buttermilk
1 cup finely chopped apples

Cream butter and sugar until fluffy. Beat in egg, molasses and
lemon peel. Mix and sift flour, baking soda, baking pow-

der and spices. Stir into butter mixture alternately with buttermilk. Stir in apples. Fill greased melon mold ⅔ full. Cover mold tightly. (If mold does not have cover, use aluminum foil, pressed tightly against sides.) Steam 1½ hours on rack in large covered kettle. Water should reach halfway up the mold and should be kept boiling. Add more boiling water as level drops. Makes 6 servings.

For Christmas: Prepare hard sauce according to any favorite recipe; shape into small balls; roll in flaked coconut; chill. Place "snowballs" around pudding and decorate top of pudding with holly sprigs, real or artificial.

DANISH APPLE PUDDING 1

2 cups sweetened applesauce	1½ cups graham cracker crumbs
1½ tablespoons lemon juice	1 teaspoon nutmeg
1 tablespoon grated lemon peel	2 teaspoons cinnamon
	½ cup chopped walnuts
	¼ cup melted butter or margarine

Combine applesauce, lemon juice and peel. Combine graham cracker crumbs, nutmeg, cinnamon, walnuts and melted butter or margarine, mixing lightly. Place ⅓ crumb mixture in greased baking dish. Add ½ applesauce mixture. Add another ⅓ crumb mixture, then remaining applesauce. Top with remaining crumbs. Bake at 350° about 25 minutes, or until crumbs are brown. Serve warm, with light cream. Makes 6 servings.

DANISH APPLE PUDDING 2

4 cups sweetened applesauce	½ teaspoon cinnamon
2 cups toasted bread crumbs	¼ cup sugar
3 eggs yolks, beaten	3 egg whites
⅓ cup melted butter or margarine	6 tablespoons sugar
	½ teaspoon rum flavoring

Combine applesauce, toasted bread crumbs, beaten egg yolks, butter or margarine, cinnamon and ¼ cup sugar. Bake in greased 2-quart casserole at 325° for 45 minutes. Remove from oven. Beat egg whites until stiff; add 6 tablespoons sugar gradually, continuing to beat until mixture stands in peaks. Add rum flavoring. Top casserole with this meringue and return to oven for 15 minutes, or until brown. Serves 6.

STEAMED APPLE RAISIN PUDDING

1½ cups sifted all-purpose flour
1 teaspoon baking soda
½ teaspoon salt
½ teaspoon cinnamon
¼ teaspoon crushed cardamom seeds

¼ cup soft shortening
1 cup sugar
2 eggs, well beaten
2½ cups shredded apples
½ cup golden raisins
Hard sauce
Fresh cranberry sauce

Mix and sift flour, baking soda, salt and spices. Combine shortening, sugar and eggs; beat until smooth and light. Stir in apples and raisins. Add flour mixture; mix well. Spoon into well-greased 1½-quart pudding mold, filling ⅔ full. Cover tightly. Set on rack in large kettle. Add enough boiling water to reach halfway up the mold. Cover kettle; bring to boil. Reduce heat. Boil gently for 2 hours. Remove mold to cake rack; let stand 5 minutes. Loosen edges; invert on serving dish. Serve with hard sauce and fresh cranberry sauce. Makes 6 to 8 servings.

HOLIDAY APPLE PUDDING

⅓ cup shortening
1 cup sugar
2½ squares (2½ ounces) unsweetened chocolate, melted
2 eggs
3⅓ cups sifted cake flour

2 tablespoons baking powder*
¾ teaspoon salt
1 cup milk
2 teaspoons vanilla
½ cup chopped walnuts
1½ cups grated raw apples

Cream shortening and sugar. Blend in melted chocolate. Add eggs 1 at a time, beating well after each addition. Mix and sift flour, baking powder and salt; add alternately with milk. Add vanilla. Fold in walnuts and grated apples. Spoon into well-greased 2-quart pudding mold. Cover mold; set on rack in large kettle. Add enough boiling water to kettle to come ⅓ way up mold. Cover kettle; steam 2 to 2½ hours, depend-

* 2 tablespoons is correct!

ing on depth of mold. Keep water boiling, adding more if necessary. Unmold on serving plate; surround with snowmen molded from hard sauce. Makes 10 to 12 servings.

DUTCH APPLE RICE PUDDING

¾ cup packaged precooked rice
2½ cups milk
⅓ cup raisins
1 egg, slightly beaten
⅓ cup sugar

½ teaspoon salt
¼ teaspoon cinnamon
1 tablespoon butter or margarine
2 cups warm applesauce
Nutmeg

Combine rice, milk and raisins in saucepan. Bring to full boil. Remove from heat; cover; let stand 10 minutes. Combine egg, sugar, salt and cinnamon; mix well. Add a little of the hot rice mixture to egg mixture; return to saucepan; mix well. Add butter or margarine. Simmer about 4 minutes, stirring constantly. Pour into serving dishes. Add applesauce; stir enough to streak applesauce through rice pudding, but not enough to blend. Chill. Makes 6 servings.

TIPSY APPLE PUDDING

4 eggs, slightly beaten
¼ cup sugar
Few grains salt
3 cups milk, scalded

1 teaspoon vanilla
1 loaf baker's pound cake
¼ cup sherry
2 cups applesauce

Combine eggs, sugar and salt. Add milk. Cook over hot water, stirring constantly, until mixture coats the spoon. Chill. Add vanilla. Slice pound cake thin; arrange slices in serving dish; pour sherry over cake. Top with applesauce. Pour chilled custard sauce over all. Makes 8 servings.

SPICY APPLE PUDDING

¾ cup finely chopped suet
1 cup raisins
2¼ cups sifted all-purpose flour
1 teaspoon baking soda
½ teaspoon nutmeg
1 teaspoon cinnamon

⅛ teaspoon powdered cloves
½ teaspoon salt
1½ cups grated raw apples
1 cup molasses
1 egg, beaten

Combine suet and raisins. Mix and sift dry ingredients; add with apples. Stir in molasses; add egg. Pour into 1½-quart greased casserole; set in pan of hot water. Bake at 325° for 1¾ hours. Serve hot with plain cream. Makes 6 servings.

REGAL BREAD PUDDING

3 cups applesauce
1 teaspoon lemon juice
5 slices raisin whole wheat bread

3 tablespoons butter or margarine
¼ cup marmalade
1½ teaspoons cinnamon
2 tablespoons sugar

Combine applesauce and lemon juice; place half this mixture in small casserole. Spread bread slices with butter and marmalade. Cut 4 slices into cubes; cut remaining slice in 4 triangles. Place cubes on applesauce in casserole. Combine cinnamon and sugar; sprinkle half over cubes; top with remaining applesauce. Arrange triangles in a pattern to top casserole; sprinkle with remaining cinnamon and sugar. Bake at 350° for 30 minutes. Makes 6 servings.

APPLE COCONUT CAKE

2 cups sifted all-purpose flour
3 teaspoons baking powder
½ teaspoon salt
¼ cup butter or margarine
⅓ cup sugar
2 eggs, unbeaten
¾ cup milk

¾ cup flaked coconut
4 medium tart apples, cut in slices ¼ inch thick (3½ cups)
2 teaspoons cinnamon
¼ teaspoon nutmeg
¾ cup sugar

Mix and sift flour, baking powder and salt. Cream butter or margarine; add ⅓ cup sugar gradually, cream together until light and fluffy. Add eggs, one at a time, beating well after each addition. Add flour mixture alternately with milk, a small amount at a time, beating after each addition until smooth. Add coconut; blend well. Spread batter in 2 greased 9-inch pie pans. Arrange apple slices on top of batter. Combine cinnamon, nutmeg and ¾ cup sugar; sprinkle over apples. Bake at 400° for 35 to 40 minutes. Cut in wedge-shaped pieces; serve hot with sweetened whipped cream. Makes 12 servings.

APPLE CIDER UPSIDE-DOWN CAKE

3 medium-sized tart apples
1 cup apple cider
⅓ cup butter or margarine

1 cup firmly packed brown
   sugar
1 package spice cake mix
½ cup chopped walnuts

Pare and core apples; slice thin. Simmer in cider about 5 minutes, or until just tender. Drain, reserving cider. Combine 2 tablespoons hot cider, butter and brown sugar in 13" x 9" x 2" pan. Set in 350° oven for 5 minutes; then remove from oven. Prepare cake mix. Arrange apple slices in brown sugar mixture in pan. Sprinkle with walnuts. Pour batter into pan. Bake at 350° for 55 to 60 minutes. Invert; let stand 1 minute; remove pan. Serve warm. Makes 12 servings.

APPLE PECAN CUP CAKES

½ cup shortening
1 cup firmly packed light
   brown sugar
1 egg
½ cup chopped raisins
½ cup broken pecans
2 cups sifted all-purpose
   flour

½ teaspoon salt
½ teaspoon baking soda
1 teaspoon cinnamon
1 teaspoon nutmeg
½ cup strong cold coffee
1 teaspoon vanilla
1 cup finely chopped raw
   apples

Cream shortening and brown sugar until light and fluffy. Add egg; beat well. Stir in raisins and pecans. Mix and sift flour, salt, baking soda and spices; add alternately with coffee and vanilla. Stir in apples. Fill well-greased muffin pans ⅔ full. Bake at 350° for 30 minutes. Makes 10 to 12 cup cakes. If desired, frost with confectioners' sugar icing to which a little cinnamon has been added; garnish with whole pecans.

APPLE UPSIDE-DOWN CAKE

5 tart apples
12 maraschino cherries

½ cup honey
1 package spice cake mix

Pare and core apples. Quarter and slice thin. Arrange apple slices and cherries in bottom of 9-inch-square cake pan. Pour honey over all. Prepare cake mix as directed on package.

Pour batter over fruit. Bake at 350° for 45 to 50 minutes. Serve hot, with plain or whipped cream or lemon sauce. Makes 6 to 8 servings.

APPLE UPSIDE-DOWN GINGERBREAD

¼ cup butter or margarine
½ cup firmly packed brown sugar
1 teaspoon cinnamon

3 small apples, peeled and cored
1 package gingerbread mix

Melt butter in bottom of 9-inch-square cake pan. Combine brown sugar and cinnamon; sprinkle on bottom of pan. Cut apples into rings; arrange in pan on brown sugar mixture. Prepare gingerbread mix as directed on package; pour batter over apple slices. Bake as directed for gingerbread mix. Invert on serving plate. If desired, garnish with whipped cream and maraschino cherries. Cut into squares and serve.

APPLESAUCE BOWL CAKE

1 package sponge cake layers (2 layers)
1 cup whipping cream, divided

2 cups sweetened, spiced applesauce
½ cup crushed peanut brittle

Cut each sponge cake layer in half, crosswise, making 4 thin layers. Whip ½ cup of the cream; fold into applesauce. Press 1 layer of sponge cake into small mixing bowl. Add a thick layer of the applesauce mixture. Repeat twice; then end with fourth sponge cake layer. Chill several hours or overnight. Unmold on serving plate. Whip remaining cream; spread over surface; garnish with crushed peanut brittle.

APPLESAUCE FILBERT CAKE

½ teaspoon each cinnamon, nutmeg and allspice
1 package (1 pound 4 ounces) white cake mix

1 cup canned applesauce
2 unbeaten egg whites
½ cup finely chopped filberts

Add spices to cake mix, stir to mix. Add applesauce and egg whites; beat 3 minutes, until smooth and creamy. Stir in chopped filberts. Bake in 2 greased and floured 8-inch layer cake pans at 350° for 35 to 40 minutes, or until cake tests

done. Fill and frost with fluffy white frosting; decorate with
additional chopped filberts, if desired.

APPLESAUCE WALNUT CAKE

2 cups sifted all-purpose
  flour
1 teaspoon baking soda
½ teaspoon salt
¼ teaspoon cloves
1 teaspoon allspice
1½ teaspoons cinnamon
1 teaspoon nutmeg

½ cup shortening
¼ cup sugar
¾ cup corn syrup
1 egg, slightly beaten
1 cup thick applesauce
1 cup coarsely broken
  walnuts

Mix and sift flour, baking soda, salt and spices. Cream
shortening and sugar. Add corn syrup gradually, beating after
each addition. Add egg; beat until light and fluffy. Add
sifted dry ingredients alternately with applesauce. Stir in walnuts. Bake in greased and floured square cake pan at 350°
for 50 to 60 minutes.

CHOCOLATE APPLESAUCE CUP CAKES

½ cup shortening
1 cup sugar
1 egg, unbeaten
1 cup applesauce
1½ cups sifted all-purpose
  flour

½ cup cocoa (not instant)
1 teaspoon cinnamon
¼ teaspoon allspice
¼ teaspoon nutmeg
1 teaspoon baking soda
1 teaspoon water

Cream shortening and sugar; add egg; beat well. Put applesauce through fine sieve; stir in. Sift flour, cocoa and spices
3 times; stir in. Dissolve baking soda in water; stir in; mix
well. Bake in greased muffin pans at 350° for 25 to 30 minutes. Makes 18 cup cakes, 2½ inches in diameter.

APPLESAUCE LOAF CAKE

1¾ cups sifted all-purpose
  flour
1½ teaspoons cinnamon
1 teaspoon allspice
1 teaspoon nutmeg
¼ teaspoon ground cloves
½ teaspoon salt

1 teaspoon baking soda
½ cup shortening
1 cup sugar
1 egg, well beaten
1 cup unsweetened
  applesauce

Mix and sift first seven ingredients. Cream shortening; add
sugar gradually; continue beating until light and fluffy. Add

egg; beat well. Stir in applesauce. Add sifted dry ingredients; stir only enough to blend. Pour into greased and floured loaf pan, 9" x 5" x 3". Bake at 350° for 50 to 60 minutes, or until cake springs back when lightly touched with fingertip. Cool in pan 5 minutes. Remove from pan and cool on rack. Frost, if desired.

APPLESAUCE CUP CAKES

2 cups sifted all-purpose flour
1 teaspoon baking soda
1 teaspoon baking powder
½ teaspoon salt
½ teaspoon nutmeg
¼ teaspoon cloves
1 teaspoon cinnamon
½ cup shortening

1 cup sugar
2 egg yolks
1 cup canned applesauce
1 tablespoon grated lemon peel
1 cup raisins
1 cup chopped walnuts

Mix and sift flour, baking soda, baking powder, salt and spices. Cream shortening and sugar until fluffy. Add egg yolks; mix well. Add applesauce to creamed mixture alternately with flour mixture. Fold in lemon peel, raisins and nuts. Pour into well-greased muffin pans. Bake at 375° for 25 to 30 minutes. Frost and decorate as desired. Makes 2 dozen medium cup cakes.

APPLESAUCE RAISIN CAKE

½ cup shortening
1 cup sugar
⅓ cup raisins
1 egg
1 cup unsweetened applesauce
1¾ cups sifted all-purpose flour

1½ teaspoons cinnamon
1 teaspoon allspice
1 teaspoon nutmeg
¼ teaspoon cloves
½ teaspoon salt
1 teaspoon baking soda
½ cup broken walnuts

Cream shortening to consistency of mayonnaise; add sugar gradually, while creaming. Add raisins. Beat egg until light and lemon colored; add. Mix well. Add applesauce. Sift flour, spices, salt and baking soda; add. Mix well. Stir in walnuts. Pour into 2 greased and floured 8-inch layer cake pans. Bake at 350° for 40 to 45 minutes, or until cake tests done. Fill and frost with Mocha Frosting.*

* **Mocha Frosting**

Cream ⅓ cup butter; add 1½ cups confectioners' sugar, while continuing to cream. Melt 1½ squares unsweetened chocolate over hot water; add. Add 1½ cups confectioners' sugar and enough strong cold coffee to make frosting fluffy and easy to spread on cake. Add ½ teaspoon vanilla.

APPLESAUCE RING CAKE

½ cup butter or margarine	½ teaspoon cloves
1 cup sugar	½ cup milk
3 eggs	1 cup raisins
1 cup sifted all-purpose flour	1 cup chopped pecans
¼ teaspoon salt	¾ cup sweetened canned
2 teaspoons baking powder	applesauce
1 teaspoon cinnamon	1 cup rolled oats (quick or
½ teaspoon nutmeg	old-fashioned, uncooked)

Beat butter until creamy; add sugar; beat until fluffy. Add eggs, beat well. Mix and sift flour, salt, baking powder and spices. Add to creamed mixture alternately with milk. Stir in raisins, pecans, applesauce and oats. Pour batter into greased and floured 1½-quart ring mold. Bake at 350° for 45 to 50 minutes. Loosen edges; cool in pan 10 minutes; remove from cake pan to cake rack. Cool. Frost with orange-flavored confectioners' sugar frosting. Decorate with pecan halves.

APPLESAUCE TORTE

1 cup sifted all-purpose flour	1 cup firmly packed brown sugar
½ teaspoon baking soda	1 egg
1 teaspoon baking powder	1 cup thick, sweetened
½ teaspoon salt	applesauce
1 teaspoon cinnamon	1 cup rolled oats
½ teaspoon allspice	½ cup raisins
½ cup shortening*	

Mix and sift flour, baking soda, baking powder, salt and

* Shortening must be at room temperature.

spices. Add shortening, sugar, egg and ½ cup applesauce.
Beat until smooth, about 2 minutes. Fold in remaining applesauce, rolled oats and raisins. Bake in greased oblong pan,
7" x 11", at 350° for 40 minutes. Serve warm with plain
cream or hard sauce. Makes 12 servings.

CHOCOLATE WALNUT APPLESAUCE CAKE

½ cup butter or margarine
1 cup sugar
2 eggs
2 squares (1 ounce each)
　unsweetened chocolate,
　melted
½ cup broken walnuts

1¾ cups sifted cake flour
1½ teaspoons baking
　powder
½ teaspoon baking soda
½ teaspoon salt
1 cup canned applesauce
2 teaspoons vanilla

Cream butter until consistency of mayonnaise. Add sugar
gradually while continuing to cream. Add eggs 1 at a time,
beating well after each addition. Blend in chocolate. Stir in
nuts. Mix and sift dry ingredients. Stir in alternately with
applesauce. Stir in vanilla. Spoon into greased and floured
loaf pan 9" x 5" x 3". Bake at 325° for 1 hour and 15 minutes
or until cake tester inserted in center comes out clean. Cool
in pan on rack for 10 minutes. Remove cake from pan to
rack. When cool, frost with canned ready-to-spread lemon
frosting, or any desired frosting.

HUDSON VALLEY APPLE CAKE

1 cup sifted all-purpose flour
⅔ cup sugar, divided
¼ teaspoon baking powder
½ teaspoon salt
¼ teaspoon vanilla
½ cup butter or margarine
4 cups thinly sliced apples
¾ cup slivered roasted
　almonds

½ cup raisins
1 teaspoon cinnamon
Juice and grated peel of
　1 lemon
¼ cup white wine
2 egg yolks
1 cup dairy sour cream

Mix and sift flour, 2 tablespoons sugar, baking powder and
salt. Stir in vanilla. Cut in butter until mixture resembles
coarse corn meal. Spread on bottom of greased 9-inch pie
pan. Combine apples, almonds, raisins, ½ cup sugar, cinnamon, lemon juice, grated lemon peel and wine; mix well;
heap in pie pan. Bake at 425° for 10 minutes. Combine egg

yolks, remaining sugar and sour cream; pour over apple mixture; bake at 350° for 35 minutes longer. Makes 6 servings.

MADCAP CAKE

1½ cups sifted all-purpose flour
3 tablespoons dry breakfast cocoa (not instant)
1 cup sugar
1 teaspoon baking soda
½ teaspoon salt
1 teaspoon cider vinegar
1 teaspoon vanilla
5 tablespoons vegetable oil
1 cup canned applesauce

Sift first 5 ingredients into greased 8-inch-square cake pan. Make 3 depressions in dry ingredients. Pour vinegar into one, vanilla into the second, and oil into the third. Spoon applesauce over all. Mix well until smooth. Bake at 350° for 35 minutes. When cool, cut into squares; top with whipped cream. Makes 9 servings.

APPLE CRUNCH

¼ cup biscuit mix
1 cup firmly packed brown sugar
½ teaspoon salt
1 teaspoon vinegar
1 cup water
1 teaspoon vanilla
1 tablespoon butter or margarine
5 cups sliced pared apples (about 5 medium)
½ teaspoon cinnamon
¼ teaspoon nutmeg
1½ cups biscuit mix
½ cup milk
⅛ teaspoon cinnamon

Combine ¼ cup biscuit mix, brown sugar and salt. Stir in vinegar and water. Cook, stirring, over medium heat until mixture thickens and boils. Boil and stir 1 minute. Remove from heat; stir in vanilla and butter. Cool. Place apples in 8-inch-square pan. Sprinkle with ½ teaspoon cinnamon and nutmeg. Mix 1½ cups biscuit mix and milk with fork to soft dough. Spread over apples; sprinkle with ⅛ teaspoon cinnamon. Pour brown sugar mixture over top. Bake at 400° for 35 minutes. Makes 6 servings.

DUTCH APPLE CAKE

2 cups sifted all-purpose flour
3 tablespoons sugar
2 teaspoons baking powder
1 teaspoon salt
1 cup whipping cream
3 to 4 apples
¼ cup sugar
½ teaspoon cinnamon
2 tablespoons melted butter or margarine

Mix and sift first 4 ingredients. Whip cream; blend in lightly with a fork. Spread in greased 9-inch-square cake pan. Pare, core and quarter apples; cut each quarter in 3 slices. Arrange in parallel rows on dough, pressing edges into dough. Combine remaining ¼ cup sugar and cinnamon; sprinkle evenly over apples. Pour melted butter or margarine over all. Bake at 400° for 30 minutes, or until done when tested with a cake tester. Cut in squares. Serve with a foamy sauce or plain cream. Makes 9 servings.

APPLE-RAISIN COBBLER

5 cups sliced raw apples (about 5 medium)	Dash of salt
½ cup raisins	½ cup water
⅔ cup sugar	1½ cups biscuit mix
1 teaspoon cinnamon	2 tablespoons sugar
½ teaspoon nutmeg	⅓ cup milk

Mix apples and raisins in 9-inch square pan. Blend ⅔ cup sugar, spices, salt and water; pour over apple mixture. Combine biscuit mix, 2 tablespoons sugar and milk. On lightly floured board, roll dough into 9-inch square; place over apple mixture. Bake at 400° for 30 minutes or until crust is golden brown. If desired, serve with ice cream. Makes 8 servings.

KNOBBY APPLE CAKE

3 tablespoons shortening	1 teaspoon baking powder
¼ cup sugar	½ teaspoon baking soda
¾ cup honey	¼ teaspoon nutmeg
1 egg, well beaten	1 teaspoon lemon extract
2 cups sifted all-purpose flour	3 cups diced cooking apples

Cream shortening and sugar; gradually add honey, beating constantly. Add egg; mix smooth. Sift together flour, baking powder, baking soda and nutmeg; add to creamed mixture. Add lemon extract and apples; mix well. Pour into greased 13″ x 9″ x 2″ pan. Bake at 350° for 55 to 60 minutes. Cool 10 to 15 minutes. Remove from pan; cool on wire rack. If desired, serve warm with Lemon Sauce.*

*Lemon Sauce:

2 tablespoons cornstarch	Juice and grated peel of 1 lemon
½ cup water	
½ cup light corn syrup	1 tablespoon butter or margarine
Few grains salt	

Blend cornstarch and water. Add corn syrup. Cook over low heat until boiling point is reached, then boil 5 minutes. Add salt, lemon juice, grated peel and butter or margarine; mix well.

TEXAS APPLE CAKE

½ cup shortening	Grated peel of ½ lemon
½ cup sugar	3 red apples
2 eggs, unbeaten	⅓ cup sugar
½ teaspoon vanilla	1 teaspoon cinnamon
1 cup sifted all-purpose flour	2 tablespoons butter or
¼ teaspoon salt	margarine

Cream shortening and ½ cup sugar until light and fluffy. Beat in eggs one at a time. Add vanilla. Mix and sift flour and salt; add with grated lemon peel. Beat well. Spoon into greased 8-inch-square cake pan. Core apples; cut each into 16 slices; place peel side up in rows in cake batter. Combine remaining ⅓ cup sugar and cinnamon; sprinkle over apples. Dot with butter or margarine. Bake at 350° for about 45 minutes. Makes 6 servings.

Note: The batter does *not* use baking powder or liquid.

APPLE SCOTCH COOKIES

1¼ cups firmly packed brown sugar	1 teaspoon cinnamon
½ cup soft butter or margarine	½ teaspoon cloves
2 eggs	½ teaspoon nutmeg
¼ cup milk	1½ cups chopped apples
2 cups sifted all-purpose flour	1 cup chopped walnuts
1 teaspoon baking powder	1 cup seedless raisins
½ teaspoon salt	1 package (6 ounces) butterscotch pieces

Cream together brown sugar and butter. Add eggs and milk; beat well. Mix and sift flour, baking powder, salt and spices; stir into creamed mixture. Stir in apples, walnuts, raisins and butterscotch pieces. Drop by tablespoons on well-greased baking sheets. Bake at 400° for 10 to 12 minutes. Remove from baking sheets immediately; cool on racks. Makes about 4 dozen cookies.

APPLE TREASURE COOKIES

1 cup shortening
1½ cups firmly packed brown sugar
¼ cup light molasses
3 eggs, unbeaten
3½ cups sifted all-purpose flour
½ teaspoon salt
1 teaspoon baking soda
3 teaspoons cinnamon
½ teaspoon cloves
½ teaspoon nutmeg
1 cup chopped peanuts
1 cup finely chopped apples
1 package (6 ounces) semi-sweet chocolate pieces

Cream shortening with brown sugar until light and fluffy; add molasses. Add unbeaten eggs one at a time, beating well after each addition. Mix and sift flour, salt, baking soda and spices; add. Mix lightly. Stir in peanuts, apples and chocolate pieces. Mix well. Drop by spoonfuls on greased baking sheets. Bake at 350° for 12 to 15 minutes. Makes 5 to 6 dozen cookies.

APPLE WALNUT BROWNIES

½ cup butter or margarine
2 squares (1 ounce each) unsweetened chocolate
2 eggs
1 cup sugar
1 cup sifted cake flour
¼ teaspoon baking powder
¼ teaspoon salt
1 cup broken walnuts
1 cup finely chopped apples
1 teaspoon vanilla

Melt butter and chocolate together over hot water. Beat eggs until light and lemon colored; add sugar gradually while continuing to beat. Stir in chocolate mixture; beat hard 1 minute. Mix and sift flour, baking powder and salt; stir in. Stir in nuts, apples and vanilla. Spoon into greased 8-inch-square cake pan. Bake at 350° for about 40 minutes, or until done. Cool. Cut into squares to serve.

APPLESAUCE NUGGET COOKIES

2 cups sifted all-purpose
 flour
½ teaspoon salt
½ teaspoon cinnamon
½ teaspoon nutmeg
¼ teaspoon cloves
½ teaspoon allspice
1 cup broken walnuts
½ cup shortening

1 cup firmly packed brown
 sugar
1 teaspoon baking soda
1 cup applesauce
1 egg, well beaten
1 package (6 ounces) butterscotch pieces

Mix and sift flour, salt and spices. Add nuts. Cream shortening and sugar. Add baking soda to applesauce; add egg; add
to creamed mixture. Add dry ingredients. Stir in butterscotch
pieces. Drop by teaspoons 2 or 3 inches apart on greased
baking sheet. Bake at 375° for 12 to 15 minutes. Makes about
4 dozen cookies.

JOHNNY APPLESEED BARS

1 cup sifted all-purpose flour
½ teaspoon salt
½ teaspoon baking soda
1 teaspoon cinnamon
1½ cups rolled oats (quick
 or old-fashioned,
 uncooked)
⅔ cup firmly packed brown
 sugar

½ cup shortening, melted
1 egg
1 teaspoon vanilla
¼ cup coarsely chopped
 pecans
2 cups thinly sliced peeled
 apples

Mix and sift flour, salt, baking soda and cinnamon. Add next
5 ingredients; beat until smooth, about 2 minutes. Press half
of dough in bottom of greased 9-inch-square baking pan.
Sprinkle pecans over dough. Arrange apple slices over pecans.
Roll remaining dough between 2 sheets of waxed paper to
form a 9-inch square. Remove top sheet of waxed paper;
place dough over filling. Remove other sheet of waxed paper.
Press lightly around edges. Bake at 350° for 25 to 30 minutes. When cool, sprinkle with confectioners' sugar. Cut in
bars. Makes 18 bars.

APPLESAUCE OATMEAL COOKIES

2 cups sifted all-purpose flour
½ teaspoon baking soda
½ teaspoon salt
½ teaspoon cinnamon
¼ teaspoon nutmeg
1½ cups rolled oats (quick or old-fashioned, uncooked)

1 cup firmly packed brown sugar
¾ cup soft shortening
1 egg
1 cup sweetened canned applesauce
½ cup raisins

Mix and sift flour, baking soda, salt and spices. Add remaining ingredients. Beat until smooth, about 2 minutes. Drop by tablespoons on greased cookie sheets. Bake at 350° for 12 to 15 minutes. Makes about 3 dozen.

APPLE ICE CREAM

1 cup milk
3 tablespoons sugar
¼ teaspoon salt
3 egg yolks

½ teaspoon vanilla
1 cup sieved canned applesauce
1 cup whipping cream

Scald milk; add 3 tablespoons sugar and salt; stir until sugar dissolves. Beat egg yolks slightly; add milk mixture. Cook over hot water, stirring constantly, until mixture coats spoon. Add vanilla; chill. Fold in applesauce. Whip cream; fold in. Pour into freezing tray; freeze until firm. Makes 6 servings.

APPLE MINT MOUSSE

1 can (1 pound) applesauce
½ cup sugar
1 tablespoon lemon juice
⅛ teaspoon mace

½ teaspoon peppermint extract
Few grains salt
Green food coloring
1 cup whipping cream

Combine applesauce and sugar; stir until sugar dissolves. Add lemon juice, mace, peppermint extract and salt. Tint green with food coloring. Whip cream; fold in. Pour into freezing tray; freeze until firm. Makes 6 servings.

APPLE MINT RIPPLE ICE CREAM

1 can (1 pound) applesauce
Red or green food coloring

1 teaspoon peppermint
  extract
½ gallon vanilla ice cream

Tint applesauce deep pink or mint green with food coloring. Add peppermint extract; mix well. Spread half the ice cream in double freezing tray, making a layer about 1 inch deep. Swirl half the applesauce into ice cream. Repeat. Freeze until firm. Makes 16 servings.

APPLESAUCE SHERBET

1 can (1 pound) applesauce
¾ cup light corn syrup,
  divided
¼ teaspoon salt
1 tablespoon lemon juice

1 tablespoon grated orange
  peel
¼ cup orange juice
2 egg whites, stiffly beaten

Combine applesauce, ½ cup corn syrup, salt, lemon juice, orange peel and orange juice. Beat remaining corn syrup gradually into stiffly beaten egg whites; fold into applesauce mixture. Pour into freezing tray; freeze until firm. Makes 6 to 8 servings.

FROZEN APPLE CREAM

1 cup sweetened, spiced
  applesauce
1 teaspoon butter, melted

2 teaspoons lemon juice
2 tablespoons molasses
1 cup whipping cream

Combine applesauce, butter, lemon juice and molasses; mix well. Chill. Whip cream and fold in. Pour into freezing tray; freeze until firm. Makes 6 servings.

FROZEN APPLE MAPLE PARFAIT

1 cup cooked diced apples
¼ cup sugar
1 teaspoon cinnamon

1 pint softened vanilla
  ice cream
Maple-blended syrup

Combine apples, sugar and cinnamon; mix well; combine with

softened ice cream. Fill tall parfait glasses with alternate layers of ice cream mixture and maple-blended syrup. Freeze firm. Top with whipped cream, if desired. Serves 4 to 6.

APPLE CHIFFON RING

1½ envelopes (1½ table-spoons) unflavored gelatin
¼ cup cold water
3 eggs, separated
½ cup firmly packed brown sugar
½ teaspoon salt
1 teaspoon grated lemon peel

2 tablespoons lemon juice
1 teaspoon cinnamon
½ teaspoon allspice
¼ teaspoon cloves
1 can (1 pound) applesauce
1 cup whipping cream
½ cup gingersnap crumbs

Sprinkle gelatin on cold water. Beat egg yolks slightly; combine with brown sugar, salt, lemon peel and juice. Cook over hot water, stirring constantly, until thickened. Add softened gelatin, stir until dissolved. Add spices to applesauce; mix well; add to gelatin mixture. Chill until mixture begins to thicken. Fold in stiffly beaten egg whites. Spoon into 8-inch ring mold which has been rinsed in cold water. Chill until firm; unmold. Whip cream; fold in gingersnap crumbs; spoon into center of ring. Makes 8 to 10 servings.

APPLE BAVARIAN CREAM

1 envelope unflavored gelatin
¼ cup cold water
1 cup grated tart apple
1 teaspoon lemon juice

¼ teaspoon salt
⅔ cup sugar
½ cup finely chopped nuts
1 cup whipping cream
Maraschino cherries

Sprinkle gelatin on cold water; place over boiling water, stirring until gelatin dissolves. Combine grated apple, lemon juice, salt and sugar; stir until sugar dissolves. Add to gelatin; mix well. Chill until syrupy. Fold in nuts. Whip cream; fold in. Turn into mold; chill until firm; unmold. Garnish with additional whipped cream and maraschino cherries. Makes 6 servings.

APPLE LEMON SNOW

2 envelopes unflavored
  gelatin
½ cup cold water
2 cups boiling water
1 cup sugar
Grated peel of 1 lemon

Juice of 3 lemons
2 eggs whites, stiffly beaten
1 cup coarsely chopped
  apples
Mace

Soften gelatin in cold water. Dissolve in boiling water. Add sugar; stir until dissolved. Add lemon peel and strained lemon juice. Chill until syrupy. Fold in egg whites and chopped apples. Chill until firm. Break up lightly with fork. Sprinkle with mace. Makes 6 to 8 servings.

APPLE SNOW

1 envelope unflavored
  gelatin
¼ cup cold water
1 cup chilled canned
  applesauce

½ teaspoon salt
2 egg whites
½ cup extra-fine granulated
  sugar
1 teaspoon lemon juice

Soften gelatin in cold water; dissolve over boiling water. Add to applesauce; mix well. Add salt to egg whites; beat to stiff foam. Add sugar, 1 tablespoon at a time, beating constantly until mixture forms stiff peaks. Fold in applesauce and lemon juice. Chill until firm. Serve with custard sauce or whipped cream. Makes 4 servings.

APPLE AMBROSIA

3 large red apples
3 ripe bananas
2 cups grapefruit sections

Sugar, extra-fine granulated
1 cup flaked coconut

Core apples, do not pare; cut into thin slices. Slice bananas. Combine apples, bananas and grapefruit sections; sweeten to taste with sugar. Arrange in dessert dishes, layered with coconut. Sprinkle coconut on top. Makes 6 servings.

APPLESAUCE BAVARIAN

1 envelope unflavored
  gelatin
¼ cup cold water
1½ cups sweetened
  applesauce
1 tablespoon lemon juice

¼ teaspoon salt
¼ teaspoon cinnamon
¼ teaspoon ginger
2 egg whites
1 cup whipping cream

Soften gelatin in cold water; dissolve over hot water. Add gelatin gradually to applesauce, stirring constantly. Add lemon juice, salt, cinnamon and ginger. Fold in stiffly beaten egg whites. Whip cream; fold in. Turn into mold; chill until firm. Unmold and serve with Nutmeg Custard Sauce.* Makes 6 servings.

°Nutmeg Custard Sauce:

2 egg yolks
1 cup scalded milk
¼ teaspoon salt

⅓ cup sugar
½ teaspoon vanilla
¼ teaspoon nutmeg

Beat egg yolks; add scalded milk gradually. Add salt and sugar. Cook over hot water, stirring constantly, until custard coats spoon. Add vanilla and nutmeg. Serve cold. Makes about 1⅓ cups.

CINNAMON APPLE WHIP

1 cup applesauce
2 egg yolks, slightly beaten
¼ cup molasses
¼ teaspoon cinnamon
1 envelope (1 tablespoon)
  unflavored gelatin

½ cup cold water
Juice and grated peel of
  ½ lemon
2 egg whites, stiffly beaten
Chopped nuts

Combine applesauce, egg yolks, molasses and cinnamon. Heat. Sprinkle gelatin on cold water, dissolve in hot applesauce mixture. Add lemon juice and peel. Chill until mixture begins to thicken. Fold in egg whites. Chill until set. Break up with a fork; garnish with chopped nuts and serve with chilled light cream. Makes 5 to 6 servings.

JELLIED APPLESAUCE DESSERT

1 package cherry-flavor
  gelatin
1 cup hot water
8 marshmallows, diced

1 can (1 pound) applesauce
½ cup chopped walnuts
¼ cup salad dressing

Dissolve gelatin in hot water. Stir in marshmallows; dissolve partially; chill until consistency of unbeaten egg white. Combine applesauce, walnuts and salad dressing; fold into gelatin mixture. Chill until firm. Serve on water cress with additional salad dressing. Makes 6 servings.

APPLE BANANA BETTY

2 large tart apples
3 firm yellow bananas
¾ cup sugar
½ teaspoon cinnamon

¼ teaspoon salt
3 cups soft bread crumbs
3 tablespoons butter or
  margarine, melted

Pare, core and slice apples thin. Cut bananas in ½-inch slices. Combine fruits, sugar, cinnamon and salt. Combine bread crumbs and butter or margarine. Place alternate layers of crumbs and fruit in greased baking dish, beginning and ending with crumbs. Cover; bake at 375° for 40 minutes, or until apples are tender. Remove cover; bake about 5 minutes longer to brown crumbs. Serve hot, with frozen whipped cream. Makes 6 servings.

APPLE BLOSSOM DESSERT

1 jar (5 ounces) pineapple
  cheese spread
2 tablespoons whipping
  cream
¼ cup chopped pecans

2 tablespoons sliced
  maraschino cherries
4 medium-size red apples

Combine cheese spread and cream. Whip until creamy; fold in pecans and cherries. Core unpeeled red apples; cut in eighths, almost to base of apples. Spread sections apart slightly, like petals. Fill centers with cheese mixture. Makes 4 servings.

APPLE CHEESE DESSERT TRAY

3 jars (5 ounces each) pineapple cheese spread
¼ pound blue cheese
Cream or rich milk

Unpeeled red apples, cored and quartered
Crisp crackers

Combine cheese spread and blue cheese. Beat until creamy, adding a little cream or rich milk if necessary. Serve in a bowl surrounded by apple wedges and crackers.

APPLE COCONUT BETTY

6 cups thinly sliced, cored and pared tart apples
1½ cups soft bread crumbs
1 can flaked coconut (1⅓ cups)

1 cup firmly packed brown sugar
¼ teaspoon salt
1 teaspoon cinnamon
6 tablespoons butter or margarine

Arrange 3 cups apple slices in shallow greased baking dish. Sprinkle with half the bread crumbs and ½ cup coconut. Combine brown sugar, salt and cinnamon; sprinkle half this mixture over coconut. Dot with 3 tablespoons butter. Repeat. Sprinkle top with remaining ⅓ cup coconut. Cover (use aluminum foil if baking dish does not have a cover). Bake at 350° for 35 to 40 minutes. Remove cover; bake 10 minutes longer, or until apples are soft. Makes 8 servings.

APPLE FRITTERS WITH LEMON SAUCE

3 medium-size tart apples
¼ cup white wine
½ cup sugar
¼ teaspoon nutmeg
3 eggs

1¼ cups sifted all-purpose flour
¼ teaspoon salt
½ cup milk

Core and pare apples; cut in eighths. Combine wine, sugar and nutmeg; pour over apples. Cover; chill 1 hour. Beat eggs until light; beat in flour, salt and milk to make a smooth, thin batter. Drain apples; dip in batter; cook in shallow fat, 2 inches deep, heated to 375°, until golden brown. Drain on absorbent paper. Serve with Lemon Sauce.* Makes 6 servings.

*Lemon Sauce #2:

½ cup sugar
3 tablespoons cornstarch
¼ teaspoon salt
2 cups boiling water
¼ cup butter or margarine

3 tablespoons lemon juice
1 tablespoon grated lemon peel
Dash nutmeg, mace and cloves

Combine first 3 ingredients in saucepan. Add boiling water slowly, stirring constantly to avoid lumps. Simmer, while stirring, about 5 minutes or until clear and thickened. Remove; stir in rest of ingredients. Makes 2 cups.

APPLE GINGER CRISP

4 large tart apples
½ cup water
1 tablespoon orange juice
¼ cup molasses
1 cup gingersnap crumbs

⅛ teaspoon salt
2 tablespoons melted butter or margarine
1 tablespoon grated orange peel

Pare and core apples, slice thin. Add water; cook over low heat until just tender. Pour into shallow baking dish. Combine orange juice and molasses; pour over apples. Combine gingersnap crumbs, salt, melted butter or margarine and grated orange peel; sprinkle over surface. Bake at 350° for 25 minutes. Serve warm with cream. Makes 4 servings.

APPLE DESSERT FRITTERS

4 to 6 tart apples
1 cup sifted all-purpose flour
1 teaspoon baking powder
1 tablespoon sugar
½ teaspoon salt
¼ teaspoon nutmeg

1 egg
½ cup milk
1 tablespoon vegetable oil
1 tablespoon lemon juice
½ cup flaked coconut

Peel and core apples; slice ¼ inch thick. Mix and sift flour, baking powder, sugar, salt and nutmeg. Beat egg slightly;

beat in milk and vegetable oil. Add to flour mixture. Stir in lemon juice and coconut. Dip apple slices in batter. Fry in hot vegetable oil about ¼ inch deep, until golden brown, turning to brown on both sides. Drain on absorbent paper. Serve with maple syrup. Makes 6 to 8 servings.

APPLE COCONUT CREAM PUFFS

Cream Puff Shells:

½ cup butter or margarine   Few grains salt
1 cup boiling water   4 eggs
1 cup sifted all-purpose flour Apple Coconut Filling*

Bring butter and water to boil. Combine flour and salt; add all at once; mix well. Cook and stir until mixture forms a smooth compact mass. Remove from heat. Add unbeaten eggs, one at a time, beating vigorously after each addition. Drop by tablespoons on greased baking sheet 2 inches apart, making 18 mounds. Bake at 400° for 35 minutes, or until golden brown and set. Cool. Slit each puff near bottom; fill; dust tops with confectioners' sugar.

*Apple Coconut Filling:

1 cup whipping cream   ½ teaspoon cinnamon
1 cup cooked diced apples   1 cup flaked coconut
¼ cup sugar   18 cream puff shells

Whip cream; combine apples, sugar and cinnamon; fold into whipped cream with coconut. Fills 18 cream puff shells.

APPLE GINGER FRUIT CUP

1 cup sugar   3 tart red apples
½ cup grapefruit juice   1 can (1 pound) grapefruit
½ teaspoon powdered   sections
  ginger

Combine sugar, grapefruit juice (from canned grapefruit) and ginger in saucepan. Stir over low heat until sugar dissolves. Boil 5 minutes. Chill. Core and dice apples without paring.

Combine with grapefruit sections; arrange in serving dishes. Add ginger syrup. Makes 6 servings.

APPLE JAM "CAKE"

1 loaf thin-sliced bread	¾ cup strawberry jam
⅓ cup soft butter or margarine	2 apples
	Crumb Topping*

Cut crust from 18 slices of bread. Spread each slice with butter or margarine and strawberry jam. Makes 6 stacks of three slices each, ending with spread slice up. Place stacks close together on a baking sheet. Peel apples; slice very thin. Arrange apple slices on top of bread stacks. Sprinkle with Crumb Topping. Bake at 425° for 10 minutes. Serve warm. Makes 6 servings.

*Crumb Topping:

Combine ¼ cup sifted all-purpose flour, ¼ cup firmly packed brown sugar and ¼ teaspoon cinnamon. With a pastry blender cut in 2 tablespoons butter or margarine.

APPLE KUCHEN

Dough:

1½ cups sifted all-purpose flour	¾ teaspoon salt
½ cup enriched corn meal	¼ teaspoon nutmeg
1½ teaspoons baking powder	¼ cup shortening
¾ cup sugar	2 eggs, beaten
	½ cup milk

Topping:

16 raw apple slices, peeled	½ cup sugar
Melted butter or margarine	½ teaspoon cinnamon

For dough, sift together dry ingredients. Cut in shortening until mixture resembles coarse crumbs. Add eggs and milk; stir until dry ingredients are just moistened. Pour into greased 8-inch-square baking pan. For topping, dip apple slices in melted butter. Combine sugar and cinnamon; dip apple slices in some of this mixture. Arrange 4 rows of apple slices over dough; sprinkle remaining sugar mixture on top. Bake at 400° for 35 to 40 minutes.

APPLE CRISP

4 cups sliced pared apples
  (4 to 5 medium)
2 tablespoons water
¼ cup sugar
1½ cups biscuit mix

½ cup sugar
½ teaspoon cinnamon
1 egg
¼ cup shortening, melted

Grease 8-inch-square pan. Arrange apples in pan; sprinkle with water and ¼ cup sugar. Stir together biscuit mix, ½ cup sugar and cinnamon. Beat egg thoroughly; pour slowly into biscuit mixture stirring constantly with fork until mixture is crumbly. Sprinkle mixture evenly over apples; pour shortening over top. Bake at 400° for about 25 minutes or until brown. Serve warm or cold with milk or cream. Makes 6 to 8 servings.

APPLE LIME SNOW

1 cup applesauce
Juice and grated peel of 1
  lime

3 egg whites
2 tablespoons sugar

Combine applesauce, lime juice and grated peel. Beat egg whites stiff; add sugar gradually while beating; fold into applesauce. Chill. Serve with custard sauce. Makes 5 to 6 servings.

APPLE MINCE CRISP

4 cups sliced, peeled apples
1½ cups mincemeat
⅓ cup Sauterne
1 cup firmly packed light
  brown sugar
¾ cup sifted all-purpose
  flour

½ teaspoon cinnamon
1 teaspoon mace
¼ teaspoon salt
½ cup softened butter or
  margarine

Spread half the apples on the bottom of a greased shallow baking dish; spread mincemeat over apples; top with remaining apple slices. Pour wine over all. Combine sugar, flour, spices and salt. Mix in butter until mixture is crumbly; spread evenly over the top; pat down. Bake at 350° for 1 hour, or until apples are tender. Serve warm with hard sauce shaped and tinted to look like a big apple. Makes 6 servings.

APPLE OATMEAL CRISP

5 large apples	¾ cup rolled oats
⅓ cup water	⅓ cup sugar
1 tablespoon lemon juice	⅓ cup peanut butter
½ teaspoon nutmeg	2 tablespoons butter or
¼ teaspoon allspice	margarine
3 tablespoons flour	

Pare, core and slice apples. Arrange in baking dish. Add water and lemon juice; sprinkle with spices. Blend together flour, rolled oats, sugar, peanut butter and butter or margarine. Spread over apples. Bake at 325° about 40 minutes, or until apples are tender. Serve hot with plain cream. Makes 6 servings.

APPLE PANCAKE

1 pound tart apples (3 or 4)	½ cup milk
⅓ cup melted butter or margarine	½ cup sifted all-purpose flour
⅓ cup sugar	¼ teaspoon salt
⅛ teaspoon nutmeg	5 tablespoons melted butter or margarine
¼ teaspoon cinnamon	¼ cup sugar
2 large eggs	

Pare and core apples; cut in thin slices; cook in ⅓ cup butter or margarine 5 minutes. Combine sugar, nutmeg and cinnamon; add to apples; cover; cook over low heat 10 minutes longer, or until apples are crisply tender. Remove from heat; cool to lukewarm. Combine eggs, milk, flour and salt; beat with rotary egg beater or electric mixer about 2 minutes (batter will be very thin). Heat 1 tablespoon of remaining butter or margarine in 10-inch frying pan. When hot, pour batter into pan. Bake at 450° for 15 minutes. As soon as batter puffs up in center (about 3 minutes) puncture with skewer or fork, repeating as often as necessary. Lower heat to 350° and bake 10 minutes longer, or until golden brown and crisp. (Batter will creep up on sides of pan, forming a shell.) Remove from oven; pour half the remaining butter or margarine over surface, sprinkle with half the remaining sugar. Spread apple mixture over half the surface; fold as for an omelet; remove to hot platter. Pour remaining butter on top; sprinkle with remaining sugar. Makes 6 servings.

APPLE PEPPERMINT FRUIT CUP

3 red apples	2 cups seedless grapes
2 navel oranges	Peppermint Syrup*

Core apples; do not pare; cut in thin slices. Section oranges. Arrange apple slices, orange sections and grapes in sherbet glasses. Fill glasses with chilled Peppermint Syrup. Makes 6 servings.

*Peppermint Syrup:

Combine 1 cup sugar and 1 cup water in saucepan; stir over low heat until sugar dissolves. Boil 5 minutes. Remove from heat. Tint deep pink with red food coloring. Chill. Flavor to taste with peppermint extract.

APPLE REFRIGERATOR DESSERT

6 tablespoons cornstarch	4 egg yolks, beaten
½ cup sugar	½ cup light cream
¼ teaspoon salt	Rum flavoring (optional)
¼ teaspoon cinnamon	1 package (12) lady fingers
3 cups apple juice	

Combine cornstarch, sugar, salt and cinnamon. Add a little apple juice; blend well. Add remaining apple juice slowly, while mixing. Bring to boil; boil 2 minutes, stirring constantly. Add hot mixture slowly to egg yolks; return to heat; cook 2 minutes longer. Cool slightly. Add cream; mix well. Add rum flavoring to taste, if desired. Place a layer of split lady fingers in bottom of waxed-paper-lined loaf pan,

9″ x 5″ x 3″. Cover with a layer of sauce; repeat until all ingredients are used, ending with lady fingers. Cover pan with waxed paper; chill several hours or overnight. Unmold; garnish with whipped cream and toasted coconut, if desired.

APPLES CONTINENTAL:

Simple, yet sophisticated . . . easy but delicious . . . cold, crisp, fresh apples, cheese and nuts, with perhaps one other fruit, in unlimited combinations, for dessert, after a hearty dinner. Perfect! To spark your imagination, here are a dozen highly successful combinations. You can go on from there!

APPLES	CHEESE	NUTS
Stayman	Roquefort	Walnuts
Jonathan	Swiss	Peanuts
Golden Delicious	Camembert	Brazil
McIntosh	Sharp Cheddar	Cashew
Red Delicious	Blue Cheese Spread	Salted Filberts
Northern Spy	Bel Paese	Salted Almonds
Cortland	Pineapple Cheese Spread	Salted Peanuts
McIntosh	Muenster	Mixed Salted Nuts
Golden Delicious	Brie	Walnuts
Red Delicious	Gruyère	Walnuts
Northern Spy	Bel Paese	Pecans
Stayman	Blue	Filberts

APPLE PILAFF

Boiling water	4 tablespoons brown sugar
½ cup regular rice	1 cup diced apples
3 tablespoons butter or margarine	⅓ cup chopped walnuts
	⅛ teaspoon salt
1 can (1 pound 2 ounces) pineapple juice	Few grains nutmeg
	1 cup whipping cream

Add enough boiling water to rice to cover. Cover; let stand 10 minutes. Drain. Heat butter or margarine; add rice and stir until kernels are coated with butter. Add pineapple juice;

cover; cook very slowly until rice is tender (about 50 minutes). Combine brown sugar, apples, walnuts, salt and nutmeg. Add to rice; stir until blended. Cool. Whip cream; fold in. Makes 6 servings.

APPLE RICOTTA REFRIGERATOR CAKE

1 frozen pound cake
1 pound ricotta (Italian
  cottage cheese)*
½ cup sugar
2 squares (1 ounce each)
  unsweetened chocolate,
  grated

1 cup freshly grated raw
  apple
Few drops almond extract
1 cup whipping cream
½ cup broken walnuts

Thaw pound cake; cut crosswise in thin slices. Combine ricotta and sugar; mix well. Stir in chocolate, apple and almond extract. Spread generously between cake slices, putting together in loaf shape. Chill several hours or overnight. Just before serving, whip cream; frost top and sides of cake. Sprinkle walnuts over top. To serve, slice on the diagonal. Makes 10 to 12 servings.

* Or any dry, fine-curd cottage cheese, such as farmer style.

APPLESAUCE AMBROSIA

1 can (1 pound) applesauce
2 bananas, sliced
1 can (11 ounces) mandarin
  oranges

½ cup slivered roasted
  almonds
½ cup flaked coconut
Whipped cream

Combine all ingredients except cream; chill. Serve in dessert glasses topped with whipped cream. Makes 6 servings.

AUTUMN SHORTCAKE

2 cups fresh cranberries
2 cups diced unpeeled tart
  apples
1 cup canned pineapple
  tidbits

2 cups sugar
¼ teaspoon salt
3 cups biscuit mix
1 cup whipping cream

Chop cranberries; combine with apples, pineapple, sugar and salt. Chill at least 2 hours. Prepare biscuit mix as directed on package; spread in greased deep 8-inch layer cake pan.

To glaze, brush top with slightly beaten egg yolk and sprinkle with sugar. Bake at 450° for 18 to 20 minutes, or until golden brown. Remove from pan; split in half, crosswise; butter cut surfaces. Serve with apple mixture between and on top. Whip cream; serve separately. Makes 8 servings.

APPLE RICE CREAM

2 cups cooked rice
½ pound marshmallows (24), quartered
1 cup diced apples
½ cup sugar
1 cup drained canned pineapple tidbits
1 cup whipping cream
½ cup flaked coconut, toasted
Maraschino cherries

Combine rice, marshmallows, apples, sugar and pineapple tidbits. Chill 1 hour. Whip cream; fold in. Serve in sherbet glasses, garnished with toasted coconut and maraschino cherries.

APPLE RING FRITTERS

2 eggs, separated
½ cup milk
1 cup sifted all-purpose flour
¼ cup sugar
1 teaspoon baking powder
1 teaspoon salt
1 teaspoon vegetable oil
6 apples

Beat egg yolks; stir in milk. Mix and sift flour, sugar, baking powder and salt; beat into egg yolk mixture. Beat in oil. Beat egg whites stiff but not dry; fold in. Core and pare apples; cut into crosswise slices ¼ inch thick. Dip apple rings in batter. Fry a few at a time in shallow fat or oil heated to 370° until brown, turning once. Drain on absorbent paper. Sprinkle with confectioners' sugar. Serve hot with butter or margarine and maple syrup. Makes about 24 fritters.

APPLE ROLY POLY

2 cups biscuit mix
½ cup honey
5 large tart apples
¾ teaspoon cinnamon
¼ teaspoon nutmeg
¼ teaspoon cloves
3 tablespoons sugar
2 tablespoons butter or margarine

Prepare biscuit mix as directed on package. Roll out on lightly floured board into oblong ¼ inch thick. Spread with honey to within 1 inch of edges. Pare and core apples; chop fine; spread on dough. Combine cinnamon, nutmeg, cloves and sugar; sprinkle over apples. Dot with butter or margarine. Roll up like jelly roll. Bake in greased pan at 350° for 40 minutes. Slice and serve hot with plain or whipped cream. Makes 6 servings.

BAKED APPLE ALMOND DELIGHT

1 cup sifted all-purpose flour
2 teaspoons baking powder
1/4 teaspoon salt
1 1/2 tablespoons sugar
2 tablespoons shortening
6 tablespoons milk
1 egg
2 tart apples, thinly sliced

1/4 cup honey
1/2 teaspoon cinnamon
1 tablespoon soft butter or margarine
1/2 cup canned slivered blanched almonds
Cream

Mix and sift flour, baking powder, salt and sugar. Cut shortening into flour mixture. Stir in milk and egg. Spread in bottom of greased 8-inch-square baking pan. Arrange apples over dough. Blend together honey, cinnamon, butter and almonds; spread over apples. Bake at 450° for 15 minutes. Reduce temperature to 300° and continue baking about 10 minutes, or until apples are tender. Serve warm with cream. Makes 6 servings.

COCONUT-CRUSTED APPLE DESSERT

Filling:
6 large tart apples
1/2 cup firmly packed brown sugar
1 1/2 teaspoons cinnamon

1/2 teaspoon mace
2 tablespoons flour
1/4 cup orange juice

Topping:
1/2 cup firmly packed brown sugar
1/4 cup butter or margarine

1/3 cup sifted all-purpose flour
1/2 cup flaked coconut

Pare, core and slice apples. Heap in greased 8-inch baking dish 2 inches deep. Combine 1/2 cup brown sugar, spices and 2 tablespoons flour; sprinkle over apples. Pour orange juice over all. For the topping, blend ½ cup brown sugar, butter or margarine and ⅓ cup flour with fork until crumbly. Stir in coconut. Spread over apples. Cover with aluminum foil. Bake at 425° for 20 minutes. Remove foil; bake 15 minutes longer, or until apples are tender. Makes 6 to 8 servings.

APPLE SCOTCH

4 cups sliced pared apples
4 cups soft bread cubes
¾ cup melted butter or margarine
½ cup sugar
½ teaspoon cinnamon
2 tablespoons lemon juice
Brown sugar

Combine apple slices and bread cubes. Combine melted butter or margarine, sugar, cinnamon and lemon juice; pour over apple mixture; toss with fork until thoroughly mixed. Turn into casserole; cover; bake at 350° for 30 minutes. Remove cover; sprinkle with brown sugar. Return to oven for 10 minutes. Serve warm, with additional brown sugar and plain cream. Makes 8 servings.

BRAZIL NUT CHEESE SPREAD

2 jars (5 ounces each) pimiento cheese spread
¼ cup chopped Brazil nuts
2 tablespoons mayonnaise
1 teaspoon Worcestershire sauce
1 teaspoon grated onion

Combine all ingredients; mix well. Serve with crisp rye wafers and apples as dessert or as an evening snack.

BAKED APPLE SLICES WITH CHEESE

5 cups apple slices
1 tablespoon lemon juice
¾ cup firmly packed brown sugar, divided
½ teaspoon cinnamon
½ cup sifted all-purpose flour
¼ teaspoon salt
¼ cup butter or margarine
1 cup grated sharp Cheddar cheese

Arrange apple slices in shallow baking dish; sprinkle with lemon juice and ¼ cup brown sugar. Combine remaining brown sugar, cinnamon, flour and salt; cut in butter or margarine; stir in cheese. Spread over apples. Bake at 350° for 35 minutes, or until apples are tender. Serve warm, with plain cream. Makes 6 servings.

BAKED SLICED APPLES VIRGINIA

6 tart apples
½ cup golden raisins
⅓ cup orange juice
3 tablespoons flour
⅓ cup firmly packed light brown sugar
½ teaspoon cinnamon

3 tablespoons butter or margarine
1 tablespoon grated orange peel
⅛ teaspoon salt
2 tablespoons peanut butter
½ cup chopped peanuts

Pare and core apples; cut in eighths; arrange in shallow baking dish. Add raisins and orange juice. Combine flour, sugar, cinnamon, butter or margarine, orange peel, salt and peanut butter; mix until crumbly. Add peanuts. Sprinkle over apples and raisins. Bake at 375° for 30 minutes, or until apples are tender. Serve warm with plain cream. Makes 6 servings.

CREAMY PEANUT SPREAD

1 package (8 ounces) cream cheese
¼ cup creamy peanut butter
½ cup chopped peanuts

¼ cup chopped chutney with syrup
Tart red eating apples

Whip cheese until soft; beat in peanut butter. Stir in peanuts and chutney. Use as a spread for crisp apple slices for dessert. Makes about 1½ cups.

CRÊPES AUX POMMES

1 cup sifted all-purpose flour
1 tablespoon sugar
Few grains salt
3 eggs

1 cup milk
2 tablespoons melted butter or margarine
1 cup hot spiced applesauce

Mix and sift flour, sugar and salt. Beat eggs; add. Add milk; stir until smooth. Add butter. Strain through a fine sieve. Let stand 2 hours. Melt ½ teaspoon butter in 7-inch skillet. Pour in a thin layer of batter. Cook over low heat until underside is golden brown. Turn and brown other side (about 1 minute each side). Repeat until batter is used. Spread each "crêpe" with hot applesauce. Roll up. Sprinkle with powdered sugar. Makes 12 crêpes, or 6 servings. If desired, pour 1 ounce apple-jack over all and ignite.

DOUBLE-A MERINGUE

6 medium apples	¼ cup boiling water
1 cup firmly packed light brown sugar	3 egg whites
	Few grains salt
¼ teaspoon cloves	½ cup sugar
¼ teaspoon cinnamon	1 tablespoon grated lemon peel
¼ teaspoon nutmeg	
1 tablespoon melted butter or margarine	⅓ cup slivered blanched almonds

Core and pare apples; slice thin. Pour into shallow baking dish. Combine brown sugar, spices and melted butter. Sprinkle over apples. Add boiling water. Bake at 350° about 20 minutes, or until apples are just tender, stirring occasionally. Remove from oven. Cool slightly. Beat egg whites until foamy; add salt; beat until stiff. Beat in sugar, 2 tablespoons at a time. Continue beating until the meringue is satiny and stands in peaks; fold in lemon peel. Spread over apples; sprinkle with almonds. Return to oven and bake 15 minutes longer or until meringue is golden brown. Serve hot or cold. Makes 6 servings. If desired, make a custard sauce with the 3 egg yolks; chill; serve with the meringue.

DUTCH APPLE PANCAKES WITH SYRUP

2 cups sifted all-purpose flour	¼ cup melted butter or margarine
1 cup light cream	1 large apple, cored, pared and thinly sliced
½ cup milk	
¼ teaspoon salt	
1 tablespoon sugar	

Combine all ingredients except apples. Beat until fairly smooth. Melt about 2 teaspoons butter in an 8-inch skillet. When butter is hot, spoon in batter to a depth of about ¼ inch. Sprinkle with ¼ the apple slices; spoon a little more batter over apples. When pancake is browned underneath, turn to brown on other side. Repeat until all batter is used. Makes about 4 large pancakes. Serve with syrup.

GINGER APPLE SQUARES

2 packages gingerbread mix
3 or 4 large tart apples, sliced in eighths
¼ cup sugar
½ teaspoon cinnamon
¼ teaspoon nutmeg
2 tablespoons melted butter or margarine

Prepare gingerbread mix according to directions on package; pour into greased and floured 9" x 12½" x 2" pan. Pare, core, and slice apples; arrange in rows on gingerbread batter. Combine sugar, cinnamon and nutmeg; sprinkle on apples. Pour melted butter over apples. Bake at 375° for 50 to 60 minutes. Cut in large squares. Serve warm with hard sauce. Makes 8 to 12 servings.

OLD-FASHIONED APPLE PAN DOWDY 1

8 thin slices day-old bread (about)
4 tablespoons butter or margarine
6 cups sliced apples
½ teaspoon nutmeg
1 teaspoon cinnamon
¼ teaspoon salt
2 tablespoons brown sugar
2 tablespoons light molasses
½ cup water
Cinnamon-sugar

Trim crust from bread slices; butter each slice. Line 1½-quart baking dish with bread, cutting to fit, and saving enough slices for top. Fill dish with apple slices. Combine spices, salt, brown sugar, molasses and water; pour over apples. Top with remaining bread slices, buttered side up. Cover; bake at 350° for 30 minutes. Remove cover; sprinkle with cinnamon-sugar; bake 20 minutes longer, or until golden brown. Serve hot with plain cream. Makes 6 servings.

OLD-FASHIONED APPLE PAN DOWDY 2

10 medium-size tart apples
½ cup molasses
2 tablespoons lemon juice
1 teaspoon cinnamon
½ teaspoon salt
3 tablespoons butter or margarine
Pastry for 1-crust pie

Pare, core and slice apples. Place in casserole; add molasses, lemon juice, cinnamon, salt; mix with a fork. Dot with butter or margarine. Cover; bake at 300° for 2 hours, removing cover and stirring about 3 times during cooking. Turn into shallow pan and top with layer of pastry made from pie crust mix, and rolled ⅛ inch thick. Cut slashes in pastry. Bake at 425° for 15 minutes, or until pastry is golden brown. Makes 6 servings.

GLAZED APPLE ROLY POLY

2 cups biscuit mix
1 egg
½ cup water
3 cups chopped tart apples
½ cup sugar
2½ teaspoons cinnamon, divided

2 cups firmly packed brown sugar
1½ tablespoons cornstarch
¼ cup vinegar
¾ cup water
1 tablespoon butter or margarine

Measure biscuit mix into bowl. Break egg into ½ cup water; mix well. Add to biscuit mix; blend with a fork. Turn out on floured board; knead gently until smooth. Roll out in rectangle ⅓ inch thick. Cover dough with apples. Combine ½ cup sugar and 1½ teaspoons cinnamon. Sprinkle over apples. Roll up like jelly roll. Cut in 1½-inch slices. Place slices, cut side up, close together in greased 8-inch-square cake pan. Bake at 450° for 15 minutes. Meanwhile, combine brown sugar, cornstarch, and remaining 1 teaspoon cinnamon. Combine vinegar and ¾ cup water; add; boil 5 minutes. Add butter or margarine. Pour over roly poly, pulling biscuits away from sides of pan so syrup will run underneath. Reduce heat to 375°; bake 15 minutes longer. Makes 9 servings.

OLD-FASHIONED APPLE SLUMP

4 cups thinly sliced apples
⅔ cup firmly packed brown sugar
⅔ cup sugar

½ cup water
1 teaspoon cinnamon
1 recipe dumpling dough*

Combine first 5 ingredients in deep frying pan; bring to a boil; cover; cook 10 minutes. Drop dumpling dough by

* **Dumplings:** Follow recipe for dumplings on package of biscuit mix.

spoonfuls on pieces of apples; cover; cook 12 minutes, or until dumplings are done. Transfer dumplings to deep dessert dishes; spoon apples over them. Serve with plain cream. Makes 6 to 8 servings.

OLD-FASHIONED APPLE SNOW

1⅓ cups extra-fine granu-
  lated sugar
2 large tart apples

4 egg whites, unbeaten
Few grains salt

Measure sugar into large bowl. Pare apples; grate into sugar so that apples will not discolor. Add egg whites and salt. Beat with rotary beater or electric mixer until mixture is very stiff and light (this takes a long time by hand). Serve with Custard Sauce.* Makes 8 servings.

° Custard Sauce:

1½ cups milk
3 tablespoons sugar
¼ teaspoon salt

4 egg yolks, slightly beaten
½ teaspoon vanilla

Scald milk; add sugar and salt; stir until sugar dissolves; pour slowly on egg yolks. Cook over hot water, stirring constantly, until mixture coats spoon. Remove from heat; add vanilla. Chill.

SPANISH APPLE FLAN

3 cups milk
1½ cups sugar, divided
1 teaspoon grated lemon
  peel
Few grains salt
1-inch stick cinnamon

¼ cup water
4 eggs, beaten
1 can (20 ounces) pie-sliced
  apples

Combine milk, ½ cup sugar, lemon peel, salt and cinnamon in large saucepan. Bring to boil; lower heat; simmer 15 minutes. Let cool. Combine remaining 1 cup sugar and water. Bring to boil; boil 8 minutes without stirring; lower heat; simmer until caramel color. Meanwhile, arrange apple slices in bottom of 12-inch pizza pan or 10-inch pie pan. Pour syrup immediately over apples. Strain cooled milk mixture; add to beaten eggs; mix thoroughly; strain over apples. Set in pan of hot water and bake at 400° for 45 minutes for pizza pan, 1 hour for pie pan, or until knife inserted near rim comes out clean. Let cool, then chill. Makes 8 servings.

SWEDISH APPLE MERINGUE "CAKE"

Crust:
⅓ cup butter or margarine
3 tablespoons sugar
2 egg yolks
¾ cup sifted all-purpose flour
⅓ cup chopped roasted almonds
1 tablespoon grated lemon peel
1 tablespoon lemon juice

Filling:
4 to 6 medium apples
⅓ cup sugar
1½ tablespoons lemon juice
½ cup raspberry jam

Meringue:
2 egg whites
Few grains salt
4 tablespoons sugar

For crust, cream butter or margarine; add 3 tablespoons sugar while continuing to cream. Add egg yolks; mix well. Add flour, almonds, lemon peel and 1 tablespoon lemon juice; blend well. Press on bottom and sides of 9-inch pie pan. Brush with a little unbeaten egg white. Bake at 350° for 15 minutes, or until golden brown. For filling, pare and core apples; cut in eighths; combine with sugar and lemon juice in a saucepan; cover; cook over medium heat until tender. Spread jam evenly over baked crust; arrange apples on top. For meringue, beat egg whites with salt until stiff but not dry; add remaining sugar, 1 tablespoon at a time, while continuing to beat. Mound over apples. Return to oven for about 18 minutes or until meringue is lightly browned.

VIENNESE APPLE CHARLOTTE

Kuchen Dough:
1 cup sifted all-purpose flour
½ teaspoon baking powder
¼ teaspoon salt
2 tablespoons sugar
2½ tablespoons butter or margarine
2 eggs, beaten
2 tablespoons milk

Mix and sift flour, baking powder, salt and sugar. Work butter into mixture smoothly with wooden spoon. Beat in eggs.

Stir in milk. Grease 8-inch spring form pan. With rubber spatula or spoon, spread dough on bottom and partly up side of the spring form pan (top edge of crust will be ragged).

Apple Filling:

5 cups sliced apples	1 teaspoon cinnamon
½ cup golden raisins	1 tablespoon grated lemon
⅔ cup sugar	peel

Cook apple slices and raisins in enough water to cover until apples are just tender, but have not lost their shape; drain. Combine sugar, cinnamon and lemon peel; stir gently into apples and raisins. Spoon into dough-lined spring form pan. Bake at 425° for 50 to 60 minutes, or until crust is deep golden brown and filling is firm. Serve hot, topped with almond-flavored whipped cream.

FINNISH APPLE MERINGUE

2 tablespoons butter or margarine	2 cans (20 ounces each) pie-sliced apples
½ cup firmly packed brown sugar, divided	3 egg whites
2 teaspoons cinnamon, divided	½ cup sugar
	Few grains salt

Melt butter in bottom of shallow 1½-quart baking dish. Sprinkle with half the brown sugar and cinnamon. Arrange apple slices evenly in pan. Sprinkle with remaining brown sugar and cinnamon. Beat egg whites until foamy. Slowly beat in sugar and salt. Continue beating until mixture stands in stiff peaks. Swirl on top of apples. Bake at 325° for 35 to 40 minutes or until the meringue is golden. Makes 8 servings.

SAUCES AND TOPPINGS

APPLE CRANBERRY PANCAKE SAUCE

1 cup water
1½ cups sugar
Dash nutmeg

4 cups diced tart apples
2 cups fresh cranberries

Combine water, sugar and nutmeg in deep saucepan; stir over low heat until sugar dissolves; bring to boil. Add apples and cranberries; cook, stirring often until apples are soft and cranberries have burst open (10 to 15 minutes). Put through food mill or sieve. Serve hot or cold with apple pancakes. Makes about 4 cups sauce.

APPLE PECAN SYRUP

3 tablespoons butter or margarine
¼ cup chopped pecans
1 cup maple syrup

½ teaspoon cinnamon
Few grains salt
2 cups thinly sliced peeled apples

Melt butter, add nuts; brown lightly; remove nuts. Add maple syrup, cinnamon and salt to butter in saucepan; add apples; cover; simmer slowly 10 minutes. Remove cover; simmer about 3 minutes longer. Remove from heat; add nuts. Makes 6 servings. Serve with pancakes, waffles or French toast.

APPLESAUCE

8 tart apples
¾ cup water (about)
½ cup sugar
¼ teaspoon nutmeg

Dash cinnamon
1 teaspoon grated lemon peel (optional)

Pare and core apples; slice thin. Add just enough water to prevent scorching. Bring to boil; lower heat to simmer; cover.

Cook about 20 minutes, or until apples are soft. Put through food mill or sieve. Add sugar (amount depends upon tartness of apples) and spices. Stir in lemon peel.

NOTE: If apples are quite sweet, add a little lemon juice.

Some cooks prefer to cut up apples without paring or removing cores. The apples are then cooked and sieved as above. Unpared red apples will impart a faint pink tint to the applesauce, and these cooks feel that cores and peel impart added flavor to the sauce.

BAKED APPLE TOPPING

6 to 8 tart apples
½ cup sugar
½ cup firmly packed brown sugar
½ teaspoon nutmeg

Grated peel of 1 lemon
Grated peel of 1 orange
3 tablespoons butter or margarine

Pare and core apples; cut into ¼-inch slices. Place in deep greased baking dish. Combine sugars, nutmeg and grated fruit peel. Sprinkle over apples. Dot with butter or margarine. Cover; bake at 425° for 40 to 45 minutes, or until apples are tender. Stir occasionally during baking. Makes about 2 cups. Serve for dessert or as a sauce for ice cream.

CRANBERRY APPLESAUCE

2 cups cranberries
2 cups sliced tart apples
1 cup sugar

¾ cup water
¼ teaspoon nutmeg

Combine all ingredients in saucepan. Cook over low heat until fruit is soft. Put through food mill or sieve. Makes 6 to 8 servings.

BAKED APPLESAUCE

5 pounds tart apples
1¼ cups currant jelly
10 tablespoons water

⅓ cup lemon juice
¼ teaspoon nutmeg

Pare and core apples; slice in eighths. Place in 2 large baking dishes. Heat jelly and water until jelly is partially melted.

Finnish Apple Meringue: A delicious dessert made with canned pie-sliced apples, brown sugar and spice and crowned with meringue. You'll find the recipe on page 186.

Hungarian Stew (above): This savory main dish combines a trinity of favorites—apples, pork and sauerkraut. Page 62.

Rosy Glow (below, left): A tall, cool drink based on apple juice. The recipe for this crowd-pleaser is on page 105.

Apple Salad Julienne: A new, interesting way to enjoy crisp, fresh apples. The recipe for this tempting salad is on page 90.

A tasty duo: Hot, crunchy Grilled Apple-Cheese Sandwiches (see page 94) with savory green pea soup. This chill-chaser can be served for a hearty lunch or supper.

Appetite tempter: Chunks of unpared apples on picks stuck in big, bright red apples are removed and then dunked in a tasty cream dip. The recipe is on page 37.

Remove from heat; add lemon juice and nutmeg; pour half into each baking dish. Cover; bake at 350° for 45 minutes to 1 hour, or until apples are soft. Break up with fork to desired consistency. Serve hot or cold. Makes about 3 pints.

BAKED CIDER APPLESAUCE

5 pounds apples
1 cup firmly packed light brown sugar
1 cup apple cider
2 tablespoons lemon juice
½ teaspoon nutmeg

Pare and core apples; slice in eighths. Place in large baking dish. Heat sugar and cider, stirring until sugar dissolves. Remove from heat; add lemon juice and nutmeg; pour over apples. Cover; bake at 350° for 45 minutes, or until apples are soft. Break up with a fork to desired consistency. Makes about 3 pints.

CIDER APPLESAUCE

8 apples
½ cup apple cider
½ cup sugar (about)
⅛ teaspoon salt
¼ teaspoon nutmeg

Pare, core and slice apples; place in saucepan with cider. Simmer until apples are tender. Stir in sugar, salt and nutmeg, adding more sugar if desired. Cook 1 minute longer. Makes 6 servings.

SPICY APPLESAUCE

8 apples
⅓ cup water
Strip of lemon or lime peel
1 2-inch piece stick cinnamon
3 allspice berries
8 whole cloves
½ cup sugar (about)

Core apples; cut in eighths; do not peel. Add water, lemon peel and spices; simmer about 15 minutes, or until soft. Press through a food mill or sieve. Add sugar 2 tablespoons at a time, tasting after each addition. Chill. Makes about 4 cups.

UNCOOKED APPLESAUCE

½ cup water
½ cup sugar*
1 teaspoon ascorbic acid
   and citric acid mixture

¼ teaspoon salt
1 pound tart apples

Combine first 3 ingredients in electric blender. Add salt. Slice peeled and cored apples into blender. Run blender at high speed about 30 seconds (or less). Makes 6 to 8 servings.

* If apples are sweet, add less sugar.

CANDIES AND CONFECTIONS

CANDIES AND CONFECTIONS

Perhaps you never thought of apples in connection with confections; but, for children especially, they can be used as a sweet with happy results.

APPLE CANDY

8 medium apples
½ cup cold water, divided
2 cups firmly packed light brown sugar
2 envelopes unflavored gelatin

1 cup chopped walnuts
1 tablespoon lemon juice
½ cup confectioners' sugar
1 tablespoon cornstarch

Core and pare apples; cut in small pieces. Add ¼ cup of the water. Cook until tender; put through food mill or sieve. Add sugar. Cook over low heat until thick (about ½ hour) stirring often. Soften gelatin in remaining ¼ cup cold water; add to hot apple mixture; stir until dissolved. Chill until slightly thickened; stir in walnuts and lemon juice. Pour into square pan to a depth of about ½ inch. Chill thoroughly. Cut into squares. Combine confectioners' sugar and cornstarch; roll squares in this mixture.

CARAMEL APPLES

1 pound dairy caramels
2 tablespoons hot water

4 or 5 medium-size apples

Place the caramels and water in top of double boiler. Heat, stirring frequently until caramels are melted and the sauce is smooth. Stick a wooden skewer into the stem end of each apple. Dip into the hot caramel sauce and turn until the surface is completely coated. If desired, dip in flaked coconut, chocolate or multicolor sprills, chopped nuts, etc. Place on waxed paper and set in the refrigerator for a few minutes, until the caramel is firm.

CHOCOLATE APPLE NIBBLES

Core red apples, do not pare; cut in eighths. Melt semi-sweet chocolate over hot water; stick wooden picks into peel of apple; dip in melted chocolate, leaving peeled side uncoated. Place on waxed paper; chill.

BUTTERSCOTCH WALNUT APPLES ON STICKS

6 medium apples	2 tablespoons butter or
1 cup sugar	margarine
1 cup light corn syrup	Few grains salt
1 cup light cream	½ teaspoon vanilla
	18 walnut halves

Wash and dry apples; insert wooden sticks. Combine sugar, corn syrup and cream in a large saucepan. Cook rapidly, stirring constantly, to 245° (firm ball stage). Remove from heat at once. Stir in butter, salt and vanilla. Dip apples quickly. Garnish each apple with a trefoil of walnut meats placed around stick.

JELLY APPLES

2 cups sugar	Red food coloring
⅔ cup light corn syrup	6 small red apples on
1 cup water	wooden sticks
1 2-inch stick cinnamon	

Combine first 4 ingredients in small saucepan. Stir constantly over medium heat until mixture begins to boil. Cook without stirring to 300° (brittle), using low heat after 280°. Wipe away sugar crystals from sides of pan with damp cloth wrapped around fork. Remove from heat; remove cinnamon stick; color syrup bright red, stirring as little as possible. Holding each apple by stick, dip quickly in hot syrup, covering apple completely. Remove and twirl, to spread syrup evenly. Place upright in rack to dry (a cake cooler may be used). Be sure apples do not touch while drying.

DECORATIONS FOR JELLY APPLES

1. Immediately on removing from syrup, dip into large bowl containing ready-to-serve cereal (the sweet coated cereals are best).
2. Using leftover syrup as "glue" make "funny faces" on apples with tiny gumdrops, miniature marshmallows, Life Savers, raisins, nuts, licorice strips, gumdrop "fruit" slices and strips. Shredded or flaked coconut, plain or tinted, makes a fine head of hair!
3. Tiny lace paper doilies slipped over the stick make pretty "collars."
4. To cool dipped apples upright, use pin flower frogs if available, or cut slots in top of sturdy cardboard box, such as a shoe box. Or use a block of styrofoam, if available.
5. Wooden meat skewers or flat wooden blades (tongue depressors) make good sticks.

HINTS FOR SUCCESS WITH JELLY APPLES

1. Crisp, firm red apples are best for jelly apples.
2. Work fast when dipping and twirling apples.
3. If syrup gets thick, set it over very low heat or boiling water to keep it fluid.
4. Tip the pan to make a well of syrup for easier coating.

FROSTED APPLE CIRCLES

Prepare penuche quick fudge mix as directed on package. Cool in refrigerator 5 minutes, stirring occasionally. Meanwhile core red apples; do not peel; slice crosswise about ½ inch thick. Fill centers with penuche, then spread entire surface. Top with finely chopped nuts. Makes about 2 dozen.

CANNING, FREEZING, JELLY-MAKING AND PRESERVING

With all the fine processed apple products available at groceries and supermarkets, home canning and freezing may not be in wide practice nowadays. But for those who delight in their own apple trees, and cannot bear to waste any of the lovely fruit, directions may be helpful. And it's fun, too, to see rows of glasses holding sparkling, colorful jellies, jams and conserves, made in the home kitchen.

HOW TO CAN APPLES

Make light or medium syrup in amount needed, using 2 cups sugar to 1 quart water to yield 5 cups light syrup, or 3 cups sugar to 1 quart water to yield 5½ cups medium syrup.

Wash, drain, core, pare and slice cooking apples (or cut into halves or quarters), dropping prepared apples immediately into an ascorbic acid and citric acid solution made according to manufacturer's directions, to keep apples from discoloring. Or add 2 tablespoons each salt and vinegar to 1 gallon of water. If the latter solution is used, do not leave apples in it longer than 20 minutes, and rinse well before packing.

Boil drained apples in syrup 5 minutes. Pack, hot, into hot jars, leaving ½-inch head space. Cover with boiling syrup, leaving ½-inch head space. Add ascorbic acid and citric acid mixture according to manufacturer's directions. If pure ascorbic acid is used, sprinkle ¼ teaspoon over fruit in each quart jar before capping.

Adjust caps according to manufacturer's directions. Process pints and quarts for 20 minutes in boiling water bath. Complete seal, if necessary. Cool upright, away from drafts.

HOW TO CAN APPLESAUCE

Wash, quarter and core apples. Add just enough water to prevent scorching; cook over low heat 15 to 20 minutes, or until tender. Put through food mill or sieve. Add sugar to taste; heat until sugar dissolves. Bring to boiling point. Pack boiling hot applesauce in hot sterilized jars, leaving ½-inch head space. Partially seal; process 5 minutes in hot water bath. Be sure to keep water at least 1 inch above tops of jars. Cover kettle; bring to boil. Begin counting processing time as soon as water starts to boil. Keep water boiling constantly. When processing time is up, remove jars to a cooling rack or folded towels, out of drafts. Complete seal immediately. Self-sealing jars do not need tightening. When jars are cool, wipe off the outside, and label. Applesauce may be spiced to taste before canning, but many authorities feel that flavor is improved if applesauce is canned without spices and these seasonings added when the jar is opened for serving.

HOW TO FREEZE APPLES

Select firm, tart apples. Core, pare and slice into a brine made with 2 tablespoons salt to 1 quart water. Prepare sugar syrup, using 1 cup sugar to 2 cups water. Add ½ teaspoon powdered ascorbic acid to each quart of syrup, to prevent discoloration. Drop drained apple slices into simmering syrup (180°); simmer 3 minutes. Cool quickly. Pack apple slices with syrup in which they were cooked, leaving head space of ½ inch for pint containers, ¾ inch for quart containers. Seal. Freeze at once.

HOW TO FREEZE APPLESAUCE

Prepare applesauce (pages 187–190) but, if spice is used, increase amount by about ¼, as flavor lessens during frozen storage. Cool quickly. Package, seal, label, freeze at once.

HOW TO FREEZE APPLE PIES

Unbaked: Do not slit the top crust. To bake, slit top; place, frozen, in 425° oven; bake 40 to 60 minutes.

Baked: Cool thoroughly before freezing. To bake, place, frozen, in 375° oven; bake 30 minutes.

SPICED CRAB APPLES

8 pounds crab apples
8½ cups sugar
1 quart cider vinegar
2 cups water

7 3-inch sticks cinnamon
2 tablespoons whole cloves
2 tablespoons whole allspice
Red food coloring

Wash crab apples; do not remove stems, but scrape out blossom ends. Combine sugar, vinegar and water. Tie spices in cheesecloth bag; add. Cook, covered, 10 minutes. Tint bright red with food coloring. Add crab apples; cover; boil 10 minutes, or until tender. Let crab apples stand in syrup overnight. Drain; remove spice bag. Pack crab apples at once in clean hot jars. Bring syrup to boil; pour at once over crab apples. Adjust covers as manufacturer directs. Set jars on wire rack in deep kettle, with enough boiling water to cover tops of jars 1 inch. Cover kettle. Process (boil) 30 minutes, counting time after active boiling begins. Remove jars, adjust seals at once as manufacturer directs. Makes 4 to 5 quarts.

SPICED APPLE PIE FILLING FOR CANNING

5 cups sliced apples (about
    7 medium-size apples)
Large bowl salted water
    (1 tablespoon salt for each
    quart of water)
½ to ¾ cup sugar (depending on sweetness
    desired)

¼ teaspoon cinnamon
⅛ teaspoon nutmeg
1 tablespoon tapioca
¼ to ½ cup water (depending on juiciness of apples)
1 tablespoon lemon juice

Wash, core, peel, slice and measure apples into salt water. (Do not leave in salt water longer than 20 minutes; rinse before cooking.) Mix sugar, spices, tapioca and water. Stir over low heat until sugar is dissolved. Add apples; bring to boil over moderate heat; lower heat; cover and simmer 10 to 15 minutes, or until slices are barely tender. Add lemon juice. If juice is thick, add a little boiling water to thin to consistency of honey. Pack hot apple mixture to within ½ inch of the top of 1½ pint fruit jar. Run knife down between apples and side of jar to remove air bubbles. Adjust lid according to manufacturer's directions. Process 20 minutes in boiling water bath. Remove jars; complete seal, if necessary. Cool upright, away from drafts. Label. Each jar makes enough filling for 8-inch pie. Dot filling with 1 to 2 tablespoons butter or margarine before putting on top crust.

APPLE BUTTER

5 pounds tart apples	½ teaspoon allspice
2 cups apple cider	3 teaspoons cinnamon
Sugar	½ teaspoon nutmeg
¾ teaspoon ground cloves	

Wash, remove stems and quarter apples. Add cider; cook slowly until apples are soft. Put apples through food mill or sieve. Measure. Add ½ to ⅔ cup sugar for each cup of pulp, depending on the tartness of the apples. Add spices; mix well. Cook over low heat, stirring constantly, until sugar dissolves. Continue to cook, stirring often, until mixture sheets from spoon. Ladle into hot sterilized jars. Seal at once. Makes about 3 pints.

APPLE CHUTNEY

2 pounds apples	¼ teaspoon cayenne
2 medium onions	1 tablespoon ground ginger
2 pounds ripe tomatoes	1 teaspoon ground allspice
1 pound seedless raisins	1 teaspoon ground nutmeg
1 pound brown sugar	¼ teaspoon ground cloves
1 quart vinegar	2 teaspoons salt

Peel and chop apples, onions and tomatoes. Add remaining ingredients. Bring mixture to boiling, lower heat and simmer 1 hour, or until thick. Ladle into clean hot half-pint jars. Seal and label. Makes about 4 half pints.

APPLE RELISH

1 pint cider vinegar	1 teaspoon ground cinnamon
3 cups honey	
1 teaspoon ground cloves	5 pounds cooking apples, peeled, cored and quartered

Heat together the vinegar, honey, cloves and cinnamon; then add the apples. Boil for 45 minutes, stirring frequently. Pour into sterilized jars; seal at once. Serve with cold meat of any kind.

SPICY APPLE RELISH

4 pounds onions	1 teaspoon powdered cloves
3 pounds green apples	1 tablespoon cinnamon
4½ cups brown sugar, firmly packed	1 teaspoon allspice
1 pound raisins	1 tablespoon salt
2 teaspoons ginger	¼ cup molasses

Put onions and apples through food chopper, using coarse knife. Combine all ingredients in large kettle; simmer, uncovered, about 2 hours, or until mixture is thick and dark. Stir occasionally to prevent sticking. Pour into hot sterilized half-pint jars. Seal at once. Makes about 3 quarts.

APPLE CARDAMOM JELLY

Cut 4 pounds tart cooking apples into quarters; do not pare or core. Add 2 quarts water and 2 tablespoons cardamom seeds (removed from pods). Cook until apples are soft— about 25 minutes. Strain through dampened jelly bag. Makes about 7½ cups juice. Measure juice; tint a delicate pink with pure food coloring; add 1 cup sugar to each cup juice. Stir over low heat until sugar dissolves. Boil rapidly to 221°– 223° on a candy-jelly thermometer, or until a good jelly test results. Skim. Pour into hot sterilized jelly glasses at once. Paraffin at once. Let cool. Put on covers and label. Makes about eight 8-ounce glasses of jelly.

APPLE HERB JELLY

Wash 4 pounds ripe apples; do not peel or core. Cut in eighths. Add 6½ cups water; bring to boil; simmer, covered, 10 minutes, or until apples are soft. Crush with masher; simmer, covered, 5 minutes longer. Strain through cheesecloth. There should be about 5 cups. Measure 2½ cups of juice into saucepan. Bring to a boil and pour over ¼ cup dried herb.*

* Sage, tarragon, thyme, marjoram, savory or mint.

Let stand 15 minutes; strain through cheesecloth into large enamel or agate saucepan. Add ¼ cup vinegar and 4 cups sugar; mix well. Place over high heat; bring to a boil. (While mixture is coming to a boil, add a few drops red or green food cloring, if desired.) Add ½ bottle fruit pectin. Bring to a *full rolling boil;* boil hard 1 minute, stirring constantly. Remove from heat; skim off foam; pour quickly into jelly glasses. Cover jelly at once with ⅛ inch hot melted paraffin. Makes about 6 medium glasses. Repeat, using remaining juice and a different herb.

APPLE JUICE BASE FOR JELLIES

Cut 4 pounds (3 quarts) tart apples into quarters. Do not pare or core. Add 2 quarts water. Cook 20 to 30 minutes, or until apples are tender. Strain through a dampened jelly bag. Makes about 6 cups juice.

APPLE JELLY

Measure apple juice (above). Add 1 cup of sugar to each cup. Stir until sugar dissolves. Boil rapidly until a good jelly test results. Skim; pour into glasses at once. Paraffin. Cool. Put on covers and labels.

APPLE MINT JELLY

Measure apple juice. Add a large bunch of fresh mint. Boil 15 minutes, skimming frequently. Remove mint. Add ¾ cup sugar to each cup of juice. Stir until sugar dissolves. Add enough food coloring to tint deep mint green. Boil rapidly until a good jelly test results. Skim. Pour into glasses at once. Paraffin. Cool. Put on covers, and label.

APPLE PEAR CONSERVE

2 cups chopped, unpared
  cooking apples
2 cups chopped fresh pears
  (or peaches)

½ cup lemon juice
3 cups sugar
1 cup chopped walnuts

Combine all ingredients except nuts; cook slowly until apple is transparent—about 20 minutes. Add walnuts. Pour into hot sterilized glasses. Seal immediately. Makes seven 6-ounce glasses.

QUICKIES

Cheese-Topped Apple Pie:

Start with a freshly baked apple pie; grate sharp Cheddar cheese over the top. Set in a 325° oven until cheese melts.

Blue Cheese Apple Canapés:

Core apples, slice in rings. Mix three parts cream cheese with one part blue cheese; add enough mayonnaise for a spreading consistency. Spread on apple rings; serve as dessert with crackers and coffee.

Curry Sauce:

For delicious curry, cook one or two chopped raw apples in the curry mixture.

Breakfast Idea:

Top ready-to-serve cereal or hot cereal with thin apple slices. Add sugar and cream or milk as usual.

Fried Apple Pies:

Prepare your favorite recipe for doughnut dough. Roll out ¼ inch thick. Cut in 6-inch rounds. Place 2 tablespoons thick, sweetened, spiced applesauce in center of each round. Moisten edges; fold over; press edges firmly together with tines of fork. Fry in shallow fat (1½ inches deep) heated to 365°, until puffed and brown. Drain on absorbent paper. Serve with sharp cheese.

Apple Pie with Cheese:

Prepare your favorite apple pie and put it together except for the top crust. Spoon Cheese Whiz on top of apples—about 1 generous tablespoon per cut of pie. Adjust top crust and bake as usual. The cheese spread will melt and permeate the whole pie.

Garnish for Fish:

When serving fish fillets, garnish the platter with fresh parsley, lemon wedges, and raw apple slices.

Company Apple Cup:

Prepare sweetened, spiced applesauce. Chill. Fill sherbet or parfait glasses with applesauce to within ½ inch of top. Crush gingersnaps into fine crumbs. Fill glasses to top with crumbs. Add a swirl of sweetened, almond-flavored whipped cream. Garnish with broken walnuts.

Apple Goobers:

An after-school treat for the younger set—crisp slices of un-peeled red apples spread lavishly with peanut butter and ac-companied by mugs of chocolate milk.

Happy Idea for the Lunchbox:

Apples and peanut butter are natural affinities. Add rasp-berry jam and you achieve a flavor combination beloved by the younger set. Try combining equal parts of peanut butter and jam in quantities needed. Core a big red apple. Cut in 8 wedges or cut crosswise in circles about ¼ inch thick. Spread with jam mixture and put together again in original shape. Wrap in heavy waxed paper, aluminum foil or Saran wrap and tuck in the lunchbox.

Pudding Topping:

Crown rice pudding or tapioca with a spoonful of apples cooked with raisins and grated lemon peel.

Quick Casserole:

Alternate layers of diced, cooked pork, applesauce and canned baked beans in a casserole. Bake at 350° for 30 min-utes.

Dessert Suggestion:

For a delightful summertime dessert for two or twenty,

serve chilled red apples accompanied by cream cheese peanut balls. To make the latter, roll cream cheese into balls about 1 inch in diameter, then coat with chopped peanuts.

Snow-Capped Apple Slices:

Core red apples; cut crosswise in ½-inch slices. Spread generously with whipped topping. Sprinkle with toasted flaked coconut. If desired, spread apples with tart red jelly or preserves before adding topping. A fine dessert to top off a hearty dinner.

Apple Gingersnack:

Core unpeeled red apples; cut crosswise in ¼-inch slices. Spread slices with jam; top each with gingersnap. Serve with mugs of cool milk for an after-school snack.

Apples Saigon:

For dessert, serve each person a shiny red apple on a plate with a mound of cream cheese sprinkled with cinnamon and sugar. Have additional cinnamon and sugar on hand.

Applesauce à la Mode:

Chill canned applesauce. Spoon into individual serving dishes; sprinkle with nutmeg. Top with scoop of vanilla ice cream.

Apple Cream:

Fold together equal quantities applesauce and whipped cream. Top with chopped walnuts.

Strawberry Surprise:

Defrost 1 package quick-frozen strawberries. Add 1 cup diced apple. Top with dairy sour cream and a sprinkle of nutmeg.

In-a-Wink Dessert:

Chill canned applesauce. Serve in sherbet glasses; top with dairy sour cream; sprinkle with sugar, cinnamon and nutmeg.

Danish Appetizer:

Add 1 cup chopped raw apple to 1 cup cottage cheese; season with 1 teaspoon celery salt and ½ teaspoon curry powder. Spread on crackers or toast, add a slice of smoked salmon or an anchovy fillet. (Or use a generous spoonful of the cheese mixture in the center of a fish salad plate.)

Crumb Top Pie:

Bake deep-dish apple pie; top with grated cheese and buttered crumbs; brown under broiler until bubbly.

To soften brown sugar:

Put hardened brown sugar in a container that has a tight cover. Place a slice of apple on a bit of waxed paper and set on top. Cover. After a few days the sugar will be moist again.

Gala Sunday Breakfast or Brunch:

Top 1 slice of hot French toast with 2 strips of bacon and a generous spoonful of hot, sweetened, spicy applesauce. Add another slice of French toast, 2 more strips of bacon and more applesauce. Serve at once.

Apple Herring Appetizer:

Arrange marinated herring (pickled herring in sour cream) on individual plates with wedges of crisp, unpeeled red apple slices.

Apple Hors d'Oeuvres:

Cut neat slices of unpared red apples. Top each slice with a ball of sharp Cheddar cheese spread. Secure with cocktail picks.

Apple-Ring Canapés:

Core unpeeled red apples; slice crosswise in rings about ¼ inch thick. Top with blue cheese spread. Dust with paprika.

Baked Apples India:

Core apples; peel ⅓ of the way from top. Fill generously with drained chutney (save syrup). Set in deep baking pan or casserole. Add enough hot water to cover bottom of pan; cover baking dish; bake at 375° about 30 minutes, or until apples are tender. Remove cover; brush peeled surfaces with syrup from chutney; run under broiler for a few minutes to glaze. Serve with curried meat or chicken.

Apple Rings with New Flavor:

Core red apples, but do not pare. Cut in rings about ½ inch thick. Dip in lemon juice; sprinkle lightly with sugar. Top with a mixture of chopped parsley and water cress. Serve with crisp brown 'n' serve pork sausages, frizzled ham, smoked pork butt, baked pork chops, roast loin of pork, broiled ham slice or baked ham.

Tropical Apple Salad:

Arrange crisp salad greens on individual salad plates. On the greens, arrange thin slices of unpared apples, canned Kadota figs and pitted dates stuffed with peanut butter. Serve with a dressing made of equal parts mayonnaise and dairy sour cream, with a few chopped walnuts added.

Snow-Cap Apple Parfait:

Spoon alternate layers of sweetened applesauce, vanilla ice cream and crushed sweetened raspberries into chilled parfait glasses. Top with whipped cream.

Apple Iceberg Pie:

Spread 2 cups sweetened applesauce on bottom of baked and cooled 9-inch pie shell. Spoon in 1 quart pistachio ice cream. Place in freezer or freezing compartment of refrigerator. Ten minutes before serving time, remove from freezer. Top with whipped cream or whipped dessert topping.

Apple Snow-Cap Brownies:

Make and bake rich brownies, using your favorite recipe or a packaged mix. Cut in squares. Soften cream cheese with a little heavy cream; spread on brownies. Top with thin slices unpeeled red apples.

Pork Chop with Jellied Apple Slices:

Broil, pan-fry or bake 6 loin pork chops. Core red apples; do not pare; cut in 12 thick slices. Place in large frying pan.

Dissolve 1 glass (8 ounces) currant jelly in ½ cup boiling water; pour over apples. Cook over low heat turning occasionally, until slices are tender and well glazed. Place pork chops on a hot platter; surround with apple slices; garnish with parsley. Makes 6 servings.

Apple "Champagne" Fruit Cup:

Combine diced, unpeeled red apples, orange sections, fluted banana slices and melon balls in any desired proportion. Arrange in sherbet glasses. Combine equal quantities of chilled apple cider and club soda; pour over fruit; serve at once.

Apple Dessert Platter:

On a large tray place a bowl of mincemeat. Arrange around it rows of thin unpeeled red apple slices; squares of cream cheese; pitted dates stuffed with peanut butter and topped with thin, peeled apple slices; crisp butter crackers.

Savory Apple Sandwiches:

Core red apples; do not peel. Cut crosswise in half-inch slices. Cut bacon strips in half; cook until crisp. Cook apple rings over low heat in bacon fat until soft, turning to brown each side *lightly*. Split and lightly toast English muffins. Place an apple ring on each muffin half; cover generously with shredded sharp Cheddar cheese. Arrange 3 half slices of bacon on top; broil until cheese melts and bacon is crisp. Serve at once.

Petal Fruit Cup:

Select large red apples. Quarter, core and slice thin (do not pare). Arrange apple slices and grapefruit sections (canned, quick-frozen or fresh) alternately around outer edge of sherbet glasses, to resemble flower petals. Inside the petals, place banana slices and halved, seeded Tokay grapes. Fill glasses with grapefruit juice.

Gouda Apples:

Pare red coating from Gouda cheese; cut cheese into ½-inch wedges. Cut cored unpeeled red apples in eighths, dip in lemon juice; alternate 5 cheese wedges and 5 apples slices to form a ball or sphere. Secure with wooden picks if necessary. Serve garnished with water cress or other greens, radishes, olives, or small stuffed prunes or onion-stuffed olives.

Hard Sauce Apples:

Prepare any favorite recipe for hard sauce; tint pink or green, if desired. Shape into "apples"; insert whole cloves for stem and blossom ends.

Last Minute Applesauce Dessert:

Combine 2 cups applesauce, 1 teaspoon cinnamon, dash nutmeg, ¼ cup firmly packed brown sugar, and 1 teaspoon lemon juice. Cut baker's pound cake in ½-inch slices; toast. Top slices with applesauce mixture and whipped cream.

Serve-Yourself Salad Platter:

Fill cornucopias of cooked ham with chive cream cheese. Dip thin slices of unpeeled red apple in lemon juice or French dressing. Cut balls from cantaloupe and honeydew melons with ball cutter. Arrange cornucopias, apple slices and melon balls on platter; garnish with water cress. Serve additional salad greens separately. Combine 1 cup mayonnaise and ½ cup dairy sour cream; sprinkle with paprika. Serve with salad.

APPLE BUYING GUIDE

(An abbreviated guide for buying and using apple varieties. Supplies are, of course, more limited toward the end of the indicated period of availability and available longer for those varieties stored in controlled atmosphere storage, which extends the market season by several months. Some varieties are more universally distributed than others. In the final analysis use is a matter of preference. All varieties can be eaten fresh for snacks, for salads, etc.; all can be baked and cooked. Our suggested uses are based on the characteristics of each variety and our experiences with each variety in our Apple Kitchen.)

VARIETY	WHEN AVAILABLE	WHERE AVAILABLE IN U.S. & CANADA				VARIETY CHARACTERISTICS	RANGE OF USES	BEST USES	SPECIAL NOTES
		EAST	CTRL	SOUTH	WEST				
SUMMER & EARLY FALL VARIETIES	July–September	x	x	x	x	Numerous varieties, Red, Green and Yellow. Tender, tart and juicy	Snacks, salads, fruit cups and all culinary uses	Sauce and all culinary uses except whole baked apples	Numerous summer and early fall varieties are available; distribution limited from area to area—none is universally distributed. (Lodi, Puritan, Summer Rambo, Williams Red, Crimson Beauty, Early McIntosh, Julyred, Starr, Melba, Tydeman's Red, Summer Champion and many others)
WEALTHY	Aug.–October	x	x			Two-toned Red and Green, usually striped or blushed with red. Tart and spicy	Snacks, salads, fruit cups and all culinary uses	Sauce and all culinary uses except whole baked apples	Declining production; limited fresh availability and distribution—mostly New York, Ontario, Michigan, Wisconsin. Major supply is commercially processed

	Season				Description	Snacks, salads, fruit cups and all culinary uses	Sauce and all culinary uses except whole baked apples	
GRAVENSTEIN	Aug.–October	×			×	Red striped or blushed. Tart, spicy and juicy	Snacks, salads, fruit cups and all culinary uses	Sauce and all culinary uses except whole baked apples	Limited fresh distribution except in California. Limited availability in northeastern U.S. and Canada. Major production is commercially processed.
GRIMES GOLDEN	Sept.–Feb.	×	×		×	Green-Yellow to Golden Yellow. Mildly tart, sweet and flavorful	Snacks, salads, fruit cups and all culinary uses	Snacks, fruit cups and all culinary uses	An old favorite which is rapidly declining in production. Limited fresh distribution in Appalachian area and central areas of U.S. Major supply utilized for commercial processing.
RED DELICIOUS	Sept.–June	×	×	×	×	Bright Red. Sweet and juicy	Snacks, salads and fruit cups	Snacks, salads and fruit cups	Most universally grown and available of all apple varieties
GOLDEN DELICIOUS	Sept.–June	×	×	×	×	Yellow-Green to Bright Yellow, often light burnished or russeted when grown in East. Sweet and juicy	Snacks, salads, fruit cups, baking and all culinary uses	Snacks, salads, fruit cups, baking, sauce and all culinary uses	Most universally available all-purpose variety
McINTOSH	Sept.–June	×	×	×	×	Two-toned Red and Green. Slightly tart, tender, juicy, spritely, aromatic	Snacks, salads, fruit cups, sauce, all culinary uses	Snacks, salads, fruit cups, sauce and all culinary uses except baked whole apples	Less generally available in western and southern U.S., but increasingly available in all areas of U.S. and Canada from November to April

209

APPLE BUYING GUIDE (cont.)

VARIETY	WHEN AVAILABLE	WHERE AVAILABLE IN U.S. & CANADA				VARIETY CHARACTERISTICS	RANGE OF USES	BEST USES	SPECIAL NOTES
		EAST	CTRL.	SOUTH	WEST				
JONATHAN	Sept.–April	x	x	x	x	Bright Red. Slightly tart, rich flavored and juicy	Snacks, salads, fruit cups and all culinary uses	Snacks, salads, fruit cups, sauce and all culinary uses	Less generally available in Northeast and Southwest during early and late months of the season. Well distributed during much of season except in Northeast
CORTLAND	Sept.–April	x	x			Red and Green two-toned color with purplish undertone on red. Snow-white flesh, mildly tart, juicy and tender	Snacks, salads, fruit cups, all culinary uses	Snacks, salads, fruit cups, baking, sauce and all culinary uses	Distribution and availability, mostly in northeastern U.S. and Canada and in Midwest. Excellent snack, salad and fruit cup apple and excellent but tender baking and cooking variety
STAYMAN	Oct.–May	x	x	x		Deep Red with purplish undertone, often slightly burnished or russeted. Rich flavored, moderately juicy	Snacks, salads, fruit cups, and all culinary uses	Snacks, salads, fruit cups, sauce and all culinary uses	Distribution and availability, mostly in Middle Atlantic and southeastern U.S.—Pennsylvania to Florida

Variety	Season				Color / Taste	Eating uses	Cooking uses	Remarks
ROME BEAUTY	Oct.–June	x	x	x	Bright Red, sometimes striped. Very mildly tart	Snacks, salads, fruit cups, baking and all culinary uses	Baking and all culinary uses	Produced and available in all areas of U.S. Less available in Canada. A fair fresh eating apple, but best for baked and cooked uses
YORK IMPERIAL	Oct.–June	x		x	Green with varying degrees of Red. Lopsided in shape, mildly tart	All culinary uses; snacks, salads and fruit cups	Baking, sauce, all culinary uses	Limited fresh distribution and availability—mostly in Appalachian area and Southeast. Major supply is utilized for commercial processing
RHODE ISLAND GREENING	Oct.–April	x	x		Green to Yellow-Green. Mildly tart	All culinary uses	Baking, sauce and all culinary uses	Limited fresh distribution and availability, mostly in New York, New England, Michigan and other upper central states. Major supply is utilized for commercial processing. Variety sometimes confused with Northwest Greening, which is an earlier maturing variety, more generally available, particularly August—December
NEWTOWN PIPPIN	Oct.–May			x	Green to Yellow-Green. Mildly tart. Less juicy than some other varieties	Snacks, salads, baking and all culinary uses	Baking, sauce and all culinary uses	Very limited local supply seasonally in Virginia, major fresh distribution and availability in California, Oregon, Washington. Large part of supply utilized for commercial processing

APPLE BUYING GUIDE (cont.)

VARIETY	WHEN AVAILABLE	WHERE AVAILABLE IN U.S. & CANADA				VARIETY CHARACTERISTICS	RANGE OF USES	BEST USES	SPECIAL NOTES
		EAST	CTRL	SOUTH	WEST				
SPARTAN	Oct.–April	x	x		x	Bright Red. Mildly tart, crisp and juicy	Snacks, salads, fruit cups, culinary uses	Snacks, salads, fruit cups	One of newer varieties (McIntosh x Yellow Newtown, 1935), excellent dessert quality. Limited distribution and availability, mostly British Columbia and West Coast, but some in Northeast
WINESAP	Nov.–July	x	x	x	x	Deep Red. Moderately tart, rich wine-like flavor, juicy	Snacks, salads, fruit cups and all culinary uses	Snacks, salads, fruit cups, sauce and all culinary uses	A late season apple available in most markets from December through June, but declining in production and distribution
BALDWIN	Nov.–April	x				Dull Red (sometimes burnished or russeted)	All culinary uses	Baking, sauce and all culinary uses	Limited fresh distribution and availability, mostly in New York and New England. Major supply is utilized for commercial processing

| NORTHERN SPY | Nov.–May | | x | x | | | Two-toned Red and Green. Moderately tart, rich flavored, crisp and juicy | Snacks, salads, fruit cups, baking and all culinary uses | Snacks, salads, fruit cups, baking and all culinary uses | Like Golden Delicious, Northern Spy is one of the finest all-purpose varieties grown. Unfortunately it is declining in supply. Limited fresh distribution and availability, mostly in New York, Michigan and Ontario, Canada. Major supply is utilized for commercial processing |

A number of other excellent old varieties—and a number of fine new varieties—are available in all producing areas. Distribution is generally limited to the area of production, hence we have not charted them. They include:

Twenty Ounce, excellent culinary apple, seasonally available (September–January) in western New York. N. W. Greening, late summer and early fall culinary apple, seasonally available in Appalachian and Great Lakes areas; Haralson and Connell Red, good all-purpose varieties generally available (October–February), Minnesota and Wisconsin. Macoun, excellent dessert quality, McIntosh type, highest flavor rating; limited availability in Northeast and North Central areas, Idared, a relatively new late-season Jonathan-type variety, good all purpose, available in Northeast and North Central areas. Mutsu, a Golden-Delicious-cross of Japanese origin, available locally in Northeast and North Central areas. These and a number of other old and new varieties seasonally available in areas of production.

INDEX

MAIN DISHES